The History of the East Riding Yeomanry
VOLUME 1
Wenlock's Horsemen

The History of the East Riding Yeomanry

VOLUME 1
Wenlock's Horsemen
The East Riding Yeomanry in the First World War
1902–1930

Neil Hutty

The History of the East Riding Yeomanry
VOLUME 1
Wenlock's Horsemen
The East Riding Yeomanry in the First World War 1902–1930
By Neil Hutty

FIRST EDITION

Leonaur is an imprint of Oakpast Ltd
Copyright in this form © 2025 Oakpast Ltd
Neil Hutty identifies himself as the author of this book for copyright purposes

ISBN: 978-1-917666-00-8 (hardcover)
ISBN: 978-1-917666-01-5 (softcover)

http://www.leonaur.com

Publisher's Notes

The views expressed in this book are not necessarily those of the publisher.

Contents

Foreword	7
Acknowledgements	9
Chapter 1: The Pre-War Years, 1902-1914	11
Chapter 2: The Home Front, 1914-1915	37
Chapter 3: Egypt, 1915-1916	81
Chapter 4: Palestine, 1917	111
Chapter 5: The Western Front, 1918-1919	185
Chapter 6: The Inter-War Years, 1919-1930	229
Appendix A	241
Appendix B	255
Appendix C	260
Appendix D	266
Appendix E	269
Appendix F	272
Notes	275
Bibliography	282
Index	288

Foreword

Herbert Brandon, 'Grampy', was my much-loved Grandfather who inspired my interest in history, especially military history. He joined the East Riding Yeomanry (Territorial Army) in April 1939, serving throughout World War Two. After his death I set out to find out more about the East Riding Yeomanry and came across references to the Regiment's service as a cavalry regiment in the First World War and so I wanted to read about that too. That in turn led to photographs and illustrations of magnificent pre-war uniforms (complete with impressively plumed helmets) and some rather primitive looking armoured cars. I wanted to know more about those as well. However, it soon became clear that whilst there were a few scarce books covering the Second World War, there was no 'Regimental History' detailing the rest of the East Riding Yeomanry story, including the First World War period. I decided to attempt to rectify the situation.

Wherever possible I have tried to use first-hand accounts to corroborate the events recorded in the War Diaries and other works. The recollections of veterans vary, depending on their point of view and level of participation in particular situations, even contemporaneous with the events, and especially when they have been set down after an interval of many years. I have tried to reconcile these accounts as best as possible; all errors and misinterpretations are my own.

Acknowledgements

I am deeply indebted to all those 'Yeomen' who took the time to record their experiences, either through interviews, diaries, letters, or memoirs without which this book would be impossible. Similarly, I would like to thank all the relatives of yeomen who I have corresponded with over the years in person, online, via email or social media and who have shared invaluable snippets of information, letters, diaries, personal memoirs, and photographs. There are too many to mention individually here, but particular thanks must go to Tony Robinson for his permission to publish extracts from the letters of Major J. F. M. Robinson and Dominic Rogan for copies of Clement Rogan's postcards.

I would like to thank the staff of the following institutions for their help and assistance with my research: The East Riding Archive and Local Studies Service; the Imperial War Museum (Library & Research Room Services and the Media Sales & Licensing Team); the Tank Museum, Bovington; the National Archives, Kew; the Liddell Hart Centre for Military Studies, King's College, London; the Parliamentary Archives, Westminster; the York Castle Museum; and the Liddle Collection at the Brotherton Library (University of Leeds). Particular thanks also go to Brian Mulrine at the Crimlisk Fisher Archive, Filey.

I would also like to express my gratitude to Doctor David Marchant, Museums Registrar of the East Riding of Yorkshire Council. His 2011 talk on the regiment showed me (and him) the depth of interest locally in the East Riding Yeomanry and led directly to a number of projects and ultimately this book, and I am grateful for all his help, enthusiasm and support since.

For me, the East Riding Yeomanry has become an obsession. I offer my sincerest apologies and thanks to all my family, friends and work colleagues who have had to endure twenty years of me rambling on about the East Riding Yeomanry, the latest acquisition to my collection, or my dreams of starting a museum or writing this book—thank you all. Particular thanks go to my friend Dave Alderton, who read all the chapters (often more than once) and provided many valuable comments and corrections. I must also thank Richard Waterhouse for his generosity, encouragement, and help; and to John Lewis at Leonaur, for his advice, encouragement, and for making this book a reality.

My final and most heartfelt thanks go to my long-suffering wife, Lu, for her continued love and support, both at home and when dragged around museums and cemeteries when we are supposed to be on holiday.

Neil Hutty

Cottingham,
East Riding of Yorkshire,
2024

Chapter 1: The Pre-War Years, 1902-1914

To this day the yeomanry form the cavalry component of the British Army's part-time reserve forces (now called the Army Reserve but better known by its former title, the Territorial Army). Yeomanry Cavalry regiments were originally formed in the late 18th and early 19th Centuries during the French Revolutionary and Napoleonic Wars for the purposes of home defence in case of a French invasion. The name 'Yeomanry' derives from the 'Gentleman' and 'Yeoman' classes from which their members were originally drawn; members were volunteers who had to provide their own horses which were expensive, restricting volunteers to those men who owned, or could afford to rent, a suitable horse. The title of 'Yeoman' originally referred to a man holding and farming a small estate (as freeholder or tenant) and ranked below a 'Gentleman' (typically one who did not need to work for a living but ranking below the Aristocracy). Although there was an East Riding Yeomanry Cavalry at this time, no such unit had survived into the second half of 19th Century.

Formation

The Boer War in South Africa, fought between 1899 and 1902, taught the British government several significant lessons, one of which was the importance of cavalry and mounted infantry. The shortage of these mobile troops during the war had been alleviated to some extent by the establishment of an all-volunteer force known as the Imperial Yeomanry. This new force was however separate and independent of the established home-based yeomanry units that had survived from the Napoleonic era. Nevertheless, initially at least, most of its volunteers came from the existing yeomanry regiments (who 'sponsored' companies of the new force); later recruits were drawn directly from the civilian population.

At the conclusion of the war the Imperial Yeomanry force was disbanded, the reason for its existence over, but even before the war ended in May 1902 the government had encouraged the formation of more regiments of yeomanry at home, in order to increase the strength of the force from 10,000 to 40,000 men. All the yeomanry regiments subsequently adopted the honorary title of 'Imperial Yeomanry', although the force remained one for intended for home defence only (as opposed to Imperial service, i.e. overseas).

It was decided that there was capacity to raise one of these new regiments in the East Riding of Yorkshire and Lord Wenlock of Escrick (Beilby Lawley, 3rd Baron Wenlock GCSI, GCIE, KCB, VD, PC, of Escrick Park, York), Chairman of the East Riding County Council, took it upon himself to raise it. At a meeting in Beverley (the county town of the East Riding) on 1st March 1902, chaired by Lord Herries, the Lord Lieutenant of the East Riding, a number of former and current officers put their names forward as being willing to serve, although there was a certain amount of scepticism as to whether it would be possible to raise a new cavalry unit, even from Lord Wenlock himself, who wrote:

"it is very uncertain as to the possibility of raising men in sufficient numbers, the full number of a complete regiment being 596" [1]

The formation of a regiment of Imperial Yeomanry in the East Riding was nevertheless approved by the War Office in April 1902. Lord Wenlock then convened a series of public meetings across the county to enlist the support of local organisations and notables (such as the Mayors of Hull and Beverley) in promoting the idea. In addition to those gentlemen who had already offered their services, Lord Wenlock hoped to attract more members of the local landed gentry to serve as his officers, there being a good number of them who had seen active service with the Regular Army, including in South Africa during the Boer War, or had seen prior service with other auxiliary units across the country. Lord Wenlock himself was the Honorary Colonel of the 2nd East Riding of Yorkshire Royal Garrison Artillery (Volunteers) and a former officer in the Yorkshire Hussars Yeomanry.

The enlisted men on the other hand would be drawn from the yeoman classes: small scale or tenant farmers, workers and craftsmen from the many estates of the East Riding or the clerks and urban middle classes of Hull. The yeomanry were still expected to provide their own horses and that generally meant that only those who had access to, or owned, a horse, or could afford to rent one for duty, were likely to join the regiment (although men could also present for duty with a bicycle in lieu of a horse).

Throughout April meetings were held in the major towns and villages of the county, including Beverley, Hull, Driffield, Pocklington, Bridlington and Market Weighton. Initial attendances were disappointingly low, not helped by that fact that several of the meetings were held during market day or at other inconvenient times.

Lord Wenlock's appeals made a great deal of the fact that the East Riding, with a long history of agriculture, horses and fox hunting, didn't have a cavalry regiment of its own and pointed out that those men from the region who had volunteered for service with the Imperial Yeomanry in South Africa had had to serve in units from the neighbouring counties. It was also emphasised that the East Riding was, in the event of war, a natural target for enemy landings and that the Boers had demonstrated the defensive value of small numbers of mounted men with intimate knowledge of the local countryside.

Leaflets were distributed outlining the conditions of service and there were numerous letters in support of the proposed regiment published in the local newspapers. Lord Wenlock offered

LORD WENLOCK, IN THE FULL-DRESS UNIFORM OF THE EAST
RIDING OF YORKSHIRE IMPERIAL YEOMANRY C. 1903
(Author's collection)

the opportunity for all those joining to learn to ride and shoot, though for many of the enlisted men the main attraction would be the annual two-week training camp which, in the time before official paid holidays, offered the chance of an escape from their daily lives and to partake in sports and other pursuits. The social aspect of membership of a unit was also important in an era of widespread working men's clubs and social clubs, and of course the men were not immune from the prestige associated with being a member of a 'dashing' cavalry regiment.

The campaign was obviously successful, as despite the slow start, the Yorkshire Post was reporting that nearly 300 men had promised to join the new unit by the end of the month.

A number of names for the regiment were suggested, including the "Yorkshire Mounted Regiment" and the "East Riding Imperial Yeomanry"; Lord Wenlock wished the regiment to be known as "Wenlock's Horse", named for its founder in a fashion resurrected during the Boer War.

Public meetings continued to be held throughout the summer and into the autumn, and the proposed regiment began to take shape. Beverley was suggested as the location of the Regimental Headquarters, it being centrally positioned, with three Squadrons headquartered in Beverley, Driffield and Howden or Selby, with Troops (detachments) in Hull, Hedon, Beverley, Driffield, Market Weighton, Pocklington, Selby and Howden. It was also hoped that a Troop would be formed from the workers of the Sledmere estate near Driffield.

The first seven officers for the new regiment were officially appointed on 6th December 1902 and formal recruiting for the men was finally opened. The East Riding members of the Yorkshire Hussars held a meeting to discuss their future (now that recruiting for the Hussars in the county had been stopped) however a vote held resulted in a decision not to transfer. This meeting did not address the views of the Hull members and at a second meeting a few days later they almost unanimously agreed to transfer to the new unit, 21 members immediately volunteering.

Lord Herries was appointed Honorary Colonel of the Regiment in February 1903 and further officers were commissioned, including the Quartermaster and Veterinary Officer, and by April 1903 it was reported that in addition to 12 officers, a total of 340 men had enlisted, including 145 in the Hull Squadron and 111 in the Squadron to be headquartered in York.

The Regiment was formally accepted for service by the government on 15th May 1903 as the 'East Riding of Yorkshire Imperial Yeomanry' (ERYIY), with Lord Wenlock as Colonel-in-Chief. Nevertheless, the regiment continued to be unofficially known locally as Wenlock's Horse.

The official establishment of the regiment was to be 30 officers and 566 other ranks, organised into a Regimental Headquarters and 4 Squadrons. The plans submitted to the War Office in July 1903 comprised:

'A' Squadron, to be located in Hull, under the command of Major Arthur Stanley Wilson (at Morpeth Street)

'B' Squadron, to be located in Beverley, under the command of Major Benjamin Booth Haworth-Booth, with detachments planned at Hotham (North Cave), Newport, Rolston (Hornsea) and Patrington

'C' Squadron was planned for Escrick (the seat of Lord Wenlock) outside York under the command of Major Philip Joseph Langdale, with detachments at Fulford, Riccall, East Cottingworth, Pocklington and Hexby

'D' Squadron was intended to be headquartered at Bridlington under the command of Captain Charles Oswin Hall with detachments at Hunmanby, Driffield and Norton (Malton)

Second-in-Command of the regiment was to be Major John Bouchier Stracey-Clitherow and Captain Calvert, 1st Royal Dragoons, was confirmed as Adjutant. There were also five Non Commissioned Officers (NCOs) attached from regular regiments as instructors, known as the 'Permanent Staff': a Regimental Sergeant Major (RSM) and four Squadron Sergeant Majors (SSM).

Each Squadron would have been organised along the lines laid out in the Imperial Yeomanry Training Handbook of 1902:

> "The squadron is the tactical and administrative unit, capable of independent service at all times. The squadron should be divided into four troops, each complete in itself, and capable, in its turn, of independent service. The troop is further divided into permanent groups of four men, with their horses, one of whom will be selected as leader. Each troop should be composed of men raised in the same locality, or, if detachments from existing corps, are associated together, of men belonging to the same regiment. The permanent groups similarly should be formed of men who live in the same vicinity in civil life, or who have some association in common." [2]

There typically seems to have been four 'permanent groups' (also known as sections) to a Troop, with the sergeants, the artificers and trumpeters of the Troop being outside the group system. The organisation is however a theoretical one, and the actual organisation used for exercises and annual camp depended entirely on the numbers of men actually enlisted or attending.

The regiment chose a running fox as their cap badge, a motif popular with the fox hunting fraternity of which they were members; likewise, they chose the well-known hunting song 'D'ye Ken John Peel' as the Regimental march. Major Stracey-Clitherow later wrote:

> "It is really difficult to say why we took 'The Flying Fox' as a badge, except to catch the fox hunting farmers of the East Riding. It was difficult to find something different in a badge and I had the door of the hind boot of the Brighton Coach hanging up in my room and suggested taking that as our badge. The flying fox was what the original Nimrod coach had on it and nothing else. Anyhow the badge was of good service to us, in spite of the whole country saying it was impossible to raise a regiment in the East Riding and having the Yorkshire Hussars and the Yorkshire Dragoons in opposition to us, as the East Riding was used by them for recruiting and they always considered the East Riding men were the best recruits in Yorkshire. In spite of everything we very shortly filled the Regt up to full strength with first class recruits and are now as quality a yeomanry Regt as there is in the whole of the United Kingdom". [3]

The regiment was outfitted with khaki uniforms inspired by those of the Imperial Yeomanry in Boer War, consisting of a khaki serge tunic, Lancer-style, with a French Grey (actually light blue) plastron (triangular chest piece), collar patches and shoulder straps (epaulettes), worn over khaki overalls with a broad light blue stripe along the outer seam. Brass collar badges were worn on the collar patches comprising mirrored versions of the cap badge fox (i.e. facing towards each other) and brass shoulder titles, comprising the letters 'E.R.Y.I.Y.', were worn on the shoulder straps.

The headdress was a khaki felt 'slouch hat' with the brim pinned up on the left side by a small button. A light blue pugree (cloth scarf) was wound around the hat and there was a light blue patch on the turned-up brim on which was mounted the cap badge.

The men's uniforms were provided by the regiment (except boots, which the men were required to purchase themselves), funded by a grant from the government, whilst the officers were expected to provide their own. Rifles, bayonets and saddlery were provided by the War Office. Horses were expected to be provided by the officers and men; there was an allowance of £5 paid for attendance at annual camp which would cover the cost of hiring a suitable steed.

The Imperial Yeomanry at this time were officially roled and equipped as Mounted Infantry and were therefore primarily armed with a rifle (as opposed to the cavalry, who were armed with swords or lances). Nevertheless, there is ample evidence that the Officers and senior NCOs carried swords, certainly in full dress; the senior NCOs at least appear to have worn Sam Browne belts.

Many of the men joining the regiment, particularly in the rural districts, could already ride but many could not, especially in Hull. The regiment had some difficulty in finding suitable accommodation and training facilities in the city and therefore decided it would have to construct its own. Consequently, the City Corporation was approached in February 1903 for planning permission to erect a 100ft long riding school on land adjoining the fairground in Walton Street in Hull. Permission was granted, provided the Ambulance Corps were permitted to use the building and that it would be made available for public functions.

In the meantime, despite the lack of suitable facilities in Hull, training commenced as the new regiment started to get up and running. Lord Wenlock and Major Stracey-Clitherow attended a course at Aldershot in March and the first drills were held; amongst the earliest was a drill held in Newport (for the recruits from Newport and Gilberdyke) which took place on Friday 27th March 1903 (in a field lent by local landowners).

During the formation of the regiment, it had been promised that all recruits would be taught to ride and shoot. Plans were already in hand for the building of the riding school in Hull so after annual camp the regiment turned its attention to shooting, building on the musketry training carried out there. The regiment soon began to establish an excellent reputation, there being a number of excellent shots amongst the recruits, including several members of the Hull Patriotic Rifle Club. Teams from the regiment took part both inter and intra Regimental shooting competitions with some success.

Construction of the new Riding School commenced in April on the Walton Street site in Hull, although the project suffered a setback the following month when high winds damaged the unfinished building, bringing down some 100ft of the 120ft northern wall, fortunately with no injuries to the builders.

The Riding School was completed in March 1905, despite the earlier weather-related setbacks. The building, designed by Messer's Thompson and Kirton of Lowgate, Hull, in fact comprised two adjoining buildings: the riding school itself and a club building. The larger of the two comprised an indoor arena for riding instruction with saddle stores and stabling for 12 horses, whilst the club facilities included a recreation room with billiards table, a non-commissioned officers' room, a reading/committee room, bar, gymnasium and shower-bath for use after

A GROUP OF **ERYIY** OFFICERS AND SERGEANTS
IN FULL DRESS UNIFORM C.1903
(Author's collection)

A GROUP OF **ERYIY** OTHER RANKS
IN FULL DRESS UNIFORM C.1903
(Author's collection)

training, as well as a Morris 'Tube' range for shooting practice.

Lancers

When the regiment was initially raised in 1902 it was equipped with the mounted infantry role in mind, in light of the experiences of the Boer War. One consequence of this was the khaki uniform worn by the regiment when in full dress, rather less impressive than the elaborate uniforms of other cavalry and yeomanry regiments, not least the neighbouring Yorkshire Hussars and Yorkshire Dragoons. In September 1905 Lord Wenlock wrote to the War Office on the subject of the regiment's full dress, petitioning for a new, more impressive uniform:

> "*This regiment has been formed 3 years so a very serious consideration now arises, namely the re-engagement of over half the men; the question of a full dress is a great point they all raise when approached on the subject as there is no doubt that both officers and men are at a disadvantage when brought in contact with the other two Yorkshire Regiments of Yeomanry who have a full dress; this naturally tells on recruiting. His Majesty has expressed his disapproval of officers appearing at court functions in khaki, so my officers are unable to obey his Majesty's command to attend such functions.*" [4]

At the time the War Office replied that the whole subject of yeomanry uniform was under review and subsequently it was decided to re-designate six regiments of yeomanry, including the East Ridings, as Lancer regiments (although the East Ridings may not in fact have ever been issued with lances) and as a result a new full-dress uniform for the regiment, in the Lancer style, was approved in January 1906.

The new uniform for the officers, designed by the regiment, consisted of a lance cap or helmet, with the upper portion covered in French grey cloth, to match the facings (collars, cuffs and plastron) and finished with gilt metal edges and ornaments. On the left front side was a silvered Yorkshire rose, which formed the socket for the plume of 14" French Grey over shorter 7" white cock or swan's feathers. The gilt helmet plate, mounted at the front, consisted of a silver-plated crown, royal cipher, a running fox, laurels and the full regimental title over a Yorkshire rose.

The tunic consisted of a double-breasted lancer-style jacket made from maroon cloth with the collar, pointed cuffs, shoulder straps and plastron of French Grey cloth, with 1" gold lace trim on the collar and cuffs. Collar badges were worn as before. There were two regimental buttons above each cuff, two rows of six buttons on the front of the tunic, with two flat buttons at the waist to sit beneath the girdle. At the rear there were two more buttons at the waist and three on each of the three-pointed flaps, which were edged with gold cord. Along the back and sleeve seams there were welts of French Grey ending at the waist.

The tunic was worn with dark blue overalls with a 2" wide stripe of French Grey along the seams, black Wellington boots and steel spurs (with boxes for spurs when dismounted). The sword belt was worn under the jacket with 1" gold slings lined and edged with leather and with a gold sword knot, corn and acorn.

There was also a shoulder belt, worn over the left shoulder, of gold lace and leather lining and edging with a tip and slide of regimental pattern. Mounted on the rear of the shoulder belt was a black leather pouch with a crown above a running fox, both in gilt metal. Side ornaments were also of gilt or gilding metal. Around the waist gold lace girdle with two crimson silk stripes was worn with white gloves to complete the uniform.

The uniform for other ranks was similar to that of the officers, except for the lack of lace trim and the headdress. All other ranks wore an all maroon staff pattern forage cap with French Grey piping and cap band and a black patent leather peak. There was also a 'pillbox' type forage cap, which was maroon with a broad light blue stripe and topped with a gold button. This type of hat seems to have only been worn by the trumpeters.

1908 – A YEAR OF CHANGE

The year 1908 was a momentous one for the regiment with several significant changes taking place. The first change of the year occurred on the 14th May when the Colonel and founder, Lord Wenlock, officially retired after 6 years in command. His hard work and dedication had seen the regiment, from somewhat uncertain beginnings, grow to become one of the best in the country in a relatively short space of time, laying the foundations of many more years of commendable service. His deputy, Major Stracey-Clitherow, was promoted to Lieutenant Colonel the following day and succeeded to the command.

The next change arrived on the 1st April 1908 when the Imperial Yeomanry was abolished and replaced by the new Territorial Force.

At the end of 1905 Richard Burdon Haldane had become the Secretary of State for War and instigated a series of sweeping reforms of the army. Once the reorganisation of the Regular Army and the Army Reserve was complete attention turned to the auxiliaries that supported it.

The auxiliary forces comprised the Volunteers and the Imperial Yeomanry. These were very different independent organisations with separate command structures, differing terms and conditions of service and of varying degrees of effectiveness.

The Volunteers (which included units of infantry, artillery, and engineers) dated from the Victorian era and lacked a coherent command, administrative or logistic structure. The Imperial Yeomanry was a cavalry only formation and similarly lacked a coherent command, administrative or logistic structure. Many in the Regular Army and the War Office doubted the fighting capabilities of part-timers who must, by implication, have insufficient training and whose units typically struggled to recruit to their full establishments and therefore it was accepted that the auxiliary forces would require a major reorganisation.

This was achieved by the Territorial and Reserve Forces Act of 1907 which established the new combined Territorial Force (TF), essentially merging the Volunteers and the Yeomanry, on 1st April 1908. The new force was to consist of 14 Infantry Divisions and 14 Cavalry Brigades, together with associated support units such as artillery, signals, engineers, medical and supply. The existing Yeomanry and Volunteer units would, in fact, be abolished and those men wishing to join the Territorial Force would

A GROUP OF OTHER RANKS IN LANCER FULL-DRESS AT ANNUAL CAMP, C.1907
(Author's Collection)

A GROUP OF OFFICERS IN LANCER FULL-DRESS AT ANNUAL CAMP
(Author's Collection)

have to enlist in the new organisation.

Haldane had wanted the Territorial Force to act as the second-line to the Regular Army and to be deployed overseas, however this was unpopular with the Volunteers and Yeomen (who had enlisted for home service only) and therefore as a compromise, although the new force was intended primarily for home defence, provision was made for individuals to take a pledge to serve overseas in times of crisis.

For the yeomanry the effect of the changes included the dropping of the 'Imperial' from their unit titles (the regiment becoming the East Riding of Yorkshire Yeomanry (TF), usually abbreviated to ERYY or ERoYY) and a slight reduction in the strength of a regiment to 25 officers and 449 men. Revisions to the terms of service meant that men now enlisted for a term of 4 years instead of 3 (although a man could 'buy himself out' for £5 with three months' notice).

There were also decreases in pay (other ranks pay was reduced from 5s 6d to only 1s 2d), although yeomen now received free rations whilst on training (a messing allowance of 1s per day paid to the regiment).

There was some nervousness and concern amongst the yeomen of the impact of Haldane's scheme; nevertheless, despite the unease and pay reductions, eventually all but 41 men from the East Riding of Yorkshire Imperial Yeomanry elected to transfer to the new Territorial Force regiment. Of those that did not, some were no longer eligible on account of their age whilst others simply chose not to re-enlist.

The new Territorial Force units were placed under the administrative control of recently created County Associations, each under the Lord Lieutenant of the county (rather than the War Office). The Yeomanry Regiments were to be permanently brigaded together to create the planned 14 Cavalry Brigades; the 'new' East Riding of Yorkshire Yeomanry (TF) joined the Yorkshire Dragoons and Yorkshire Hussars in the newly created Yorkshire Mounted Brigade, with the West Yorkshire Battery of the Royal Horse Artillery (TF).

LIEUTENANT COLONEL JOHN BOUCHIER STRACEY-CLITHEROW
IN LANCER FULL-DRESS, C.1908
(Author's Collection)

Uniform Changes

The next series changes of 1908 were related to Regimental insignia. On his appointment as the Commanding Officer, Lieutenant Colonel Stracey-Clitherow instigated a change to the Regimental cap badge, remodelling the fox to be more fox-like (he felt the original design looked too much like a dog) and introducing a scroll beneath with the hunting cry 'Forrard' as a motto. The revised fox was, it has been suggested, inspired by the frontispiece of 'Sport' by W. Bromley-Davenport (published in 1888). Initially at least it appears that the scrolled badge was used primarily as the cap badge, with the scroll-less badges continuing to be used for the collar badges and Sergeants' arm badge (worn on the right sleeve above the chevrons ("Sergeants stripes"), fox facing forwards) until sufficient quantities of the new badge were available, although photos show a mix of badges remained in use right up until the First World War.

The second insignia modification was a change to the shoulder titles as a consequence of the formation of the Territorial Force. The existing straight 'E.R.Y.I.Y.' Imperial Yeomanry brass title was replaced by a three-tier pattern, 'T/Y/E.RIDING' (the 'E.RIDING' being curved), although again it was some time before the old titles were completely supplanted by the new and both types remained in use up until WW1.

The final change of the year resulted from the death, in October, of Lord Herries, aged 71, the Honorary Colonel of the Regiment and a staunch supporter of Lord Wenlock in his efforts to raise the regiment. He was succeeded as Honorary Colonel of the Regiment by Lord Wenlock.

Although the regiment had coordinated annual training with neighbouring units in previous years, annual camp for 1909 was the first camp of the newly created Yorkshire Mounted Brigade. The training took on a more serious military tone, with for example, no caterers being engaged. This left the preparation of food to the enlisted cooks who were only allowed army rations, consisting of 1lb of bread and 1lb of meat per man per day, although this was supplemented by an allowance of 1s per man per day paid by the Territorial Association. To assist the Territorials, the Sergeant-Cooks of the Regular 5th Lancers were attached for the duration of camp.

One notable feature of the camp was the use, for the first time by Territorials, of a wireless telegraph, which enabled communications between the regimental camps and provided valuable experience in using this still new technology.

Driffield and 'D' Squadron

The Territorial Force units often struggled to recruit enough men to fill their establishments and after reaching peak strength in 1910, numbers steadily declined. The East Ridings were fortunate and were generally able to recruit sufficient men, at least as far as enlisted men were concerned. It was more difficult to attract officers (or perhaps the 'right sort of officers') however and the regiment was always under strength in that regard.

In 1910 the regimental strength was 21 Officers and 452 men compared to the establishment of 25 Officers and 449 other ranks. This was not the entire picture however, as the establishment allowed for four Captains but there was only one, and there was no Veterinary Officer at this time either. This situation was exacerbated by the retirements of Major Charles Hall (March 1910) and Major Arthur Wilson (June 1910), the transfer of 2nd Lieutenant Oswald Sanderson to the Regular 4th (Royal Irish) Dragoon Guards (June 1910) and the resignation of 2nd Lieutenant Alan P. Slingsby (June 1910) with no new officers joining to replace them.

One consequence of this was the transfer of 'D' Squadron's headquarters from Bridlington to Driffield. Major Hall, who resided in Malton, had commanded the Squadron since its formation and on his retirement was succeeded by Captain Guy Wilson, who lived at Warter Priory near Pocklington. Driffield was the nearest 'D' Squadron location to Warter (12 miles away) whereas Bridlington is 25 miles away.

The lack of Captains in the regiment may also have influenced Major Clive Wilson's decision in 1911 to revert at his own request to the rank of Captain.

Imperial Service

Within the original Territorial and Reserve Forces Act of 1907 was provision for men of the Territorial Force to individually commit to serve overseas in times of crisis. It had been hoped that as many as 25% of those enlisting would sign up to the 'Imperial Service' pledge although actual uptake was far lower than this. Army Order No. 3 of 1910 therefore introduced a new Imperial Service Badge to be worn by those officers and men who had agreed to serve overseas. In addition, any unit that achieved a 90% take up would have, "that fact recorded in a suitable manner under its title in the Army List". However, being mindful of the Territorial Associations' fear that the Territorials would simply be used as a pool of manpower for reinforcing the Regular Army, and to encourage as many men to sign up as possible, the Army Order contained the proviso that Imperial Service volunteers could not be drafted as individuals to any unit other than their own.

Annual Camp 1912

Annual Camp for 1912 took the form of the second Yorkshire Mounted Brigade camp and was held at Bulford Camp on Salisbury Plain. A total of 17 officers and 370 men with their horses made the journey to Amesbury station (just 2¼ miles from the camp) by train; altogether some 17 trains were required to transport the entire brigade.

For many of the men this would have been the furthest they had travelled away from home, and it would have been an exciting adventure. There was however some disquiet amongst those yeomen owning their own horses at the prospect of transporting valuable animals over such a long journey in cattle trucks. Lieutenant Colonel Stracey-Clitherow had raised the issue at a general meeting of the East Riding Territorial Association, where he requested that 20% of the horses required be transported by horse box. The Transport and Supply Committee declined to pay any additional allowances but conceded that if there were

East Riding Yeomanry Private Jack Smart wearing the Imperial Service Badge. He is wearing new pattern cap badge with motto but scroll-less collar badges.
(Author's Collection)

sufficient funds available, they would look to refund the cost of the horse boxes.

The local press of the period was full of adverts for horses for hire for training and annual camp, the adverts frequently emphasising the subject horse's suitability and experience of yeomanry training. This gave rise to concerns that the same horses were being used for multiple regiments' camps, masking the fact that in times of mobilisation there would be insufficient horses available. An anonymous correspondent to the Hull Daily Mail, 'One Who Knows' wrote:

> "*The Territorial horse is a noble animal. He attends every camp which he can fit into his programme, accepts his fee and is reckoned each time as a possible equine unit on the strength. But if he were to die the public would be astonished to learn how few and far between he really was. In the case of war too, he could only be in one camp at a time, but then the Territorial Force isn't equipped on a war basis.*" [5]

The weather during camp was poor; Private Harold Lyon recalled in his post-WW1 lectures that:

> "*throughout the two weeks rain fell almost constantly and the camp became a veritable quagmire*" [6]

It was so bad that the usual regimental sports day at the end of the camp, usually a highlight, had to be abandoned. The camp did however provide an insight into a new emerging technology. The Hull Daily Mail noted that:

> "*while at Salisbury Plain, the East Riding Yeomanry learnt much as to the possibilities of aviation in times of war*". [7]

Aviation was at this time still in its infancy; the Wright Brothers had only achieved the first heavier-than-air powered flight in December 1903, but progress was rapid, and Louis Bleriot succeeded in flying across the channel in July 1909. The Royal Flying Corps (RFC) was established as the aviation branch of the British Army in April 1912, based at Larkhill Aerodrome on Salisbury Plain (close to the Brigade camp). Undoubtedly the exciting new field of flying was of interest to the men, and particularly the officers, who were members of the upper classes

The ERYY watering the horses on the way to annual camp by train, May 1912
(Author's Collection)

The Yorkshire Mounted Brigade Camp, Salisbury Plain, May-June 1912
(Author's Collection)

from which many of the early aviation pioneers were drawn. One yeoman wrote home:

> "*there is plenty to see and do, there is some flying machines near hand, there is one up now...*" [8]

There was also of course a professional interest, the units sharing a common role of scouting and reconnaissance.

This camp was to be the last under the command of Lieutenant Colonel Stracey-Clitherow, who resigned his commission and retired on the 5th June 1912. Lieutenant Colonel Stracey-Clitherow had played a major part in the formation of the regiment, not least the selection of the Regimental badge, and had been in command since 1908. He was succeeded by his second-in-command Major Philip Langdale, who was promoted to full Lieutenant Colonel. Colonel Stracey-Clitherow was subsequently appointed to the position of Honorary Colonel of the Regiment, in succession to the late Lord Wenlock.

Horses of course were at the absolute core of the regiment's identity, but the very earliest signs of the eventual replacement of the horse in war arrived in June 1913, with the authorisation of a section of seven motorcycle dispatch riders for each Yeomanry regiment. Motorcycles had the potential to allow urgent messages to be delivered more quickly than on horseback, improving command and control, although perhaps being restricted to the roads. As was the case with the horses, riders were expected to provide their own mounts, receiving an allowance of 8s a day to cover expenses, including petrol.

THE LAST SUMMER

The momentous year of 1914 began much like any other. The regiment held the customary round of balls, dinners and prize givings to mark the achievements of the previous year and the usual training programmes continued, including a substantial weekend exercise for 'A' and 'B' Squadrons in April held at Newbald, near Market Weighton.

The exercise was great preparation for annual camp, which was held at York during the latter part of May 1914. The camp site was on the Knavesmire (Bustardthorpe Field), adjacent to the racecourse and around 390 men, under the command of Lieutenant Colonel Langdale, assembled at the site over the opening weekend, although not without mishap. Unfortunately, as 'C' Squadron marched to camp, one of the horses was spooked by a tram and bolted, running some 100 yards out of control before colliding with a tram stand and falling on the rider, a Private Sidney Deighton. He suffered a broken leg and had to be taken to York Military hospital whilst the horse had to be shot.

Following the rather inauspicious start, the first week proceeded with a horse inspection and then the individual, Troop and Squadron drills were carried out. For the new recruits there were lessons in fitting saddles and horsemanship.

As befitting the idea of a long glorious Edwardian summer, the weather was excellent, reported as astonishingly good. As was normally the case when encamped close to a racecourse, there was ample opportunity for the men to attend the various race meetings when not on duty, and the Regimental band played every evening, drawing crowds from York and becoming very popular. The Hull Daily Mail reported:

"in York, garrison town as it is, there seems to be doubt in the minds of many as to who the yeomanry are, and many yeomen come back to camp proud of the fact that they have been taken for regulars". [9]

The second week was rather less enjoyable. The weather took a decided turn for the worst with torrential rain for the majority of the week and, although the campgrounds were reasonably well drained, 'A' Squadron were obliged to move their lines owing to the churned and slippery state of the ground.

Towards the end of the week the weather dried up somewhat, only to be replaced by bitterly cold nights with the plentiful standing water turning to ice. Nevertheless, the training programme continued, progressing to the customary large-scale Regimental field days.

During the period of the camp the Knavesmire was also home to a detachment of the Royal Flying Corps, equipped with four aeroplanes, and the yeomen took the opportunity to gain more knowledge of these still very new flying machines, first encountered during the annual camp of 1912, at close quarters.

With annual camp completed, the men of the East Riding Yeomanry returned to their homes and their places of work as they had done after every annual camp, settling back into the familiar routines of their lives. However, tensions in Europe, which had been rising for several years, were about to reach boiling point and soon nothing would ever be the same again.

THE EAST RIDING YEOMANRY AT CAMP, YORK, MAY 1914
(Author's Collection)

'A' SQUADRON, EAST RIDING YEOMANRY IN FULL-DRESS,
ANNUAL CAMP, YORK, MAY 1914
(Author's Collection)

Chapter 2: The Home Front, 1914-1915

Author's Note:
In contemporary documents the East Riding of Yorkshire Yeomanry was referred to as the 'East Ridings' and this convention has been followed. The regiment itself effectively dropped 'Yorkshire' from their title during the war.

Europe during the summer of 1914 was a powder keg waiting to explode. The continent was, in effect, one huge armed camp simmering with tension as the various empires and newly created nation-states vied for political, military, and economic domination across the world. The industrialisation of Europe in the 19th century had provided the great continental powers of France, Germany, and Russia the means to finance, equip, feed and transport huge armies the likes of which had never been seen before. In 1914, the army of the German Empire was 1.5 million strong and France matched it despite her smaller population; the Russian Army numbered 1.2 million. In times of war, millions of reservists would swell these numbers. The German Empire was also in the throes of a provocative naval arms race with Great Britain, still the world's pre-eminent naval power.

The spark that ignited the world was the assassination, by Gavrilo Princip, of the heir to the Austro-Hungarian throne, Archduke Franz Ferdinand, at Sarajevo in the Austrian province of Bosnia, on 28th June 1914. The assassination itself caused little concern initially (the Archduke was not a popular character, even at home) but through a series of seemingly inevitable events was to lead the world into long and devastating war.

There had long been trouble in the Balkans. There were two wars in the region immediately prior to the First World War, the first in 1912 and another in 1913, during which time Serbia almost doubled her territory. The Slavic people, supported by Russia, were demanding self-determination, and dreaming of a pan-Slavic state in the Balkans (Greater Serbia). This nationalism was causing some unrest in the southern (Slavic) provinces of the Austro-Hungarian Empire, which Vienna feared could spread to the many other ethnic and religious groups within the Empire.

Austria therefore resolved to use the assassination to stamp her authority on the region and forestall any possible action by Serbia. After nearly a month of deliberations, on 23rd July, Austria issued Serbia with an ultimatum. Austria claimed that Serbia was behind the assassination and that the assassins must be brought to justice. The ultimatum was severe, and its demands effectively violated Serbia's sovereignty. In spite of all this, the Serbs essentially agreed to all the demands, except for a few minor clauses.

Nevertheless, the Austrians, who had never intended the ultimatum to be accepted, broke off diplomatic relations with Serbia on the 25th July. After consultations with their ally Germany, who agreed to back Austria (the so-called 'blank cheque'), they declared war on Serbia on the 28th July 1914. Now a tangled web of treaties and alliances came into play.

The Outbreak of War

On the 30th July 1914, Russia, allied to Serbia by a treaty of 1909, began to mobilise her vast army as a precaution. The Germans, as allies of the Austrians, demanded the Russians stand down and that France remain neutral. The Russians refused; unable to only partially mobilise (i.e. against Austria) due to the logistical and organisational difficulties that would entail, Russia felt she had no choice but to continue with a general mobilisation.

This was a major threat to the Germans. Germany had long feared a war against both Russia and France (who were bound together by treaty). What would happen if Russia attacked Austria? Germany would have to support their ally, but then what would France do? Events seemed to be leading inexorably towards Germany having to fight both France and Russia.

The German High Command had already devised a plan to deal with a war on two fronts, however. Originally drawn up in 1906 by Alfred von Schlieffen, the German Army Chief of Staff, the so-called 'Schlieffen Plan' called for a rapid strike at France in the west, knocking her out of the war before the huge Russian Army could mobilise (it was thought, accurately, that it would take 6 weeks for Russia to fully mobilise). To this end, the German mobilisation plan required large numbers of troops to be deployed in an attack on France in the west and not on Russia to the east. To change the plan, reorganise the mobilisation and re-route the trains earmarked to transport the army to France would take many months.

The Germans therefore decided to strike first and declared war on Russia on 1st August. The German Army began mobilisation and occupied neutral Luxembourg to secure the railways required for the fulfilment of the mobilisation plan. In response, the French also began mobilisation. This led, in accordance with the 'Schlieffen Plan', to Germany declaring war on France on the 3rd August.

The 'Schlieffen Plan' relied on an advance through neutral Belgium (a 'right hook') to outflank the French armies positioned on the Franco-German border and to strike at Paris. The Germans issued an ultimatum to Brussels demanding unhindered passage through Belgian territory. They expected Belgium to agree but considered that they would be unable to put up much resistance if they did not. However, the Belgian government immediately ordered the mobilisation of its little army and began the destruction of the bridges along the border with Germany.

Britain, though only loosely allied to France and Russia,

had signed a treaty in 1839 protecting Belgium's neutrality. She therefore issued her own ultimatum on the 3rd August demanding Germany respect Belgian neutrality. Britain was concerned about the prospect of a continent dominated by the German Empire and the threat to the Royal Navy should the Germans secure the channel ports. Ignoring the British ultimatum, German troops crossed into Belgium on the 4th August 1914 and once this was known in London, Britain declared war on Germany.

BRITAIN GOES TO WAR

The mobilisation of the regular British Army was ordered during the afternoon of the 3rd August as it became apparent that a German invasion of Belgium was imminent. News of the subsequent declaration of war on the 4th was met across Britain with a wave of patriotism and pride, echoing what was happening on the continent. Enthusiastic crowds gathered outside Buckingham Palace and across the country, singing the national anthem and waving the union flag. It was all going to be a big adventure, and few believed it would be a long war: it would all be over by Christmas.

The tiny British Army (*'contemptibly small'* according to an often miss-quoted German Kaiser) was put on a war footing. Unlike the continental powers, who had large conscript armies, Britain maintained only a small professional army of volunteers, primarily designed for policing the Empire; in 1914 at least one third of the regular army was stationed abroad, mostly in India. The defence of Britain was, and always had been, largely the responsibility of the Royal Navy, backed up in 1914 by the part-time volunteers of the Territorial Force. However, Britain had not been blind to the increasing military power of Germany and had established a British Expeditionary Force (the 'BEF') consisting of 150,000 men (6 divisions), which could be deployed to the continent should such a necessity arise.

All over the country, reservists began arriving at their depots on the 5th August and the first embarkation orders were issued for the transportation of the BEF to the continent. The initial advanced units would arrive in France, in secret, on the 7th August, followed by the bulk of the BEF, which landed at Dunkirk, Le Havre and Boulogne between the 12th and 17th August. The troopships transporting the BEF across the English Channel were heavily protected by the warships of the Royal Navy. Although there were no treaty obligations establishing what part the BEF would play in any European conflict, it had long been expected that it would take up position on the left of the French line, opposite the Belgian border.

Mobilisation of the Territorial Force

The onset of war caught most Territorial Force units away from home at annual summer camp. The increasing tension in Europe had become apparent over the bank holiday weekend and, following the mobilisation of the regular army on August 3rd, the decision was taken to end the camps early and send the Territorials home. The declaration of war on the 4th led to notices being hastily posted in prominent locations, such as railway stations and public houses, ordering the mobilisation of the Territorials and that evening telegrams were sent out instructing the men to report for duty the following day. Fortunately, the East Ridings had completed their annual camp at York in May and so were spared some of the confusion caused by sending the men home from camp only to call them out again immediately.

The East Ridings began assembling at their mobilisation stations on the 5th August as ordered; 'A' and 'B' Squadrons congregating at Beverley, whilst 'C' Squadron assembled at Fulford in York and 'D' Squadron at Driffield. The Driffield Times reported that:

> "*the yeomanry were ordered to assemble at the Drill Hall, at noon on Wednesday and loyally responded. The greatest enthusiasm has prevailed among the men, and some former members have willingly offered their services and been accepted.*" [1]

With little or no accommodation available in their drill halls, the men were billeted in local pubs or, if they lived locally, sent home on an evening, reporting for duty again the following morning.

One of the most pressing tasks at this time was to equip the regiment with sufficient horses and transport. During peacetime many men (particularly those of the largely urban Hull Squadron) had hired horses for duty and camps or attended on a bicycle and consequently officers were dispatched across the county to purchase enough horses to bring the unit up to strength. Around the country some 165,000 horses would be requisitioned for the Army in the first few weeks of the war. Sergeant Frank Wood remembered:

> "*On August 5th Jack and I went off in good time to the barracks where already small parties of khaki clad figures had gathered and more came in every hour. Oh, the excitement! One officer detailed to buy horses, another to buy or requisition transport, another to find billets and stable room, mobilisation stores issued etc. Several of us had horses to sell, and although we belonged to the regiment and had to ride the horses we sold, we did not get good prices, but who cared, war was declared. The next two days were busy ones, horses and transport had to be collected from the county district, branded and numbered*".[2]

After a few days completing the formalities of mobilisation, the Troops and Squadrons of the regiment began to deploy to their various war stations along the east coast of the county for coastal defence duties. This was the established plan for the regiment which formed part of the York-headquartered Yorkshire Mounted Brigade. Large and enthusiastic crowds gathered to see the men off as they rode out from their hometowns and villages; the Driffield Times reported that as the men of 'D' Squadron left they "*caused (a) considerable stir as they rode through the streets*"[3].

Regimental Headquarters were initially established at Patrington, but soon moved to Withernsea, where the men were billeted in the Queens Hotel and the Pier Hotel. Individual Troops were deployed along the coast, from Flamborough Head in the north to Spurn Point at the mouth of the Humber. The York Troop of 'C' Squadron, for example, occupied the Coastguard station at Aldborough, being billeted in the Temperance

Hotel there, whilst the Pocklington Troop of 'D' Squadron was billeted at Sewerby Park, just north of Bridlington.

With a German landing on the east coast considered a real possibility, sentries were posted at night and mounted patrols, each consisting of a section of four men, were dispatched from the various outposts every hour from dusk until dawn to reconnoitre the coast. Everyone expected a German landing almost immediately and there were numerous alerts, false alarms, and reports of spies signalling ships offshore by flashlight. Sergeant Wood wrote:

> "*knowing the country very well I was often sent out to investigate the origin of flashing lights, usually some lover returning home with a bright bicycle lamp*". [4]

Private Norman Green, of the York Troop, wrote to his brother:

> "*our sentry captured a suspicious looking tramp and handed him over to me while he went for Scottie. I had my rifle cocked and kept him covered. We untied his bundle and searched him but he was alright, so we let him go. We then got a message to say that 2 men had been seen on motor bikes signalling out to sea with the Morse code. They also reported that they had seen somebody signalling from a house window.*" [5]

On another occasion a York Troop patrol spotted what appeared to be two boats, resembling barges or lighters, moored close to the shore near Withernsea and raised the alarm. The 5th Battalion, The Yorkshire Regiment, billeted nearby, stood to and deployed to their action stations. However, a local yeoman soon identified the two suspect 'boats' as an old wreck and the alert was called off. Similarly, on August 12th the Hull Daily Mail reported that 'A' Squadron had been turned out after firing was heard off the coast at Spurn Point:

> "*for nearly an hour they remained on duty, before being ordered back to the various hotels and licensed houses where they are billeted. The usual armed men were left on duty all night, their work in the present crisis being to patrol the coast on horseback for many miles.*" [6]

Private Green, further along the coast, was also turned out:

"we had another scare last night. We intercepted a message saying that heavy firing could be heard 10 miles S.E. of Spurn Head. We nearly all heard it. Lieut. Scott made us stand to our arms and had us all out on the cliffs. It occurred at 1.30 this morning... tell mother she would have been proud of her little sonny to see him buckling on his 100 rounds of ammunition and standing to arms yawning and shivering at 1.30 this morning. I heard Jock Inglis came galloping in, in the moonlight about 2 o'clock to report that he had heard the firing and then away he went again back to his post at Hook's Farm, about 7 miles down the coast" [7]

After about a fortnight, on August 24th, the regiment was ordered to concentrate at Beverley to get properly organised and commence training for war, and the scattered Squadrons and Troops began trekking to their Regimental hometown. Sergeant Wood recalled:

"we enjoyed our duty on the coast, treating it as a game, but now it was work, returns to be sent in by the score". [8]

Unfortunately, at this critical time, the Regimental Sergeant Major, Wilkinson Brown, a member of the 1st Royal Dragoons serving on the permanent staff, died at Railway Street. RSM Brown was a veteran of the Boer War but had been ill with a liver complaint for some time. The adjutant, Captain Tylden-Wright considered:

"his loss to the regiment at a time of crisis like the present is great, and is felt by all ranks". [9]

RSM Brown was buried in St. Martin's Cemetery in Beverley with full military honours on the 26th August, with 'A' and 'B' Squadrons in attendance. As the outlying Troops and Squadrons arrived the men were again billeted in local hotels and hostelries, but this was far from an ideal situation and even before the entire regiment could assemble orders were received to move to a camp at Kilnwick Percy, near Pocklington in the East Riding.

Whilst the Territorials were sorting out the confusion of their mobilisation, elements of the still mobilising German 1st and 2nd Armies (together 'The Army of the Meuse') had already crossed into Belgium. The city of Liège quickly fell, surrendering on the 6th August, but the Belgian Army put up surprisingly stiff resistance, centred on the 12 forts that surrounded the city. The Germans had brought up heavy artillery by the 8th and began the systematic destruction of forts one-by-one. On the 12th the Germans brought in a pair of huge 420mm (16½") Austrian siege guns and the final fort was battered into submission by the 16th. The German 1st and 2nd Armies were now free to resume their march and were soon pouring into central Belgium, rapidly advancing towards Brussels and Namur, and forcing the Belgian Army to withdraw to Antwerp.

On the 20th August the Germans entered Brussels and were shelling the fortified towns of Charleroi and Namur. Facing this onslaught was the overstretched French Fifth Army and on its left, concentrated around Mauberge, the newly arrived BEF. The Germans did not know the British were there, nor did the British know the location or strength of the Germans. Early on the morning of the 23rd August, the BEF cavalry screen stumbled into the lead elements of the German 1st Army in front of the Belgian town of Mons, and the first British shots of the war were fired. The two divisions of the BEF's II Corps now found themselves in the path of six German divisions.

The British soldiers in their positions before Mons were highly trained professionals, pre-war regulars many of whom were veterans of the Boer War and of service in numerous colonial campaigns. They had learnt the lessons of the Boer War the hard way; they had adopted Khaki uniforms to be less conspicuous (unlike many units of the French and Belgian Armies that still wore bright coloured tunics or trousers); appreciated the firepower afforded by machine guns and magazine-fed rifles accurately used; and the importance of 'digging in' for protection. The BEF of 1914, the 'Old Contemptibles', were (and still are) considered by many to be the best trained, best prepared, and best equipped force to ever leave the shores of Britain.

The Germans advanced towards Mons in close order, not much different from their forefathers in the Franco-Prussian War

A PAIR OF EAST RIDING YEOMANRY CORPORALS, KILNWICK PERCY,
POCKLINGTON, OCTOBER 1914
(Author's Collection)

A GROUP OF YEOMEN AT MEALTIME AT KILNWICK PERCY, POCK-
LINGTON, SEPTEMBER 1914
(Author's Collection)

45 years before. They presented easy targets and suffered heavy casualties at the hands of the BEF, famously trained to fire 15 *aimed* rounds a minute from their rifles (whose magazines contained only 10 rounds, necessitating a reload). There are many accounts of the Germans believing they were being attacked by numerous machine guns or by units much larger than those actually involved. Nevertheless, the BEF were outnumbered and after the Germans brought up artillery and machine guns, they were forced to give ground. To the south the commander of the French Fifth Army had given the order to withdraw from Charleroi and the British, who had hoped to continue the fight the following morning, were forced to pull back to prevent being left exposed.

As the outnumbered Allies fell back the BEF's I Corps, who had escaped action at Mons, mounted a day-long stand at Le Cateau on the 26th and the French likewise at Guise on the 29th August, but these were nothing more than delaying actions and the retreat continued.

The Expansion of the Territorial Force

As the opening battles of the War on the Western Front began, the East Ridings assembled at their new camp at Kilnwick Percy Hall to reorganise and commence training for war service. Here the horses were picketed in the open, as at annual camp, and the men were housed in various outbuildings, such as the granaries and cart sheds, whilst the officers were billeted in the hall itself.

The men were full of enthusiasm and wanted a chance to join the war before it was over. There was however, one significant issue that had to be addressed. Generally, men enlisting in the Territorial Force were volunteering for Home Service only, although they were encouraged to sign the 'Imperial Service' pledge, whereby they would serve overseas in a national emergency. This meant that the regiment contained a mix of men that would serve aboard and men that would not. Harold Lyon recalled:

"now came the time for the separation for those of us who had offered to serve overseas, from those who had chosen otherwise. At first there were only enough men to form one Service Squadron – three parts or so of which I'm proud to say came from the peacetime 'D' Squadron". [10]

Sergeant Frank Wood also recalled:

"they started to pick out the volunteers for foreign service and put them into one squadron which was called the first Service Squadron, most of these were 'D' Squadron men. Then came recruits from Beverley and the second Service Squadron was formed, then 'A' Squadron volunteered and became the 3rd Service Squadron". [11]

It seems that at least some of the men were asked to volunteer by their Squadron leaders prior to arriving at Kilnwick Percy; Sergeant Wood remarked that, whilst still at Beverley:

"an order came round asking for volunteers for foreign service. I am pleased to say my section volunteered to a man although quite a number in the squadrons held back, but to give the men credit I think it was through not being properly asked by their officers". [12]

The result was three new 'Service Squadrons', containing those agreeing to serve overseas and a 'Reserve Squadron' for Home Service, consisting of those men that did not volunteer or were considered unfit, too young or too old for foreign service. The horses and equipment of the Home Service men were taken and used to equip the 'Service Squadrons'. The 'Reserve Squadron' was sent back to Beverley where some of those deemed unfit or too old for continued service were discharged from the Army.

Shortly after the declaration of war the new Minister of War, Field Marshal Lord Kitchener (who predicted a long conflict which would require a large continental-style army), issued a call for 100,000 volunteers to form a 'New Army' (also commonly known as 'Kitchener's Army'). Encouraged by the famous recruiting poster featuring the Field Marshal, hundreds of thousands answered the call, swamping recruiting offices, town halls and Police stations. The response was overwhelming, and the required number of men came forward in only three weeks;

over 750,000 had volunteered by September and one million by December 1914.

In fact, a substantial number of those who volunteered chose to join their local Territorial Force unit; because it was their local unit, to join friends or family already serving, or because of the perceived home defence role of the force. The Hull Daily Mail reported on the 4th September that since mobilisation 250 men had joined the East Ridings and that there were another 100 at the depot awaiting orders.

Consequently, there were soon enough new volunteers and returning ex-members to expand the Reserve Squadron to full regimental strength. The three Service Squadrons therefore formed a new Service Regiment under command of Lieutenant Colonel Guy Wilson, to be designated the 1/1st East Riding of Yorkshire Yeomanry, whilst the new second-line regiment would become the 2/1st East Riding of Yorkshire Yeomanry (pronounced as the First-First and Second-First respectively) under the command of Lieutenant Colonel Philip Langdale. The intention was that the second-line regiment would provide training and replacements for the first-line regiment, which would proceed overseas.

The new 1/1st East Riding of Yorkshire Yeomanry comprised a Regimental Headquarters, a Machine Gun Section and the three Service Squadrons (now identified as 'A', 'B' and 'C' Squadrons). Regimental Headquarters was the home of the support services such as the Medical Officer and his orderlies, the Veterinary Officer, the Signals Officer and his Signallers, the Orderly Room Clerk and the Quartermaster and his storemen (responsible for supplies and provisions). Headquarters also controlled the Machine Gun Section (consisting of two Maxim Machine Guns and their crews under a Subaltern).

Each of the Squadrons was commanded by a Major, with a Captain as his second-in-Command and comprised four Troops (numbered 1–4). Each Troop was commanded by a Subaltern and was made up of four Sections of four men each. In total the approved strength, including attached personnel, was 26 Officers

A GROUP OF NEW RECRUITS C. SEPTEMBER 1914. MANY OF THE MEN WEAR ERY CAP OR COLLAR BADGES ON THEIR LAPELS AS AN INDICATION OF THEIR AFFILIATION; THERE WERE INSUFFICIENT UNIFORMS FOR THE INFLUX OF VOLUNTEERS (Author's Collection)

and 523 Other Ranks (ORs).

With the regiment now reorganised for overseas service an intense training programme could begin. Private Hairsine, although ultimately wrong on the timescales, summed up the situation of the regiment when he wrote to a friend:

> "*I hope many of my old school chums are on the same footing. We are for foreign service after 3 to 6 months of training*". [13]

In the case of the East Ridings this training was badly needed. The regiment had been somewhat under strength in 1914 (for example, there were only 19 officers at the outbreak of war compared to the pre-war establishment of 26) and their ranks had been swollen with recent volunteers, including several young officers, who had little or no previous military, and in some cases, riding, experience. Private Jimmy Seddon, himself a raw recruit, considered that:

> "*the officers in charge, although accomplished horsemen themselves were young and inexperienced at manoeuvring troops.*" [14]

This was amply demonstrated during an exercise when two Troops collided during manoeuvres, which resulted in Private Seddon being thrown from his horse and leaving him in hospital for seven weeks. This meant the novice horseman missed the all-important Regimental riding school arranged for the less experienced riders.

As well as a riding school and drill there was training in the other basic military skills required of a cavalryman: musketry and sword drills. Swords had not officially been part of the equipment of a pre-war yeomanry regiment, but there is ample photographic evidence that swords were carried (and presumably sword drills practiced) in the years preceding the war, so they would not have been entirely foreign to the yeomen.

Despite the rigours of living in rough conditions (at Kilnwick Percy Private Seddon's Troop was billeted in an old cowshed) and the constant training, life for the yeomen was good; summertime training close to home was just like an extended annual camp. Sergeant Eric Burch noted:

A SECOND GROUP OF NEW RECRUITS C. SEPTEMBER 1914. MANY OF THE MEN WEAR ERY CAP OR COLLAR BADGES ON THEIR LAPELS AS AN INDICATION OF THEIR AFFILIATION; THERE WERE INSUFFICIENT UNIFORMS FOR THE INFLUX OF VOLUNTEERS (Author's Collection)

"we had quite a good time there and father used to motor Gerry and I home nearly every Sunday". [15]

Fellow Sergeant Frank Wood, with the Machine Gun Section at nearby Warter Priory recalled:

"what a pleasant time we had here although we did a lot of training which was very necessary, most of the men being new to the guns. I had two or three days off duty with the Colonel's shooting parties. How I so enjoyed leading for the pheasant drives in the famous golden valley and at times having the privilege of a few shots".[16]

On the Western Front

In France the Allied retreat continued in good order and with the delaying actions at Mons, Le Cateau and Guise slowing the pace of the German 'right hook', a gap was beginning to develop between the German 1st Army (on the far right of the advance) and the 2nd Army on its left. The 1st Army therefore had to turn south-eastwards to close the gap and maintain contact with the 2nd Army. This meant that they would pass to the east, rather than to the west, of Paris, as was intended by the 'Schlieffen' Plan. In addition, the Germans believed that the BEF had been destroyed at Le Cateau (it hadn't) and that by moving south-east they could turn the flank of the French line. In fact, this manoeuvre unwittingly exposed the flank of the German advance to a possible attack from the area around Paris.

The Battle of the Marne began of the 5th September 1914 when elements of the French Sixth Army encountered the German 1st Army north of Meaux. Sensing the danger to the German flank the local German commander, General von Gronau, launched an immediate counterattack by his Reserve Corps (the only German forces facing the French in this sector) the following day. These attacks forced the French Sixth Army to halt. Reinforcements from the Paris garrison were rushed to the battlefield in commandeered Parisian taxis; the situation was saved, and a legend was born.

The Germans, aware of the threat to their flanks, began to redeploy the 1st Army to meet the unexpected French attacks.

This finally broke any links with the 2nd Army on the left and opened a 30-mile gap between them. It was into this gap that the now reinforced BEF and the French Fifth Army advanced on the 9th September. News that the BEF had crossed the river Marne and were advancing virtually unopposed led the German High Command to order a retreat to the line of the river Aisne. The 'Schlieffen' Plan, with its hopes of a swift victory in the west, was dead.

The Germans reached the high ground to the north of the river Aisne on the 13th September and began to dig in. Fresh troops arrived to plug the gap between the 1st and 2nd Armies and by the time the advancing Allies arrived a basic trench line had been established. During the initial attacks, the BEF managed to get across the river, but little real progress was made and by the 14th September the Allies had begun to dig in themselves. Trench warfare had arrived.

With the main forces entrenched opposite one another each side now attempted to turn the open flank (to the north) of the other. The series of encounters that followed would become known as 'The Race to the Sea' although the sea was the ultimate target of neither side. Throughout September and into October the opposing armies moved north trying to advance faster than the other and make it into the ever-decreasing gap between the front lines to the south and the Channel coast.

Further north the Germans finally captured Antwerp on October 10th whence the Belgian Army had retreated in August. This thorn in their side removed, the German High Command now resolved to capture the channel ports of Dunkirk, Calais and Boulogne, ports vital to the BEF. The German 4th Army attacked the new Belgian positions along the Yser River, from Nieuport on the coast to Dixmunde, on the 16th October, eventually forcing King Albert to order the locks along the Yser opened, flooding the area north of Dixmunde. This forced the German advance to turn south in search of firmer ground, towards the Belgian town of Ypres.

Ypres, a medieval market town set on the wet plain of Flanders, sat in the midst of the narrow open corridor that remained between the Belgian positions on the coast and the Allied lines to the south, behind Lille. It held the key to the Channel ports and in consequence, between the 8th and the 19th October the BEF (again reinforced and expanded to five Corps) was deployed to plug the gap.

Heavy fighting commenced on 20th October as a major German offensive was launched along the whole Flanders front. The outnumbered BEF (seven infantry and three cavalry divisions against fourteen German) held a salient around Ypres that was exposed to German fire on three sides. During fierce fighting they succeeded in defeating repeated German assaults, their professionalism and marksmanship again taking a terrible toll on the German attackers, comprised mostly of fresh, barely trained volunteers who had joined up in August 1914. The German Army lost 50,000 dead, compared to 24,000 British killed.

The fighting continued into November (the official date for the end of the battle is the 22nd November) but eventually exhaustion and the onset of winter brought the fighting on the Western Front in 1914 to a close. Everywhere everyone began to dig in. An almost continuous line of trenches now stretched from the Belgian coast at Nieuport south to the Swiss border.

The First Battle of Ypres signalled the end of the original pre-War BEF. The intense fighting throughout the summer of 1914 had left almost half the pre-War BEF as casualties; some 30,000 had been killed and 50,000 wounded. Severe as these figures were for the British, they pale into insignificance when compared to the losses of the Germans and the French; 240,000 and 300,000 dead respectively.

THE EAST RIDINGS MOVE NORTH

As winter approached it was apparent that, since Kitchener's Army was still largely untrained and ill equipped, if equipped at all, Territorial Force units would have to make good the losses suffered by the BEF. As more units prepared to leave for France and Flanders, the Yorkshire Mounted Brigade was broken up and its constituent units dispersed. The Yorkshire Hussars and Yorkshire Dragoons were themselves split up and their squadrons distributed between various infantry divisions destined for the continent.

The East Ridings, their ranks filled with a substantial number of recent volunteers, were not considered ready for deployment and were to remain together as a unit, becoming the divisional cavalry regiment of the 2nd Northumbrian Division which was headquartered at Newcastle. They were destined to remain at home for a while longer. After a lavish send off at Warter Priory (home of Charles Wilson, 1st Baron Nunburnholme, father of the Colonel, Guy Wilson) the regiment moved to north, to Northumberland, on the 4th November. Sergeant Wood wrote:

> "we had to pack up and be at Pocklington station to entrain at 8am... On arrival at the station, I entrained the section on the headquarters train and away we started. It was awfully foggy that day so we could not tell where we were going except that we were heading north. At 4.30pm our train stopped at a small station which we discovered to be Chester-le-Street near Durham. We detrained and trekked away down the road, what a country; imagine a colliery district at 4.30pm on a November day, with a thick fog - however, we soon reached our destination which proved to be at Bowes House Farm, the home farm of the Lampton Castle estate. The horses were stabled in wagon sheds and we slept in granaries over them while the officers took up their quarters at Bidwick Hall, a mile away. How cold it was here, sometimes snow on the ground and we had to wash out in the yard in the early mornings, but we were soldiers now and although we groused – which is a soldier's privilege – we took it all as we found it and didn't really mind the discomforts." [17]

Whilst Regimental Headquarters was located at Bowes House Farm near Fencehouses, the remainder of the regiment was stationed at various locations along the coast, with Squadrons being based (at various times) at Seaham Harbour (Seaham Hall), Bedlington, Shotton Hall (the horses were stabled at the nearby Castle Eden Brewery) and Newbiggin-by-the-Sea.

The regiment was now part of the Tyne Garrison, which had responsibility for the defence of the Northeast coast from

Seaham Harbour to Newcastle. Consequently, the East Ridings spent the winter of 1914-1915 on coastal defence duties, much the same as they had along the East Yorkshire coast in the autumn, digging trenches and gun positions and mounting patrols along the coast.

Coastal Defence duties might have lacked the perceived glory and adventure of the war on the continent, but they were nevertheless seen as important. The threat of German invasion was foremost in the minds of the government and the general population. The threat of German invasion reached its peak in mid-November 1914; the fighting around Ypres threatened the Channel ports (a suitable base from which to mount an invasion) and several German ships had bombarded Great Yarmouth on the 3rd (although without much effect).

There was a major scare on the 20th November when a German invasion fleet was reported to have left Kiel and many units along the southern and eastern coasts were turned out to man their positions during the night. The reports were false however and the men were soon stood down again. There was another alarm on the 1st December when at 1:30am the regiment was called out, *"saddle up and turn out was the order,"* remembered Sergeant Wood:

> *"and away we trekked in the darkness, our first experience of night marching and we had little thought then how many weary hours we should spend night marching in future – at about 5am we arrived at Sunderland where we put our horses under the football grandstand and waited with what patience we could command. No one seemed to know what the game was, some said an invasion, but no, at 1.30pm 'A' Squadron and the MG section trekked off again to Seaham Hall on the coast, while headquarters returned to Bowes House farm."* [18]

Then on the 16th December the German Navy returned, this time to bombard Scarborough, Whitby and Hartlepool. Several ships shelled Scarborough, damaging the castle, before moving onto Whitby whilst a second force consisting of 2 Battlecruisers and a light Cruiser made for the more important port of Hartlepool. At around 4am the alarm was raised and once again the

A GROUP OF 1/1ST EAST RIDING YEOMANRY OFFICERS, SEAHAM
HALL, C. DECEMBER 1914
L–R: 2nd Lieutenant J Lee Smith, 2nd Lieutenant H D P Francis,
Lieutenant H P Parker, Captain J D White, Lieutenant R W R Scott,
2nd Lieutenant J R Lloyd (Author's Collection)

MEN OF THE 1/1ST EAST RIDING YEOMANRY 'SHAVING'
AT SHOTTON HALL, C. DECEMBER 1914
(Author's Collection)

garrison stood to, including the East Ridings.

'B' Squadron, stationed not far from Hartlepool at Shotton Hall near Peterlee, received the order to saddle up with all haste and make for the village of Blackhall Rocks as fast as their horses could carry them. The German warships were able to get in close under the cover of an early morning fog and began to bombard the town at 8:10am. The East Ridings could see the flashes of the guns from their positions on the cliff tops but could not see the ships.

The Germans withdrew 40 minutes later having fired 1,150 shells causing damage to the steelworks, the gasworks, 7 churches and 300 homes, and killing 86 and wounding 424. Another 19 were killed and 101 wounded during the bombardments of Scarborough and Whitby.

This was the first time that British civilians had been killed on home soil by enemy action in nearly 250 years. There was a public outcry, and 'Remember Scarborough' became a strong recruiting tool in the coming months. For the East Ridings however, the major consequence was the cancellation of Christmas leave. Deprived of their furlough the men went out and got drunk. According to Jimmy Seddon:

> "*on Christmas morning there was a church parade and a minor route march to a church which was an appreciable distance from the billets. What a weary looking lot! The hang-overs! The officer in charge called a halt once or twice for a rest which was grimly needed. I suspect that the officers were not feeling too good either.*" [19]

However, as the end of the year approached the failure of the German offensive in Flanders and the onset of winter weather meant that the threat of invasion diminished, at least in the short term, and the East Ridings were able to concentrate on their training. Private Leonard May remembered that:

> "*away from the mines the county was very pretty and the 'Deans' were lovely grassy hills with a stream between the two. Our Troop officer Lieut. Sykes used to take us over these Deans. It was follow my leader and it really made good riders of us*". [20]

Private James Seddon also recalled:

> "an *amusing incident which occurred while we were in that part of the country was when Charles Lyon (Captain at the time) was giving us some tips on the art of jumping. He told you that we should make up our minds that we were going over the jump and to let the horse know that we were determined about it. To demonstrate this, he put his horse at a hedge – Charles jumped but the horse didn't, and he landed on his behind in front of us. He had to grin, and he said, 'Well not exactly like that'. Needless to say, we had a hearty laugh".* [21]

In addition to honing their riding skills there was training in signalling, map reading, musketry, sword and bayonet drills, and shooting practise on the rifle range or out to sea from on the cliff tops. There were also numerous training exercises, or 'schemes' as they were known. All this was made harder by the winter weather, Sergeant Wood remarking that 'A' Squadron:

> "*turned out on parade each morning spotlessly clean and went to drill in a field which soon became six inches deep in mud, but they stuck it like men, turning out spotless clean every morning"*. [22]

As always it wasn't all training and hard work, there were numerous sports and games, including horseback sports (VC races, tent pegging etc.), for the men to enjoy, as well as concerts and trips to the local towns such as Sunderland and Hartlepool.

1915 – The Strategic Situation

By the end of 1914, it was obvious to all the major combatants that the war would not be over by Christmas. For the Germans the hope of a quick victory in the west, before turning to deal with Russia in the east, had died at the Battle of the Marne. Despite repulsing the Russian forces that had invaded Prussia on the eastern front (at the Battle of Tannenberg in August 1914), the huge Russian armies remained essentially undefeated and posed a serious threat, not only to Germany, but to the Austrians, who had performed poorly in the eastern campaigns of 1914 and were in serious danger of collapse.

As a consequence, the German strategy for 1915 was to remain on the defensive in the west, holding their positions in

France and Belgium to concentrate on the eastern front, in the hope of inflicting a decisive blow against Russia. A successful campaign in the east would also have the effect of propping up the faltering Austro-Hungarian Empire and might influence the governments of Italy, Bulgaria and Romania to either join the Central Powers or dissuade them from joining the allies.

For the French it was much more straightforward. The enemy occupied large parts of their country, including some of the most important industrial regions and that could not be allowed to continue; they must recapture their lost territory. Beginning in December the French mounted a series of winter offensives along the Western Front, but these all failed to break through the German lines and caused more than 250,000 casualties. It was apparent that it was going to take more men, more artillery, and more shells to break the deadlock.

These lessons were particularly difficult for the British. The bulk of the pre-war BEF was gone and time was needed for Kitchener's volunteer New Army to be brought to the field. The Territorials could fill the gap, together with reinforcements from India and the Dominions, but it was going to take a significant amount of time before sufficient men and materiel would be available. This effectively limited the role that Britain would be able to play on the Western Front in 1915, where most believed the war must be won. So instead, the British government began to look for other ways to use their limited resources.

The entry into the war of the Turkish Ottoman Empire, on the side of the Central Powers, in October 1914 provided one possible opportunity. Obviously, the greatest asset available to the British was the Royal Navy, undisputed master of the seas for a century but largely inactive in the war so far. Winston Churchill, First Lord of the Admiralty, championed an amphibious attack on the Dardanelles, the straits that separate Europe and Asia and control access to the Black Sea. This plan had three objectives: give the Royal Navy an offensive role in the war; knock Turkey out of the war thereby opening a supply route to the Russians; and to persuade Italy, Bulgaria, Greece, and other neutrals to join the Allies.

British attention was further drawn to the east in February 1915 when the Turks launched an attack across the Sinai desert aimed at the Suez Canal, that vital artery of Empire. A force of 20,000 made the arduous crossing of the Sinai desert, no mean feat, but the attack was repulsed with heavy Turkish casualties (2,000) and light British ones (32) but the threat from Turkey was now real.

Gallipoli

The first attempts to force the Dardanelles took place on the 19th February 1915 and again on the 26th, when the Allies bombarded the forts at the entrance to the Dardanelles. These attacks caused little damage and served only to forewarn the Turks that an attack was imminent.

The main naval attack was launched on 18th March 1915, when some 17 British and French battleships entered the straits, engaging the Turkish coastal batteries. However, as the force moved up the straits six ships hit mines laid by the Turks and the navy withdrew. Mobile artillery batteries that had escaped the naval bombardment (they were difficult to identify and could be quickly moved to new positions once they had been spotted) posed a major threat to the minesweepers and without the minefields being cleared, the navy was unwilling to risk more ships. It was decided that a full-scale landing would have to be made to clear the batteries before the minesweepers could in turn clear the minefields.

Lord Kitchener agreed to the formation of a Mediterranean Expeditionary Force (MEF) on the 26th March. It was to comprise the Australian and New Zealand units currently in Egypt en route to Britain, a French Colonial division, and a single British infantry division (the 29th Division), in all some 78,000 men. The preparations for the attack didn't go well; incorrect packing of the transport ships resulted in a month's delay and the fact that an attack was likely was hardly a secret. The Turks used the time to strengthen the previously lightly held Gallipoli peninsular, sending an additional 85,000 men commanded by a German, General Liman von Sanders, as reinforcements.

The Allies finally landed on Gallipoli on the 25th April, at a spot subsequently named ANZAC Cove (after the Australian and New Zealand Army Corps which made up the bulk of the MEF) and Cape Helles. At ANZAC Cove, 15,000 Australians and New Zealanders were put ashore largely unopposed. Unfortunately, the landing force didn't immediately press on from the landing beaches and the Turks quickly occupied the dominating high ground, pinning them in a narrow beachhead. There was stiffer resistance at Cape Helles where the Turkish defenders caused heavy casualties amongst the men of the 29th Division on the beaches. By the end of the day, the Allies had established five slender beachheads, but they were effectively blocked by the Turks.

The Allies launched a series of attacks over the next few weeks, each time they were repulsed with heavy losses and by May 8th stalemate had set in. The Turks now launched their own counterattacks aimed at driving the invaders into the sea and the battle turned into one of attrition, with heavy losses on both sides for very little gain. By the end of May 1915, the Allied force had lost nearly a third of its strength and those that remained were struggling with the summer heat, the ever-present flies, and rampant disease and dysentery. Further attacks were mounted in June which were also repulsed by the Turks.

Back on the Home Front

A world away from Gallipoli the East Ridings had spent a dreary winter in Northumberland. The ongoing demands of the Western Front for more men meant that the 2nd Northumbrian Division, for whom the East Ridings were acting as divisional cavalry, was chronically under strength. Many of the best men had been drafted to the first-line battalions of the original 1st Northumbrian Division to make good the losses suffered in the Allied offensives on the Western Front in the spring. Despite this, the division was able to parade some 40,000 men on Town

Moor, Newcastle on the 20th May, before the King George V and Lord Kitchener. The Newcastle Journal described the review:

> "*There were many impressive and stirring scenes, and the march past the saluting base was a most inspiring spectacle. Public interest in the review was widespread and there were thousands of people on and in the vicinity of the Town Moor. Both the King and Lord Kitchener expressed their gratification at the conduct and bearing of the troops*". [23]

The East Ridings proudly led the parade, Jimmy Seddon recalling:

> "*I was the end man of our particular column and I got a good view of them. The horses had become restive after the long wait and mine pranced as we rode past but I had it well under control. I could not but notice how small the King appeared to be beside the Earl. The latter was a very tall and soldiery looking man*" [24]

Private Leonard May thought it was:

> "*a tiring, miserable day and* (I) *only saw the dear old General for a second as we trotted by*". [25]

According to the Deputy Lord Lieutenant of the East Riding, Colonel Lambert White, who was a member of the King's party, the King was delighted with the bearing and condition of the yeomanry and remarked that he had never seen a finer body of men.

Nevertheless, despite the impressive show, it was apparent that the division, largely untrained and short of equipment of every kind (some units had had to borrow rifles for the parade), would not be ready for deployment for a considerable time. Consequently, the divisional artillery was transferred to the new Royal Naval Division and the East Ridings were ordered south to join the North Midland Mounted Brigade, a pre-war Territorial yeomanry brigade.

Almost as soon as the parade was over the regiment began their relocation to East Anglia, mounting a week-long trek south to Filey. The regiment rode to Wolviston, north of the River Tees, where there were billeted the first night. Once across the river they were to engage in war games (referred to as 'sham fighting' at the time) with the Yorkshire Hussars; the East Ridings playing the role of the advanced guard of an invading force and the Hussars that of the defenders.

The regiment trekked to Stokesley and then onwards through the Cleveland Hills to Helmsley, all the while attempting to avoid the Hussars. By keeping off the main routes, the East Ridings managed to dodge the enemy and arrived unscathed at their camp at Duncombe Park, Helmsley. Here the CO was told that the Hussars were encamped at Gilling Castle, five miles south of Helmsley, and a sortie was mounted in order to try to surprise them. The regiment rode through the night arriving at Gilling Castle at first light and caught a Squadron of the Hussars at breakfast and promptly captured the lot.

The following day the regiment marched to Pickering and there being no encounters with the Hussars, it was a pleasant ride through the countryside. The next day the regiment began the last leg of the march, to Filey. All went well until they reached Seamer, where the Hussars, who were hiding behind some high walls, ambushed them.

The Hussars opened fire and the regiment was ordered to the gallop immediately, but the road was wet and slippery and one of the leading horses lost its footing and fell. The horse of the leading Troop Sergeant was next and, in the confusion, another 20 men and horses fell on top of one another in a heap. One sergeant, Sergeant Duffield, was dragged along the road, his foot trapped in his stirrup, and another, Sergeant Hudson, was knocked unconscious. In the end, twenty men were taken to Scarborough hospital and a number of horses were injured.

The regiment remained at Filey for around a fortnight and during their short stay the men were billeted in private homes and boarding houses which came as a welcome relief after living under canvas for several months; for Bill Austin *"it was a treat to have a proper bed, and in a bedroom"*[26]. The regiment spent their days training, both inland and on the expanse of sand at low tide, which provided ample room for the exercising of the entire

THE 1/1ST EAST RIDING YEOMANRY ON THE BEACH AT FILEY,
MAY 1915
(Crimlisk Fisher Archive)

MEN OF THE EAST RIDING YEOMANRY AT STABLES, WESTERN
AVENUE, FILEY, MAY 1915
(Crimlisk Fisher Archive)

regiment, around 500 horses.

On the 6th June 1915 the regiment continued their journey south, travelling by train to Thetford in Norfolk. The journey was very long and tiring, stopping at York, Doncaster, Lincoln (where the horses were fed and watered), Spalding and March in Cambridgeshire, taking some 12 hours.

After a few days, the regiment moved onto Diss, to join their new brigade, 1/1st North Midland Mounted Brigade, part of the 1st Mounted Division. The main memory of Diss as far as Jimmy Seddon was concerned was the local cider:

> "We had been out on an exercise all morning after which we felt hot and thirsty. A bunch of us went to a pub and started drinking the stuff. It was about the colour of dark beer and unfortunately, we had the mistaken notion that we could treat it like lemonade. We drank quite a lot of it before we returned to the billets. There we laid down for a nap. It was a little more than a nap as we passed out as though we had absorbed an anaesthetic. We could not be roused for afternoon stables and it is a wonder we were not in trouble."[27]

Around a fortnight later, the regiment moved on to Riddlesworth Hall, pitching camp in the adjoining park. Leonard May remembered:

> "this was a lovely place for me, a farmer, as the home farm of 1000 acres was just near. A few of us farmers spent our time watching the farming… the countryside around was very beautiful and we had some lovely rides. The woods were full of pheasants and partridges galore. I remember one night after leaving the girls and walking back to camp the pheasants began to cry out and when we looked up, in the distance we could discern the outlines of German Zeps (Zeppelin airships). They had been to Lowestoft. We got back to camp foot-haste and took shelter." [28]

The regiment's stay at Riddlesworth was cut short by a plague of horseflies. These tended to attack at dusk (on one evening causing a stampede amongst the horses), and so a more suitable location had to be found. That turned out to be the imposing (but until requisitioned for the war effort, abandoned) Gothic pile of Costessey Hall, on the outskirts of Norwich, to where the regiment relocated during the first week of July 1915. The regiment pitched their camp in the grounds; it would be their home for the next four months. Private Bill Austin remembered:

> *"We liked Cossey as it is called, pleasant camp, nice weather, a small river adjoining the camp where we could bathe daily".* [29]

Private Seddon similarly recalled:

> *"When we first arrived there, we erected our tents in a large field not far from the Hall. Actually, it was a meadow and the grass was long. It seemed to me that it was a pity to trample it all down. The surrounding countryside was lovely and Costessey Hall a beautiful example of the stately homes of England."* [30]

At Costessey the regiment's training continued, with cross-country rides and more 'sham fighting'. The men also had to take turns doing guard duty at Norwich railway station. During their off-duty time the public houses of Norwich were a popular destination and there was the nearby river Wensum for bathing, with diving from the bridge. There was also the nearby Norfolk Broads, for both pleasure and training. Private May recalled:

> *"One of our most enjoyable rides was to the Broads. Our training was to get across a river by stripping our horses and ourselves, we wrapped our clothes in a canvas bag, next we had to make a raft of sorts to take them over and then we had to get the horses across. We went to a place called Horning Ferry and we had to force the horses into the water from the ferry. It was a tough job; some of us took a raft across and others the horses... we managed it and dried ourselves behind a haystack or something. I remember a raft or two sinking and a job to fish them out."* [31]

Throughout the summer, the government had been deliberating over what to do about Gallipoli; should the peninsular be evacuated or reinforced? Evacuation was politically the less desirable option as it would damage the Allies' reputation within the Middle East and with those neutral countries wavering on the periphery. It would also be practically difficult during the short nights of the summer (any evacuation would have to take place under the cover of darkness) and so the decision was reached to reinforce the MEF instead and renew the campaign. Despite the demands of the Western Front, the MEF would be expanded to over 500,000 men and a new offensive launched.

Rumours that the East Ridings would be sent east were already rife. More and more units, including some yeomanry regiments, were being despatched to Gallipoli, and also to Egypt in order to bolster the defences of the Suez Canal against the Turks. And so it was that during one morning roll call in September the East Ridings were told they were to lose their horses and be retrained as infantry to reinforce the effort at Gallipoli.

The horses were taken away on the 17th September to be looked after by neighbouring units and with their horses gone, the regiment was re-equipped with new uniforms and infantry equipment. There were new infantry skills to learn including bayonet drills (rather than sword drills), and consequently a new training regime was instigated. The big differences were the route marches and the all-important trench digging. The training was physical and hard; one yeoman wrote home:

"we seem to be having a rather hard time, but it is a very nice break after having so little to do." [32]

It would stand the men in good stead in the future.

On the plus side the men were happy to be relieved of the need for grooming, cleaning saddles and all the cavalry equipment they had previously been responsible for and at the prospect of finally getting into the war. The weather was initially very wet but soon began to warm up which was a pleasant change from the Northumbrian winter. One yeoman wrote to a friend:

"the weather is getting hotter, but one consolation we are living very well indeed now". [33]

Another consolation was the chance of embarkation leave, given to those about to be sent overseas and most of the men had the opportunity to return home to visit their friends and loved ones.

Members of 'B' Squadron, 1/1st East Riding Yeomanry, Riddlesworth Park, June 1915
(Author's Collection)

The Four Troops Sergeants of 'B' Squadron, 1/1st East Riding Yeomanry, Riddlesworth Park, June 1915
(Author's Collection)

Following the arrival of 20,000 reinforcements (including some dismounted yeomanry regiments) during July, the Allies renewed their offensive on Gallipoli on the night of the 6th August 1915. An attack was to be launched from ANZAC Cove northwards towards the heights commanding the area, supported by a new landing of an additional 20,000 men further along the peninsula at Suvla Bay, in an attempt to outflank the Turkish defenders.

The initial landing at Suvla Bay went well; the beaches were largely undefended and the landings unopposed. However, once again the troops, without clear orders and lacking sufficient artillery and water supplies, failed to advance from the beachhead towards the lightly defended ridge located inland behind the beaches.

As the British dallied on the plain, the Turks rushed reinforcements to the area and secured the ridge. An attempt was made to breakout on the 8th but advancing over open terrain the British suffered heavy casualties and were forced back to their start lines.

To the south the attack from ANZAC cove (and a diversionary attack launched at Cape Helles) quickly degenerated into savage hand-to-hand fighting. Fierce fighting raged as the Turks mounted numerous desperate counterattacks. The offensive inevitably ground to a halt on the 10th August. Stalemate once again set in; the Allies once again left with little to show for the loss of 30,000 casualties.

The government was once more left wondering what to do about Gallipoli. The MEF commander, General Ian Hamilton, requested yet more reinforcements. Government support for the operation was diminishing now that it was clear that a decisive victory was not to be forthcoming, and the government offered only a quarter of those Hamilton asked for. Whilst the final decision to abandon the Gallipoli campaign and evacuate the peninsula would not be taken until the end of October, it was abundantly clear that the operation was as good as over. Hamilton was sacked.

THE MEN OF 'B' SQUADRON TAKE A DIP IN THE RIVER WENSUM,
COSTESSEY, AUGUST 1915
(Author's Collection)

THE EAST RIDING SERGEANTS ON THE NORFOLK BROADS,
SEPTEMBER 1915
(Author's Collection)

In any case, attention was now turning to affairs in the Balkans.

SERBIA

Serbia, the Balkan nation where the events that had sparked the war were played out in June 1914, had successfully defeated three Austrian invasions during 1914. Yet the country had paid a high price for these heroics and was close to collapse. The fighting had taken a heavy toll on the Serbian Army and Serbia's small population meant that these losses could barely be made up; the army in 1915 was only 20,000 men larger that it had been at the outbreak of war and seriously short of artillery and munitions.

The situation was made worse by a serious typhoid epidemic across the country.

For the Central Powers the failure of the Gallipoli campaign and the success of their operations against Russia and Italy (who had joined the Allies in May 1915 and whose advances had been checked at the hands of the Austrians) meant that they could take advantage of Serbia's weakness and knock her out of the war.

On the 6th September Bulgaria, a long-standing enemy of Serbia, signed an alliance with the Central Powers. Bulgaria coveted several areas of Serbian territory, which the Central Powers promised to Bulgaria in return for her joining the war. This meant that Serbia now faced the threat of invasion on two fronts: by the Germans and Austrians from the north and the Bulgarians from the east. Not only were they outnumbered but they were now forced to spread their forces thinly to meet both threats.

The Allies now realised it was time to send support to the Serbs. The Serbs had managed to sign an alliance with neutral Greece, under which the Greeks would offer support should Serbia be attacked. The Greeks in turn sought Allied support. The Allies began to prepare a force to be landed at Salonika in Greece, but this initially consisted of only two divisions and was little more than a token gesture. The entire process was hampered by the ambiguity of the Greek position; the pro-Allied Prime Minister was sacked on the 5th October just as the first Allied units began to land, the pro-German King (brother-in-law to the Kaiser) declaring strict Greek neutrality.

The initial Allied landings went ahead regardless, but more troops would have to be found if the expeditionary force of 125,000 men promised by the British government was to become a reality. The most obvious source was the force previously earmarked for Gallipoli.

Remounted

And so it was that at the end of September it was decided that the East Ridings and the rest of the North Midland Mounted Brigade would have their horses returned. The circumstances of the Balkans promised open plains and a return to mobile warfare, which meant that they were no longer needed as infantry; they would be going to Salonika as cavalry.

This news was met with a mixed reception. For many the news was welcomed with joy. Major Bardwell was reported to be "as excited as a schoolboy" when he broke the news to 'B' Squadron. Private Bill Austin considered that:

> "*we were lucky. After several weeks of infantry training we were told the joyful news that we were to get our horses back and become cavalry once more, preparatory to going abroad*". [34]

Not everyone felt the same way. Many men were angry at the change back to cavalry as they felt that, given the lack of employment opportunities for cavalry on the Western Front, this was a further delay to their chances of seeing action anytime soon. Private Seddon recalled:

> "*A lot of the men were very near mutiny that night and after 'lights out' they were shouting from their tents comments which were anything but flattering to those in authority.*" [35]

There appears to have also been some concerns over sarcastic comments and remarks directed towards some of the men during leave. Leonard May wrote that:

> "*a petition was got up and to a man all signed it. The Colonel, Guy Wilson, was furious. He ordered us all on parade and gave us a choice, either to take our horses back or he would abandon the regiment and we would be sent to any regiment anywhere and split up. We idolised the Colonel, so we all went back like good lads.*" [36]

The regiment soon settled down and the horses were collected from their minders on the 30th September. The horses were apparently in a terrible condition, and it took plenty of work to clean them up. Private Austin remembered, "*we then started our mounted training again, and what a treat it was.*" [37] Together with their horses, new equipment began to arrive on 7th October, including special winter clothing and new swords. "*We got re-fitted completely. New uniforms, saddlery, rifles, swords, equipment, in fact the whole lot*" according to Austin[38].

THE ADVENTURE BEGINS

Now the waiting was finally over. After a year of boredom and frustration, the men of the East Riding Yeomanry were going to war at last. On the 24th October 1915, the North Midland Mounted Brigade received secret orders to embark for the Mediterranean immediately. According to Leonard May, "*all the chaps cheered like the deuce when they got to know*"[39].

The East Ridings departed Costessey Park on the 26th October, marching through Norwich to the railway station where, after loading all the horses and baggage onto trains, they were sent off by some of the local women who came to offer refreshments, books and cigarettes. The journey was rather a tedious one, taking all night to reach their destination of Southampton where they arrived at 4am. On arrival, the East Ridings stayed in huge dock sheds, off saddled, and fed the horses.

The regiment, brigade headquarters and 11 men of the Staffordshire Yeomanry (together with 11 of their mules) were then embarked on the H.M.T. *Victorian* for the passage to Salonika. This took a little time as there was some difficulty in loading the horses. According to Private James Seddon:

> *"When we got them on deck the fun started as we then had to persuade them to go down a dark passage with a sloping floor which led to the stables below deck. A lot of them had to be pulled, pushed or coaxed."* [40]

Many of the horses would jump rather than walk down the planks and a number of men were injured.

The *Victorian* slipped her moorings and departed at 6:45pm on the 27th October, just over 12 hours after the East Ridings had arrived. As the ship got under way, the men on deck broke into song, singing the popular songs of the time and finishing with 'Auld Lang Syne'. It was a moving moment and as the ship left harbour Jimmy Seddon pondered the future:

> *"We sailed into the blackness of the night and the few lights on the docks were the last I saw of old England and I wondered – for how long?"*. [41]

For Jimmy and many of the men it would be the last time they would see England for more than 3 years. For some it would be the last time they would ever see England.

Whilst some undoubtedly considered such an eventuality, for many of the men the prospect of an overseas trip was exciting, foreign travel being beyond the means of most people during this period. This sense of adventure was perhaps heightened by the sight of their ship; the 12,000-ton *Victorian* was a modern pre-war passenger liner built for the Allan Line (one of the first turbine powered ships, she had been launched in 1905) to serve the North Atlantic routes taking migrants to Canada and the United States. The British government had provided subsidies for her construction and operation on the understanding that she would be converted into an 'Armed Merchant Cruiser' in time of war. She and many of her sister ships were duly requisitioned at the outbreak of war but were put into service as troopships.

The yeomen's excitement would have been quickly dampened, however. Rough conditions in the Bay of Biscay meant many men and horses suffered from terrible seasickness. This only added to the poor conditions onboard. The ships were carrying far more men than they had been designed for, not to mention the several hundred horses and mules also packed aboard, and they were seriously overcrowded. Although the officers lived in considerable comfort on the upper decks, waited on by stewards and residing in the cabins, the men lived in cramped and unsanitary conditions below decks that stank due to the animals and the inadequate ventilation.

Those unaffected by the rough conditions, including Bill Austin, had to take on all the duties:

> "*those of us that were go-able had to look after all the horses, not a comfortable job. Just try staggering down the centre of a narrow alleyway carrying a heavy bale of hay, the ship rolling and ravenous horses grabbing mouthfuls from each side as you passed*". [42]

For Private Seddon things were worse:

> "*I went up on to the aft deck and caught a nasty smell (improvised latrines had been erected on the deck and a large wave had splashed on board and strewn the contents all over the deck). That started it! Soon after this I went to the ship's side feeling very sick. Then I went back below decks and laid down hardly daring to move but when I did move I felt that I was going to be sick again.*" [42]

The first three days were the worst, but once out of the storm and into the Mediterranean conditions on board deteriorated further as the heat and humidity increased. The horses needed almost constant watering; according to Bill Austin:

> "*we had to keep watering the poor beggars all day long. As you got round once you had to start all over again, but we did our best and relieved their suffering to the best of our ability*". [43]

In the heat of the Mediterranean, conditions were almost unbearable, and many men chose to sleep on deck, only eight men from each Troop having to remain below to look after the horses.

The situation for the horses was appalling. The narrow stalls had been installed to house them gave little room to move around and made cleaning out the manure difficult. With so many men laid low it accumulated until it formed a thick layer in the stalls. Eventually it had to be dealt with and Bill Austin recalled:

> *"Now that most of us had got our sea legs we were are taking spells, stripped to the waist on account of the heat, digging it out as solid lumps and carrying it in large baskets to the dung port".* [44]

Dung wasn't the only thing thrown over the side. The horses were beginning to feel the effects of the voyage and a number died, their bodies had to be manhandled up on deck and thrown overboard.

Despite the conditions, many did still enjoy the voyage, taking the opportunity to sunbathe on the decks and revelling in the exotic sights and smells of Gibraltar, Malta and the North African coast. James Seddon particularly enjoyed Malta (although only officers were allowed ashore):

> *"We were near enough to land for me to see sufficient to keep me interested all the day. There was soon a babble round our ship of hawkers, in what I believe are called bum-boats, who were crying out with their peculiar accent and pronunciation to inform us what stuff they had to sell us. Most of it, to my mind, was worthless rubbish. Mingled with this noise were the pleadings of small boys in correspondingly small boats who wished us to throw silver into the water and for which they would dive. Their diving was wonderful. They would go right down out of sight under the ship and bring up a sixpence with almost unnerving precision."* [45]

The *Victorian* had passed Gibraltar on the 1st November and entered the Mediterranean Sea without an escort; the destroyer that had accompanied them through the Channel having long since departed, despite the very real threat from German submarines (*U-Boats*) in October 1915. The *Victorian* may have sighted a periscope or two on occasion, but assuming they were real, the turbine engines meant that she could outrun most *U-Boats* of the day and so the lifeboat drills were not needed in anger.

Elsewhere however, the Central Powers had in fact invaded Serbia on the 7th October. Facing offensives on two fronts and outnumbered, the Serbian Army was overwhelmed. Belgrade fell quickly on the 9th October, and despite fierce resistance by the beginning of November the Serbian Army was being pushed back towards Kosovo. The Bulgarian advance from the east effectively blocked the Serbs from retreating southwards towards the token Allied force that was now advancing northwards from Salonika.

It was clear that Serbia had been defeated and that the Allied intervention at Salonika had been too little, too late. Militarily it was now of little practical purpose (although for political expediency a sizable Allied force would be maintained there for the rest of the war) and it was decided to divert most of the troops now in transit to Egypt. Hence, after taking on fuel and stores in Valetta, the *Victorian* left Malta at 11:50am on November 6th heading for Alexandria, where she arrived 3 days later.

Sergeant Harold Lyon, 1/1ST East Riding Yeomanry in front of the Sphinx with native guide, November 1916
(ERYC)

Chapter 3: Egypt, 1915-1916

The *Victorian*, carrying the men and horses of the 1/1st East Riding Yeomanry, docked at Alexandria, Egypt, during the afternoon of 9th November 1915. The horses were disembarked after tea, but the men would have to spend another night on board before being disembarked the following morning.

Once ashore the regiment marched the short distance to Chatby Camp (Chatby-Les-Bains) in Alexandria. The regiment's horses were stiff and out of condition having spent the last few weeks in the stifling heat below decks and had to be led the 4½ miles to camp. They would require time to recover from the voyage, so for the next two weeks there was no training scheduled to allow men and horses alike to recuperate and become acclimatised to their new surroundings. The heat, even though it was winter, felt very hot to the yeomen; Private Seddon considered that:

"*although it is almost winter here it is hotter than a hot day in an English summer.*" [1]

Generally, camp life was fairly good, although Sergeant Harold Lyon noted wryly:

"*most of us soon learned the meaning of 'Gippy tummy' to our discomfort*". [2]

In camp there were locals to carry out many of the more mundane tasks and the Mediterranean offered great opportunities for bathing, although due to the risk of sunstroke this was not permitted before 4pm. The horses needed looking after of course and had to be exercised daily, which necessitated a very early start to avoid the heat of the day, but by 10am stables and exercise were complete, and the men's time was pretty much their own.

They slept, wrote letters or played cards. In the evenings the men went into Alexandria which, according to Jimmy Seddon, was:

"quite squalid, especially near the harbour, but some parts are quite pretty and presentable". [3]

Likewise, Leonard May thought it:

"not too good, very, very wicked. I dare not put down in print what went on down some of the streets. They had to be put out of bounds to us soldiers. Patrols had to be found to keep the lads out and we had some very exciting times getting them out." [4]

After two weeks the East Ridings moved by train to Mena House Camp on the outskirts of Cairo, departing from Alexandria early on the 22nd November. The regiment arrived at Cairo station at 9:30pm and quickly detrained; however. the camp was some 8 miles from Cairo station and the march took several hours as the horses were again led rather than ridden.

Life in the new camp continued to be rather pleasant despite the commencement of some routine training. The weather was a little cooler than Alexandria and it seemed less sandy. There was plenty of water and the food was very good; Sergeant Peter Thornton wrote home:

"we have a special colonial allowance here for grub and with the additional of a small subscription a native contractor runs a splendid mess for us. It really seems too ridiculously comfortable...." [5]

Private Jimmy Seddon wasn't so sure:

"There are a lot of natives working in the camp. I don't like the looks of a lot of them and would not trust them out of sight with anything of mine." [6]

The camp itself was located in sight of the Pyramids and close to the banks of the Nile. Plenty of the men took the opportunity to visit the ancient sites situated on their doorstep, many making the arduous climb to the top of the Great Pyramid with a native guide. Private Seddon noted in his diary:

"went for a ride round the pyramids and the Sphinx… what we saw was very impressive. The Sphinx naturally is greatly mutilated after all these years but still has an air of dignified grandeur about it." [7]

Private May thought:

"the old Sphinx was a good spot to sit on for a break; also, we got a good view of the Pyramids." [8]

Numerous photographs of men in front of the famous landmarks or on camels would subsequently make their way home.

The Senussi

The arrival in Egypt of a large number of troops diverted from Salonika was perhaps more than a coincidence. The Turkish attack on the Suez Canal in February 1915 might have been defeated with relative ease but the recent Allied troubles in Gallipoli and Mesopotamia (modern-day Iraq) meant that the threat from the Ottoman Empire was far from over; in fact, it was expected that the Turks would attempt to capitalise on the Allies' failings in the region. The Turkish forces remaining in Palestine and Arabia still posed a threat to Egypt and the security of the Suez Canal from the east, but now there was also trouble brewing in the desert to the west.

On the 5th November 1915 (whilst the East Ridings were at Malta, still en-route to Salonika) HMS *Tara*, an armed steamer patrolling the North African shore, was torpedoed and sunk by the German *U-Boat*, U-35. This was followed by the shelling of the British outpost at Sollum the next day. The survivors from HMS *Tara* and those of another ship had been put ashore on the North African coast and delivered into the custody of the Senussi, an Islamic tribal group residing in Italian controlled Libya, on the Western border of Egypt.

These events marked a change in the attitude of the Senussi, who initially maintained amicable relations with the British in

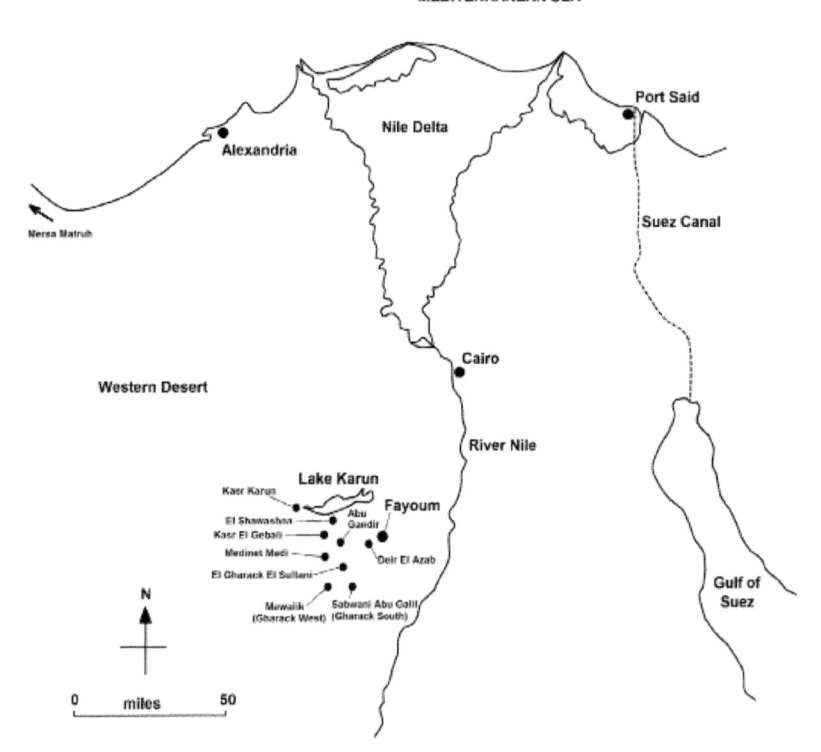

THE FAYOUM OASIS

Egypt despite their close relationship, politically and religiously, with the Ottoman Empire. Throughout 1915, German and Turkish agents had been trying to persuade the Senussi leader, the Grand Senussi Ahmed Sharif es Senussi, to take action against the British, initially without success. However, with the entry of Italy into the war on the side of the Allies in April 1915 (long-time enemies of the Senussi) and with the British defences in Egypt weakened by the demands of Gallipoli and the Western Front, the pressure on the Senussi to act increased and eventually the Grand Senussi acquiesced: he would attack Egypt.

The plan was for the Senussi to attack from the west, which it was hoped, would precipitate an uprising amongst the native Egyptians. The Turks would then launch a fresh offensive against the Suez Canal in the east. The Germans and the Turks offered money, gold and assistance, and helped smuggle substantial amounts of modern arms (including some artillery) and ammunition to the Senussi by boat and *U-Boat*.

As November wore on the Western Desert grew increasingly tense. Several thousand Senussi (regulars and Bedouin tribesmen together with some Turkish officers and men) were massed on the Libyan-Egyptian border and there were a number of Arab raids and skirmishes along the coast. Eventually the small British garrisons along the coast were withdrawn back as far as Mersa Matruh, 150 miles west of Alexandria, and their former positions were subsequently occupied by the Senussi.

Recognising the potential threat of unrest amongst the native Egyptians and the general lack of defences to the west of the Canal, additional British troops were deployed to protect the lines of communication. These included the coastal railway (which ran from Alexandria to El Daba) and various strategically important wells and oases.

The forces assembled to protect these lines of communication included the East Ridings and the rest of the 1/1st North Midland Mounted Brigade, although they were not yet considered fully recovered from their voyage. The Brigade was to be deployed to garrison the Fayoum (also called the Fayoum Oasis,

1/1ST NORTH MIDLAND MOUNTED BRIGADE CAMP, DEIR EL AZAB
(ERYC)

A GROUP OF EAST RIDING YEOMANRY OFFICERS AT DEIR EL AZAB
(ERYC)

despite not being a true Oasis) about 80 miles southwest of Cairo at the end of November.

An important agricultural area since ancient times, the Fayoum was strategically important to the defence of the Nile Valley. Consequently, on 28th November 1915, the regiment entrained at Cairo station and travelled southward to Wasya junction, then westwards to reach Medinet El Fayoum, the main town in the Fayoum, at 2am the following morning. The regiment then faced a 4-mile ride to their destination, a barren strip of stony desert at a place called Deir-el-Azab.

Garrison Duties

There may have been some action along the Mediterranean coast as the British Western Frontier Force began to push the Senussi back, but life for the men given the task of garrisoning the desert was simply boring. The 1/1st North Midland Mounted Brigade was headquartered at Deir El Azab (the site of an ancient Christian Monastery) in the Fayoum to protect the inland approach route to the Nile Valley (only 14 miles to the east) and to secure the area against Senussi agitation (there were thought to be Senussi sympathisers amongst the local population).

The men were not particularly impressed with the place. "*When we first arrived,*" recalled Jimmy Seddon:

> "*the lads were not favourably impressed by the vista before them and said so. Sergeant Dunning, who was older than us, said 'you lads will look back on this as the best days of your lives'. We were not convinced.*" [9]

The sand in the area was particularly fine and the slightest disturbance would result in clouds of sand that got everywhere, despite attempts to prevent it. The sand was also infested with lice, but the worst problem was the lack of clean water. For cooking water from a local irrigation canal was used after it had been filtered through porous earthenware vessels, but according to Peter Thornton this didn't have "*an improving effect upon the flavour of the tea*"[10]. Even the horses initially refused to drink it. Many men were laid low by illness and dysentery as a result of the sand, climate and water.

The East Ridings, in rotation with the other members of the brigade, would spend a month or so based at one of the various satellite camps located around the Fayoum, before returning to Deir El Azab for a month or two of rest. In addition, each regiment of the brigade would provide one Squadron to be detached to a smaller outpost camp from which mounted patrols were sent out and observation posts established in the desert.

Private Leonard May accurately summed it up:

> *"each Squadron of each regiment went out on outpost duty for a few weeks at a time and we spent some weary nights on guard in the desert... each outpost camp had to send out a lookout post some twenty miles into the desert. Water, wood etc. to form some shelter, was taken out. A Corporal and 4 men left camp at 2 or 3am to ride to it, so we rode in the cool of the early morning."* [11]

During their initial stay at Deir El Azab, the East Riding's initially sent 'C' Squadron to El Gharaq El Sultani (about 10 miles south west of the main camp) and then 'B' Squadron was sent to El Shawashna (about 18 miles north west).

Whilst the regiment was at Deir El Azab, once the camp had been built, the daily routine for all was training, mainly conducted at the Troop and individual level. Brigade route marches were also practised; the brigade usually accompanying one of the squadrons being detached part way to their destination. Most of the men preferred to be out in the desert, away from the 'spit and polish' of life a base camp.

The Fayoum area was thought to be in "a restless and somewhat rebellious state" and the camp guards were fully armed. One Section per Troop was expected to sleep fully dressed and be ready to turn out at a moment's notice. Route marches through the surrounding area were mounted in an attempt to impress the locals and assert British authority over the area. Again, the men were not impressed by what they saw. During one such route march Private Seddon noted houses that:

> *"in England... would be described as a hovel but thousands of such buildings in Egypt are considered to be normal dwellings"* and *"in*

every village and small town the same smell and filth is apparent." [12]

On the 18th December, after 2 weeks at Deir El Azab the East Ridings moved out and were sent to establish a new satellite camp at Abu Gandir, a native village described as a "dirty little place... fifteen miles further away from civilisation". Here, after setting out the camp, training continued and patrols were sent out into the surrounding countryside, normally two from each Squadron. Captain J F M Robinson wrote to his mother:

"we are always on the lookout for the advanced guard of a reported raiding army of Arabs so if we see anything such as a convoy of camels coming in, we rush out & hold them up until we are certain who they are. We can only stop them & wait until an interpreter comes to ask questions; so far we have not seen anyone who looks at all warlike." [13]

The weather was now a little more like home and there were showers as the winter rainy season set in. At night it was quite cold, and the heavy fall of dew soaked right through the blankets of those manning the outposts and mounting pickets (sentries), preventing them from sleeping when off duty.

On Christmas Day 1915 the East Riding's war diary blandly states "XMAS DAY usual posts sent out but otherwise no more work than necessary done". The promised turkey and Christmas puddings failed to materialise, as did the mail. Worst of all the firewood also failed to arrive but the men, with the help of some local Egyptian Policemen, were able to forage enough cotton sticks and dhoura (millet) to make a campfire. The camp at Abu Gandir was decorated with palm branches to give it a festive appearance, the effect somewhat spoilt by the bright sun! After the usual dawn stand-to there was a hunt arranged (there were desert foxes (Fennecs), jackals and wolves to be chased); practically all the officers and 10 men from each squadron took part. Despite the heavy going over sand and the few dogs, the hunt was deemed a great success. Private May recalled:

"Lieutenant Lee-Smith, a grand officer, organised a hunt through the villages and we slaughtered hundreds, I guess". [14]

The afternoon was spent sleeping and, in the evening, there

was a service given by the Brigade Chaplain and a singsong around the campfire.

For Private Seddon, with 'B' Squadron detached at El Shawashna, most of the day was spent on picket duty. When his Troop came off duty at 6:30pm they were treated to nuts, chocolate and cigarettes and:

> *"a big camp fire was lit and we had singing and fun round this until 10pm… our officers all made a short speech or gave us an item of entertainment and some did both. The evening altogether was very jolly and entirely the most unique Christmas night I have ever spent."* [15]

Christmas dinner arrived the following day. There was plenty of turkey and a pound of plum pudding per man and free beer.

> *"Considering how far we are from a large town and the means of transport available I think we did very well,"* wrote Jimmy Seddon, *"everyone was satisfied."* [16]

The much-anticipated Christmas mail finally arrived on the 29th. After Christmas 'B' Squadron returned to the Regimental camp and 'A' Squadron were sent out on detachment, to Kasr El Gebali, in their place. There followed two weeks of near torrential winter rain. On the 10th January, after a delay caused by rains making the desert impassable, the East Ridings returned to Deir El Azab.

The end of the winter rains also enabled the coastal campaigning to resume during January and into February. For the East Ridings however, back at the brigade camp at Deir El Azab, their monotonous life continued unabated. The war diary recounts a life of endless training exercises, generally taking place at the Troop level with occasional Squadron 'schemes' against an enemy simply represented with flags planted in the desert. There was a Brigade mounted sports event *"which went off champion"* according to Leonard May[17], but most exciting event was the Regimental football competition, which became the camp obsession. Peter Thornton wrote:

> *"you have no idea how this football has livened us up in this miserable place. It seems to have made quite a difference for assuredly things*

previously were so dull. Just picture a few hundred young fellows cooped up in a little space of featureless desert day and night week after week and you'll be able to imagine how exciting it was." [18]

The East Ridings also had to organise a riding school for a draft of 1 Officer and 40 men who arrived on 8th February 1916 from England. Obviously, few of them could ride a horse!

THE OASIS CAMPAIGN

Just as the tide of the coastal campaign was turning firmly in favour of the British, the Senussi launched another invasion, this time further inland. The Grand Senussi left the coastal army and withdrew to the Siwa Oasis, a Senussi stronghold deep in the desert. From there he began the second phase of the Senussi plan of action, an advance towards the Nile Valley through a string of oases. On the 11th February, the Senussi occupied the Baharia oasis, some 100 miles from the Fayoum, and before the month was out the oases of Farafra and Dakhla had also been occupied. The Egyptian authorities then abandoned the Kharga oasis (the Great Oasis) which was subsequently also occupied by the Senussi. The British now expected an attack towards Fayoum and the Nile Valley. Life for the desert garrisons looked like it might finally get interesting.

An outpost line was established along the western edge of the Nile irrigated zone to prevent the Senussi from obtaining water and supplies, stretching from Mediterranean coast west of the Nile Delta to El Minia on the Nile about 85 miles south of Fayoum. The 1/1st North Midland Mounted Brigade was responsible for that portion of the front from Kasr Karun (at the western tip of Lake Karun) to a point 4 miles south of El Gharaq El Sultani, with the East Ridings responsible for the southernmost section around El Gharaq. Brigade orders were that the outpost line must be held until the infantry could come up, after which orders for a concentration of the brigade would be issued.

The East Ridings moved out on the 24th February and established their main camp at a place called Sabwani Abu Galil ('Gharack South'), 3 miles south of El Gharaq El Sultani with

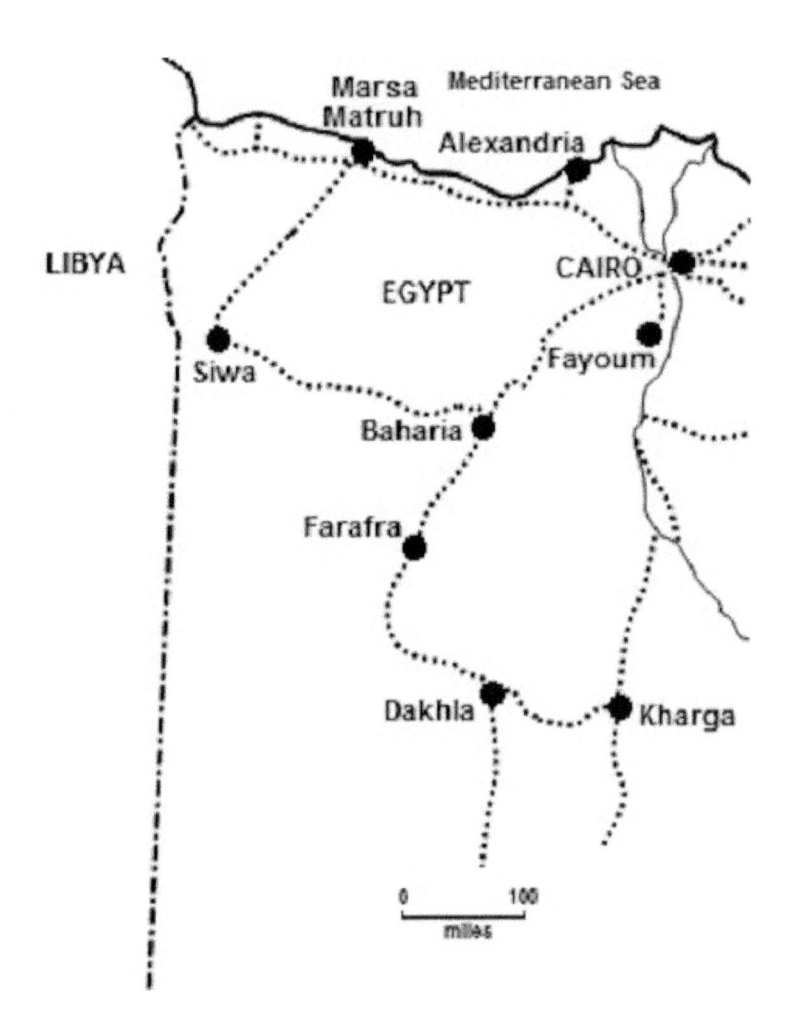

THE WESTERN DESERT OASES

'C' Squadron detached at Ezebit Mawalik ('Gharack West'). 'A' Squadron remained at Deir El Azab in brigade reserve, eventually swapping places with 'C' Squadron. The regiment immediately set about laying out the camp and building sandbagged defences. Captain Robinson considered Gharack South to be:

> *"a very nice camp on a sort of old clover field which is pleasanter and less glaring to look at than the desert."* [19]

Regimental HQ and the draft still under basic training relocated to Abu Gandir on the 7th March but 'B' and 'C' Squadrons remained around El Gharaq El Sultani.

Information was received on the 25th March that Senussi columns were moving eastwards across the desert and the entire Fayoum garrison were stood to. For four nights the whole of the 1/1st North Midland Mounted Brigade formed a cordon in the desert, manning defensive posts at 10-minute riding intervals. Captain Robinson wrote:

> *"about two weeks ago we got information that Arabs here in Fayoum were sending food etc. out to the Senussi so forthwith we prowled about the desert in a large ring about 10 miles out, at night we used to go out after dark and try and find our appointed places, then I used to trek up and down the line to visit posts... I only got to bed 11pm to 4am one night out of 5 but it was very good fun in spite of our catching nothing or even finding any tracks at daylight."* [20]

In addition to the cordon, the East Ridings also deployed several detachments further into the desert to monitor the caravan route out of the Bahariyeh Oasis. Every day a Troop of 'B' Squadron was despatched on an overnight patrol to the nearby Wadi Muellih, whilst a much larger force, consisting of 'A' Squadron less 2 Troops, was sent out to the Wadi Raiyan, from where an additional patrol was sent out to the Hagar Mashguk which offered a great vantage point view views across the desert.

Captain Robinson, now with 'B' Squadron, recalled one such patrol:

> *"I had to do one really nice trip though, about 23 miles out from us is a real desert oasis with a well. So I was ordered there at 8pm one night*

with 50 men… for 15 miles we had crossed the sand and rocks, no vegetation, all the time going down a long wide valley with big cliffs either side, then when it was light we came to patches of a sort of shrub… and saw in the distance two date palms with a spring bubbling up beneath one, the water coming up was about as quick as one fills a bath, running over the sand for 20 yards and then disappearing again in the sand, we dug a pool to bathe in and water our horses, the water was salty but good, had breakfast and slept in the shade, we stayed all night keeping a good look out and came back in daylight the next day." [21]

The information proved to be false however and with no obvious Senussi presence, the garrison was stood down.

To the north, the British resumed their advance along the Mediterranean coast towards Sollum on the 9th March, moving steadily westwards and meeting no real resistance. On the 14th March, they learnt that the Senussi had abandoned Sollum and to capitalise on this situation the Duke of Westminster was ordered to make for the town with his armoured cars. His armoured cars set off immediately and quickly caught up with the main body of the Senussi at Bir Asiso. The fighting spirit of the Senussi was now totally broken, and they were quickly overcome and Sollum reoccupied. After the action, the Duke of Westminster discovered that the survivors of the Tara were being held at Bir Hakkim inside Libya, behind enemy lines. Once again, he immediately set off with his armoured cars to rescue them, reaching them on the 17th March after a 120-mile dash across hostile and unforgiving country. They had been held captive for 135 days.

The recapture of Sollum marked the effective end of the Senussi threat, although guerrilla activity continued until April 1917, when a peace accord was signed.

Departures

Following the re-occupation of Sollum the Senussi withdrew from the Kharga Oasis, which was subsequently re-occupied by the British on the 15th April 1916, thereby greatly reducing the threat to the Nile Valley. The Senussi forces remaining in the other oases were too far from the Nile and too small to be a significant menace and so after the brief flurry of activity, life for the desert garrisons returned to the tedious routine of outpost duties and training. Once again, the promise of action and excitement was unfulfilled. Throughout April and May 1916, the East Ridings remained headquartered at Abu Gandir, with a squadron detached to El Gharaq El Sultani, and the boredom of the dreary routine and the lack of action now began to have a significant effect on the regiment. Leonard May wrote to his sister:

> *"You seem to think we have been in action, but we have not. We have expected to have a go a few times. When the Senussi hear that the East Ridings are near, they retire".* [22]

At the beginning of April Brigade HQ called for volunteers to join the Imperial Camel Corps (ICC). The ICC had been formed to patrol the Western Desert and to deny the Senussi the use of wells and cisterns, camels being found more suited to the terrain than horses. Four camel companies had been raised at the end of January 1916, drawing on volunteers from Australian infantry units returning from Gallipoli. Many of the Australians already had experience of the camels that had been imported into Australia during the nineteenth century for use in the outback. These companies had proved invaluable in the campaign against the Senussi and so the corps was to be expanded to keep the Senussi bottled up in the oases and prevent any unrest amongst the Bedouin. Perhaps unsurprisingly, a large number of East Ridings signed up to this exotic sounding unit in the hope of seeing some action and excitement. Consequently, Major Bardwell, 2nd Lieutenant Wilkinson, 2nd Lieutenant Ashlin and 57 other ranks of the East Riding Yeomanry (4 more were to join later in the month) departed Abu Gandir on the 2nd May to join the ICC. Jimmy Seddon, whose friend Jack Freeman was amongst the volunteers thought:

> *"that they had become bored and weary with what seemed to be a lot of purposeless outpost duties and 'spit and polish'.* [23]

Another volunteer, Private Ken Dodgson, agreed:

An 'A' Squadron patrol resting on the way to Hagar
Mashuk, Wadi Raiyan, 1916
(ERYC)

The Hagar Mashuk, 'Split Rock', Wadi Raiyan, 1916
(ERYC)

> *"it was a lot more exciting on a camel because you were allowed further into the desert for reconnaissance".* [24]

The tedious life of the desert garrisons also played its part in another series of departures. Men enlisting in the Territorial Force pre-war generally did so for a period of 4 years. On the outbreak of war, this was automatically extended by a year as a result of a clause in the terms of engagement. As a result, by August 1915 the first men (those who enlisted in the Territorials around 1910) began to become 'time expired' and entitled to a discharge and to return home. This would mean the loss of not just men but experienced men, and efforts were made to encourage those reaching the end of their engagements to re-join for the duration of the war. As an incentive, there was the offer of a month's leave and also a £15 bounty to those who chose to re-enlist.

At least 9 time-expired East Ridings chose to re-enlist, their return after their home leave is recorded in the war diary on the 19th July. However, a significant number did not. On April 4th a group of 24 time-expired Warrant Officers, NCOs and men left the Abu Gandir camp destined for a voyage home and discharge.

The group included 1 Squadron Sergeant Major (SSM), 2 Squadron Quartermaster Sergeants (SQMS) and 12 Sergeants and Lance Sergeants, a loss of about a third of the total number of senior NCOs, a substantial loss of experience in just one party of men and there were other groups. Lieutenant Bailey, a troop commander in 'A' Squadron wrote:

> *"we have had an upheaval owing to the departure of nearly all the sergeants in one day, either time expired or gone to take commissions. So, the juniors are having their innings. Every man promoted is transferred to another troop, so I have lost 4 of my best friends and got 4 new ones."* [25]

On arrival home time-expired men often received a cold reception from their local Territorial Force Association (the body responsible for the Territorial Force) and they were 'encouraged' to sign on again. Eventually the introduction of conscription meant that any fit men returning home would be liable to be conscripted for further service and eventually service was automatically extended 'for the duration'.

One who agreed to re-enlist once he got home was Corporal Robert 'Bob' Atkinson from York. He left the regiment with a party of time-expired men on the 14th May 1916, as noted in the diary of his friend, Harold Lyon. Bob returned to England, eventually rejoining the first-line regiment in January 1917. He was subsequently killed in action in France in October 1918 (see Chapter 5). Staff Quartermaster Sergeant (SQMS) Charles Frederick Dixon also returned home time expired. He chose to return home as he intended to obtain a commission, which he eventually did, becoming a 2nd Lieutenant with the 4th Battalion, East Yorkshire Regiment (on 24th Oct 1916).

Another time-expired yeoman who ended up in the East Yorkshire Regiment was Frederick Barr. Frederick joined the East Riding of Yorkshire Yeomanry as an 18-year-old private on 12th April 1911, being mobilised with the regiment in August 1914. He would have become time-expired in April 1915 but due to the extension that was delayed until 1916, by which time he had risen to the rank of Sergeant-Cook. On becoming time-expired, he chose not to re-enlist but to return to England. He was struck off the strength of the regiment on 10th March 1916, sailing for home on the transport HMT *Tunisian* from Alexandria on 23rd March 1916. Frederick is subsequently recorded as a sergeant with the 9th Battalion, East Yorkshire Regiment, serving for the rest of the war at home; the 9th eventually became the 7th Training Reserve Battalion and whatever the cause of his re-enlistment (conscription or voluntary), Frederick would have put his experience to good use training new conscripts.

In total, together with postings to Brigade Headquarters and elsewhere these departures represented the loss of about 25% of the East Riding's effective strength, only partly replaced by the now fully trained but inexperienced draft who had arrived back in February.

A Dreary Existence

The 1/1st North Midland Mounted Brigade became the 22nd Mounted Brigade at the end of April, following a reorganisation of the cavalry across the British Army. Then on the 9th May 1916, after two months at Abu Gandir, the East Ridings moved their headquarters a few miles to Medinet Madi, an ancient settlement (the name means 'City of the Past') about 18 miles southwest of Fayoum, setting up camp on 'Ruin Hill', the site of a ruined Middle Kingdom (12th Dynasty) temple. 'A' and 'C' Squadrons remained at Abu Gandir and Gharack South respectively.

Despite the change of scenery (metaphorically at least) the war diary details the same unrelenting routine of outpost duties and life for the men reached new lows: it was tedious, dreary, and unhealthy. Besides the lack of clean drinking water, a simple scratch or insect bite could become infected, and sepsis set in, and many of the men (perhaps as many as a third at any one time) sported bandages over wounds which could take weeks or even months to heal properly. Consequently, even the water for washing had to be disinfected before it could be used. For some it was inadvisable to shave due to a tendency to nick the skin and thus beards became common.

The Egyptian climate also contributed to the misery of the desert garrisons. In the spring, after the winter rains and cold nights came the *Khamsin*. From April onwards the *Khamsin*, a hot dry wind, blows across Egypt bringing with it violent sandstorms, lasting for days on end (reputedly for fifty days, hence the name, based on the Arabic word for 'fifty'). On the 26th April Peter Thornton wrote home to his sweetheart:

> "*it has been a terror today, the worst we have experienced yet, and they tell us today hasn't been nearly as hot as it will be later on. Most of us are going about this afternoon looking like drowned rats. Breezes keep wafting in from the desert side hot enough, I should think, to set fire to things. I'll swear they are far hotter than the last chamber in the Turkish baths, they seem almost to take one's breath away. Today has been too much for a few of the boys…*" [26]

AN OUTPOST POSITION, MEDINET MADI, 1916
(ERYC)

THE Y.M.C.A. TENT AT THE EAST RIDING'S CAMP AT MEDINET MADI, 1916
(ERYC)

During a sandstorm it was almost impossible to venture outside; visibility was no more than a few yards, often almost non-existent, and sand would fill unprotected eyes, noses, ears and mouths and scour exposed skin. Sand was everywhere and in everything; the tents, the clothes, the food, and matted in the horse's coats.

Again, Peter Thornton gives an account:

"There's simply no keeping the sand out (of the tents), *in fact it takes us all our time when a real good one starts to keep the tents up. Ordinary tent pegs of course aren't a bit of use. We have got to dig holes all round, stitch the ropes to sandbags and bury them. Then the sandy wind gets underneath the curtains and tries to make a parachute of the tent besides burying everything in sand. But it's no use worrying about it, the only thing is to sit tight and hope that the tent will hold out".* [27]

Even the landscape would have been altered, with ridges and hills shifted or swept away, depressions filled in and new ridges and hills having appeared. Captain Robinson wrote:

"we have an awfully lot of digging in the sand to do to entrench our camp, very hard work as everything has to be sandbagged up & then the sandstorms come & shift the whole bag of tricks." [28]

In May came the news of the regiment's first casualty since arriving in Egypt, when on the 17th May 1916 Corporal Harrison died in the Citadel Hospital, Cairo, having succumbed to typhoid.

As spring turned into summer the mercury continued to rise. Temperatures inside the tents could reach 120°F (49°C). Sweat would soak through clothing and literally run down the outside.

In a letter home dated 16th May 1916, Lieutenant Bailey wrote:

"It is the second day of a heat wave and such a heat wave. If I had tried to write this afternoon, I would have been dripping on the page every 15 seconds. Of course, that is our salvation. We are wet all over, running, and we can only tell when it gets hotter by the fact that we drip fastener, for instance, when I go from the double roofed mess tent into my single thickness bell tent. In the afternoon it is something over 120 in any tent..." [29]

THE SWIMMING POOL AT THE EAST RIDING'S CAMP AT MEDINET
MADI, 1916
(ERYC)

ANOTHER VIEW OF THE POOL AT MEDINET MADI
(ERYC)

There was some small respite in June when double-skinned bell tents were received, which offered some relief from the ferocious heat, the effect of which became less pronounced as the men became more acclimatised. This in fact added to their misery as they were all well aware that the climatic conditions made it very unlikely they would be relieved. It was considered that fresh troops not accustomed to the climate wouldn't be able to cope and therefore the 22nd Mounted Brigade would have to remain in the desert until the end of the summer at least.

Flies, spiders, mosquitoes and other insects were ever-present irritants. Peter Thornton wrote:

"They are dear old friends the flies; they never leave us in blazing sun or in sand storms, always about" [30]

and Robert Bailey wrote that:

"the flies stop one sleeping in the afternoon whilst it is too hot to do anything but sleep". [31]

They would crawl over every surface and on the inside of the tent walls; they would even get mixed up in the lather of those trying to shave. The Veterinary Officer discovered that fumes from heated nicotine (used on the horses' skins) would kill the flies. Fumigating the tents resulted in a carpet of flies; *"in the sergeants mess tent the floor was covered over with them"* [32] remembered Peter Thornton. However, the following morning they were back in strength and the technique was abandoned. Towards the end of May fly nets for the tents were issued and whilst that made things a little better, the flies still managed to get inside the nets. Mosquitoes conspired to keep the men awake at night with their ever-present buzzing and since it was impossible to sleep under bedding or in any clothes (on account of the heat) and despite the nets, the men were exposed to bites which were very irritating and could easily become infected if scratched.

The seemingly endless routine of training and outpost duties inevitably continued, but the High Command finally recognised the impact this was having on morale and began to take steps to improve the situation. During May, the East Riding's Sergeants Mess acquired an old gramophone and some 'well worn' records, and on the 8th June a YMCA tent was erected offering postal services and a canteen. Lieutenant Bailey wrote home:

> "*Robert Smith was just leaving for Alexandria, but we saw him for a few minutes. He does the most wonderful thing with the YMCA. This regiment alone has had a big square tent for each squadron, lots of tables and forms* (benches), *chess, draughts, quoits etc. and a small library and our squadron got a piano from them.*" [33]

There were a few concerts and the almost obligatory regimental sports including the usual foxhunts, football and boxing, as well as tent-pegging and horseback wrestling. Remarkably, there was even a pool dug (by native labourers) for swimming. It was 40 yards long by 10 yards wide (37 x 10 metres) and up to 5½ft deep (1.7m) and was filled by Nile water from a nearby irrigation canal. In addition to providing welcome relief from the heat and dust, several aquatic sports 'galas' were held.

Private Terry Ward, newly arrived from the 3/1st East Riding Yeomanry in England recalled one such event:

> "(I) *went over to 'B' Squadron in the afternoon for swimming sports (they had a bathing pool) and concert. The outpost is Medinet Madi – 8 miles away. Swam in Squadron relay team and played in Squadron water polo team. During polo game tackled one man rather hard and perhaps held him under water longer than I should have done, only to be told later by my mates he was the Regimental Sergeant Major! I don't think he ever forgave me because it took me nearly two years after this to become a Lance Corporal.*" [34]

Leave, albeit local only, was also now permitted, with up to 5% of the unit's strength permitted to be away at any one time. Initially men were granted 2 or 3 day passes to travel to Cairo. Besides the historical sites such as the Egyptian Museum, there was the Zoo and various gardens to enjoy. No one would visit without making a trip to the bazaars to purchase souvenirs and gifts to be sent home. There were several Kodak dealers which enabled the men to purchase (unofficially) pocket cameras and to get their photographs developed.

Cairo leave was replaced in June with weeklong passes to a

rest camp at Alexandria on the coast. The first group of 26 other ranks left for 7 days leave on the 21st June, with further parties leaving every few weeks. The *Kursaal* (the public area of Alexandria) offered various attractions for those on leave. There were the ubiquitous ancient ruins to visit or the Nouzha Gardens; there was a cinema, a theatre, a casino and also racetrack holding regular horse races which were undoubtedly of interest to many of the yeomen.

Like Cairo there were numerous restaurants, cafes (Harold Lyon had "*a very good tea at No. 9 Rue L'Ancienne Bourse*"[35]), bars and clubs, including one run by the YMCA. Alcohol was readily available. Many of the local establishments had belly-dancers who were much appreciated by men long separated from the company of women. Jimmy Seddon and his friend Jack Freeman:

> "*went to see what was called the "can-can" - what a sell. There was some pretty sordid stuff and Jack said he did not want to see anything like it again. I agreed.*" [36]

For the adventurous there was more; prostitution was legal in Egypt and although the red-light district was supposed to be out of bounds to military personnel, plenty simply ignored the rules, and the risk of venereal disease.

Nevertheless, there was little respite from the boredom in the field, despite the regiment moving back to Deir El Azab on the 12th August 1916. The move back to the Brigade camp was not met with enthusiasm. The regiment was being withdrawn for a rest which meant no more outpost duties; however, the men thought this no compensation for the loss of the swimming pool. In fact, there seemed to be less rest now than there had been at Medinet Madi. There were numerous lectures and classes to attend and fatigue duties to perform, and to top it off the weather seemed hotter than the old camp. Harold Lyon noted that "*everyone* (is) *sick as possible with this camp*"[37] and Peter Thornton reported that:

> "*the rest camp is a great joke… everyone seems keen to get away to*

the desert again". [38]

Added to this was an outbreak of fever that seemed to affect almost everyone and contributed to the general feeling that this was an unhealthy camp.

The frustrations of sitting in the scorching, parched desert chasing flies and mosquitoes whilst missing out on the action elsewhere were also increasing. Rumours that the East Ridings were to be sent into action abounded; to Salonika or the Sinai, or even to France, but they came to nothing, and everyone was convinced they would be forced to sit out the war without getting into action. Peter Thornton reflected the general mood when he wrote home on 16th August:

"we all out here would like to have a look in at the big game in France". [39]

The 'Big Game' in France was the Battle of the Somme on the Western Front, which had begun on 1st July. To make matters worse, this battle was the first real outing for the wartime volunteers of Kitchener's New Army. For the many pre-war Territorials of the East Riding Yeomanry, including Thornton, it seemed:

"silly to think of all these hundreds of thousands of men who had never handled a rifle before this war becoming proper war scarred veterans and we that used to fancy our chances so much years ago never having an active hand in it" [40]

These feelings were further compounded by news of the Battle of Romani, which was taking place against the Turks in the Sinai. During the battle, one of the East Riding Yeomen who had left to join the Imperial Camel Corps had been killed in action and several others wounded.

After their two month 'rest' the regiment returned to outpost duties, Regimental headquarters moving to a place called Khargat, some 25 miles north of their former camp at Medinet Madi; in fact 'A' Squadron was detached to the old camp itself, whilst 'B' Squadron was sent to Kasr Karun. With the move back into the desert, morale improved a little; the camp was healthier, despite the water having to be carried by camels the six miles from the light railway, and the fever outbreak quickly receded. The main camp had previously been occupied by the Staffordshire Yeomanry who had built mud huts for the officers and sergeants. Peter Thornton wrote:

> *"it's a great treat I can assure you getting within four walls during the heat though they are inclined to be stuffier than the canvas at night".* [41]

Initially mosquitoes were a problem, particularly effecting the horses, but 50 locals were engaged to pull out all the reeds close to the camp and the swampy area eventually dried out which greatly reduced the problem. The camp also boasted an unfinished swimming pool, although this was never really a success. Day to day life consisted of the usual outpost duties, training exercises and lectures on a range of military subjects and of course there was all manner of sports, including a Regimental cricket match with bats, balls and wickets provided by Lords.

By the beginning of November however, nearly a year after first arriving in Egypt, orders were received for the regiment to concentrate back at Deir El Azab. During October and November 1916, the Baharia, Dakhla and Farafra Oases were retaken by the British against only slight opposition and the Grand Senussi withdrew his forces back to the Siwa Oasis, effectively ending the threat to Egypt from the West. Lieutenant Bailey wrote:

> *"you may have seen in the papers 3 days ago that British troops have occupied the Dakhla and the Baharieh oases, the taking of the Baharieh oasis makes all the difference to us and now they may find something else for us to do."* [42]

The expectation was that the regiment would finally be on their way out of the desert; most people expected that to mean the Balkans, where opportunities for cavalry were perceived to be best – many though wished for France and the chance to join the war proper. These impressions were reinforced as the regiment was brought back up to full strength with the arrival of drafts totalling 4 officers and 25 men from the 3/1st East Riding Yeomanry in England.

There was some bad news though, on 25th November 1916

Private Alexander Hetherton died in Cairo. He was a friend of Leonard May who wrote home:

> "*one of my Troop pals died. It is sad. Whilst on outpost he started going sick and was in the field hospital. After getting a bit better he was sent to Cairo. When he went, he said 'I know they won't keep me long, as I am nearly better'. Well we expected he would soon be back but instead we got news of his death.*" [43]

The Move East

With the threat from the Senussi removed the troops garrisoning the western desert could now be released for service elsewhere. One division was sent to Mesopotamia (modern-day Iraq) and others to France. Those that remained, after a year of boredom and inactivity, had become demoralised and unfit, and would need time to sharpen their skills in order to become battle ready. The British commander, General Murray, therefore set about reorganising and retraining his forces. In December 1916 the East Ridings, along with the rest of the 22nd Mounted Brigade, were ordered to join the ANZAC (Australian and New Zealand Army Corps) Mounted Division in the Sinai. They were finally leaving Fayoum.

Starting on the 2nd December the Brigade moved via the light railway to a transit camp at Kantara, on the Suez Canal, arriving there over the course of the first few days of the month. The regiment set up camp in Kantara area, at a location known as Hill 40, described by Harold Lyon as "*simply a desert hillock a few miles east of Kantara*"[44]. The next few days were spent putting up tents, laying out the horse lines and unloading the regiment's kit. There was the opportunity for bathing in the canal and for trips to Port Said, and for the officers, Cairo. For the men, grown accustomed to being out in the desert and away from most signs of civilisation, there was lots of activity and interesting goings on; Kantara was in the process of expanding from a relatively small camp into a huge supply depot, and there were trains and camel convoys passing by heading east almost constantly.

After a few more days (on December 9th) the regiment moved on to Dueidar, 10 miles to the east of the canal, whilst 'A' Squadron provided four Troops detached to Hod El Aras and Hill 70 (two Troops each). These Troops were acting as flank guards to the main positions and spent their time on patrols and outpost duties. Clearly this wasn't a healthy proposition as Private Terry Ward, on relief by another two Troops on the 26th December noted in his diary:

> "(it's) *a good job we have been relieved as a lot of the men are not at all well and in need of a change.*" [45]

For the rest of the regiment camped at Dueidar there was a new intensive training programme; the war diary repeatedly refers to musketry, sword exercise and dismounted attack. Sergeant Major Peter Thornton wrote rather disparagingly that:

> "*at present* (we're) *engaged up to all sorts of silly hours crawling over loose sand*". [46]

Water here was rationed – one gallon of water per man per day ('perhaps') – four pints of which were allocated to the cookhouse leaving two pints for drinking and two pints for washing. The soft sand of the Sinai made it difficult to bring up supplies as horses and wagons would sink into the sand. Lieutenant Frank Wood thought:

> "*Dueidar was an interesting place in a hollow between large sand dunes with a lovely palm grove, which gave shelter from the blazing sun. This place had been the scene of a battle with the Turks only a few months previously, when the King's Own Scottish Borderers did good execution amongst the Jacko's, making a gallant stand against superior numbers and finally beating off the enemy*". [47]

For Jimmy Seddon:

> "*what seems to have impressed itself most on my mind regarding this camp was the canteen which was constructed of sandbags. There was a comparatively small hatch in one wall where customers came to be served and they queued outside. The different types of faces that appeared at this aperture were a study in humanity. Scotch, Irish, Welsh, Australians, New Zealanders, West Indians. This to me was seeing life*". [48]

Here they would spend their third Christmas of the war. Despite the winter rains (Lieutenant Wood noting that, "*it rained heavily all the day, but we didn't mind that, as we had seen no rain for 12 months or so*"[49]) the regiment made the best of it. There were able to enjoy turkey, plum pudding, mince pies, oranges, nuts and free beer, and the men made efforts to make their dugouts and bivouacs look festive with improvised decorations. There were of course the usual sports, including shooting competitions and horse racing, and for the officers there was the opportunity for some hunting, although the local gazelles proved cunning and elusive targets. As 1916 ended the men of the East Ridings looked forward to the coming year when they might finally get into action and make a contribution to the war.

Chapter 4: Palestine, 1917

The campaign in the Sinai during 1916 might have been successful but the Egyptian theatre was a relative sideshow, overshadowed by the Western Front, where the news was not so good for the Allies. The second full year of the war had been a year of terrible slaughter. The Allied plan for 1916 had been for concerted attacks against the Central Powers on all fronts.

The Germans inevitably had their own plans however, and had struck first, launching a major offensive against the key French position of Verdun in February 1916. The Germans realised that a decisive breakthrough was probably impossible and so adopted a policy of attrition, aiming to cause the French more casualties than they themselves suffered; 'to bleed the French Army white', in the hope of forcing the French to come to terms.

In what turned out to be an eleven month battle the French mounted a desperate and ferocious defence which ultimately cost them more than a third of a million men, with probably half that many being killed and nearly breaking their army in the process. Neither side could really claim victory though; despite their intentions, German losses at Verdun were only marginally less than the French.

The British launched their long awaited 'big push' at the Battle of the Somme in July 1916. This had originally been envisaged as a joint operation with the French as part of the Grand Plan, but was now a predominantly British operation, seeking to ease the pressure on the French at Verdun. After a week-long ar-

AN EAST RIDING YEOMANRY HOTCHKISS GUN TEAM, 1917
(ERYC)

THE REGIMENT WATERING HORSES, ROMANI, JANUARY 1917
(ERYC)

tillery barrage the attack was launched on the 1st July. The British suffered some 60,000 casualties, including 20,000 killed, on the opening day alone, the worst day in the history of the British Army. Despite the huge casualties and limited results, the battle dragged on until a state of stalemate was reached in November. Total British casualties were in the region of 420,000 men and the German casualties were just as high. Another year of war had passed and still there was no end in sight.

The Germans recognised the impact of the huge losses of 1916 had had on their ability to continue the war and therefore resolved to remain on the defensive on the Western Front in 1917. At the beginning of the year, as part of this plan, they withdrew back to a newly constructed and shorter defensive line (called the Hindenburg Line), freeing up around a dozen divisions for redeployment elsewhere. They intended to rely on a renewed *U-Boat* campaign to starve Britain into submission.

In France General Nivelle, a hero of Verdun, persuaded the French Premier that his planned offensive could end the war in 48 hours. Despite opposition the optimistic plan was given the go ahead in April 1917, together with a supporting British offensive. It was a disaster. Instead of the predicted 10,000 casualties the French suffered over 100,000 and no breakthrough was achieved. Nivelle was sacked. Throughout the French Army mutinies began to break out.

At home in Britain there was increasing disquiet at how the war was being waged in the light of the disastrous campaign on the Somme and the Easter Rising in Ireland (April 1916). Opponents laid the blame at the feet of the Prime Minister, Herbert Asquith. Eventually, on the 5th December 1916, Asquith was forced to resign, and a new coalition was formed with David Lloyd George as Prime Minister.

Whilst the general opinion remained that the war could only be won through the defeat of Germany on the Western Front, Lloyd George began to look at other, less costly, ways to strike at the Central Powers. Following his successes in driving the Turks out of Egypt, General Murray was pressing for a more active role, advocating an advance into Palestine and the capture of Jerusalem. Lloyd George saw this as an opportunity for a morale boosting victory without the huge losses that would undoubtedly accompany any offensive on the Western Front. Whilst the Western Front couldn't be ignored (a large offensive by the British at Ypres in Belgium was planned for the summer of 1917) the principle of an attack against Palestine was approved. The extra troops Murray requested for any such offensive would however not be available until the autumn. In the meantime, Murray was encouraged to do what he could with the forces at his disposal.

Preparing for war

For the men of the 1/1st East Riding Yeomanry their intensive training programme continued throughout January 1917. The emphasis remained musketry, sword drills, dismounted attacks and bayonet fighting; the men, out of shape after a year of garrison duties were to be brought back to fighting fitness.

There were a number of organisational changes whilst the regiment was at Dueidar. On the 8th January the Machine Gun section was doubled in size and the 2 Officers and 53 ORs selected (along with all the machine guns) were detached to join a new unit; the 18th Squadron, Machine Gun Corps (Cavalry). This unit was being formed from the machine gun sections of all the yeomanry units in the 22nd Mounted Brigade and would concentrate all the machine guns under brigade control. Regimental numbers were made up with the arrival of a series of fresh drafts from England; 2nd Lieutenant Tomlinson and 49 men arrived on the 2nd January, a further 80 men from England and 44 horses from the remount depot arrived on the 8th, and another group of 20 men joined in the 20th. These drafts included some men who had left in 1916 as time expired but who had chosen to re-enlist.

The winter rains meant that Dueidar was cold, wet and miserable. Acting Sergeant William 'Wass' Reader's diary entry for the 3rd January was typical:

"Wind and rain again today and several tents went away. We are not

allowed to have food in the tents so got wet through whilst getting dinner in the open and have been soaked through all day long". [1]

The weather had improved a little by the time the regiment moved onto Romani, on January 19th, but there were still cold winds and sandstorms. The area had only recently been fought over and here the East Ridings had their first real taste of the grim realities of war, which only served to add to the gloom. Private Jimmy Seddon recalled that:

"parts of bodies were exposed to view, such as a hand protruding out of the sand. The dead had been buried so hurriedly that they were not deep enough under the sand and the winds had blown much of the sand away… I noticed that a lot of them were so swollen by the heat of the sun that they looked as though they had been blown up with pumps. Birds of the vulture species hovered in the sky waiting for an opportunity to pounce. The nauseating stench of decomposing bodies was in our nostrils for days on end which was depressing." [2]

Similarly, Lieutenant Frank Wood recalled:

"Romani was very interesting owing to the fighting that took place around there in August 1916. We had to do patrol work from here to Katia and Oghratina districts, where the 5th Mounted Brigade (the Warwick, Worcestershire and Gloucestershire Yeomanry) had had such severe fighting… one came across the most gruesome sights on these patrols, on the sand, where the dead, both friend and foe had been buried. They had risen through the soft sand to the surface and there they lay in the most weird positions, close to their rough wooden crosses." [3]

The regiment was clearly being prepared for action. All the kit bags, tents and stores were packed up and sent back to the base at Kantara (and were never seen again). The firepower lost when the machine gun section was removed was addressed on the 27th January when new Hotchkiss automatic rifles were issued. These were actually light machine guns rather than rifles (the cavalry equivalent of the famous Lewis gun) and it was intended that eventually each Troop would contain one, but initially numbers were probably much lower. Nevertheless, everyone needed training on the new weapon and the associated equipment and saddlery. Wass Reader wrote:

> *"we were issued with pack saddles for our Hotchkiss guns and a most horrible time we had putting them all together".*[4]

On the 23rd January the East Ridings carried out a large tactical exercise under the watchful eyes of the Inspector General of Mounted Troops. Sergeant Reader recorded the events in his diary:

> *"were inspected by the Inspector General of the Mounted Troops in Egypt. Every man Jack in the regiment turned out and we had the biggest parade since we had been mobilised. We dismounted about 2 miles from Bushy Hill and attacked it on foot, up and down great sand hills and I was nearly beat when we finished. Most of us thought we had made a proper mess of things but it appears the General said some nice things about us and was so pleased that we have to do it again tomorrow. Curse him."* [5]

The scheme was duly repeated:

> *"Had another trying time again today in the dismounted attack for the benefit of the General and went over the very same course as yesterday"* wrote Reader. [6]

The preparations for action were lightened by a series of football matches, including one between the regiment and the West Riding Royal Horse Artillery, old friends from the pre-War Yorkshire Mounted Brigade, who were also at Romani; the East Ridings won 5-1. There was also the chance for swimming in the Mediterranean, for both men and horses.

After a two week stay at Romani the East Ridings moved further eastwards, to Bir El Abd. The camp at Romani was struck on the 30th January in the midst of a raging sandstorm, necessitating a night in the open, before the regiment departed on the 31st. Frank Wood wrote:

> *"about January 29th we started to trek to Bir El Abd in a sandstorm which lasted for three days. No one can realise the discomfort of a sandstorm unless they have experienced them as it is beyond description. Those of us who were not carrying sand goggles heartily regretted their neglect, as they suffered much with sand in their eyes. I always carry goggles with smoked glasses as a precaution against the glare of the sun and so was well equipped. We ate and drank sand and our clothes were*

full of it during the three days, for the wind even drove it through our thick riding breeches." [7]

On arrival at Bir El Abd training exercises commenced immediately, even before the camp was set up. The Regimental transport was held up however, and the train carrying all the baggage was also delayed by a breakdown, and the men ended up spending the night in the open. According to William Reader:

> *"Our transport has not turned up yet so today we again partook of bully and biscuits. It is a bit cold at night with only a saddle blanket and greatcoat but I slept with Smales again and it made it a bit warmer".* [8]

Following the repair of the line, ration trains were given priority so it meant another couple of nights sleeping in the open for the yeomen before the baggage arrived on the 2nd February. The tents could finally be pitched, but in the continuing sandstorm this was no easy task:

> *"the wind commenced to blow hard and the tents took a lot of erecting (we all wish they would do away with the blinking things)"* wrote Wass Reader. [9]

Throughout all this the preparations and build-up continued unabated. Another draft of 33 men arrived from the 3/1st East Riding Yeomanry on the 3rd February and the training programme intensified. There was the opportunity for the officers to ride out and visit the recent battlefields, and for the live firing of the new Hotchkiss guns. The training reached its climax on the 12th February with a Brigade exercise, described by Sergeant Reader:

> *"We received our final test today in the presence of General Watson and several other Generals. The regiment did a dismounted attack with ball ammunition under a cover fire of shrapnel from the four 18 pounders of the Notts R.H.A. and fire from the machine guns of the 18th Machine Gun Squadron. The shells burst about 500 yards from us and rifle volleys were flying over our heads all the time. I think I shall require a new pair of breeches".* [10]

The East Ridings and the rest of the 22nd Mounted Brigade

were now ordered forward to join up with the ANZAC Mounted Division which was in the frontline on the Egypt-Palestine frontier. The regiment was placed on a 'mobile establishment', meaning the baggage and supplies would have to be transported on pack horse or camel and the Army Service Corps wagons left behind.

After some confusion sorting and packing the stores, the East Ridings departed Bir el Abd on the 16th February. The march took in overnight stops at Salmana, Tilul, Mazar and Bardawil before arriving at El Arish during the afternoon of 20th February. Conditions along the march were basic, the men having to sleep with the horses in the horse lines or in makeshift bivouacs and dugouts during the overnight stops. The weather didn't help, it was poor, with plenty of rain and the nights were cold. However, rations were plentiful, including 'M&V' (tinned meat and vegetables, otherwise known as Maconochie's Stew) supplied by the railway line and there were issues of cigarettes too.

On arrival at El Arish the regiment camped about a mile east of the town. Here the rumble of gunfire could be heard in the distance and there were sightings of enemy aeroplanes above, although none attacked; George Lancaster noted in his diary, *"Numerous aeroplanes & gun fire discernible"*[11]. William Reader likewise wrote in his diary:

"Got our first view of an enemy aeroplane with the white puffs of the shells bursting all round it".[12]

There was an abundance of water at El Arish, considered by the men the best they had in the Sinai, and there was no rationing. After a few days rest the regiment made the final move up to the front, at Sheikh Zowaiid, only 10 miles west of Rafa, on 23rd February. This was the frontline and consequently trenches and dugouts had to be prepared, and daily patrols sent out. There was an expectant mood, noted by George Lancaster his diary;

"We are now in front line & expecting a scrap anytime."[13]

The following day the East Ridings were sent out to provide cover for parties of surveyors; 'A' Squadron and HQ to the village of Towail el Emir in the centre, 'B' Squadron to the village of Karm ibn Musleh on the right and 'C' Squadron towards Rafa on the left. The regiment soon had its first sight of the enemy, albeit a fleeting one, when a 'B' Squadron patrol spotted a distant Turkish patrol that quickly withdrew. Acting Sergeant Reader, on a patrol with 'C' Squadron noted:

> *"Left camp in line order to make a reconnaissance in force up to 2 miles behind Rafa. The Lincs formed the reserves and the Staffs stayed in camp. We reached Rafa at 11.30 to find no enemy there so made an outpost line while the surveyors behind did their work. As I sit writing this my patrol is absolutely the first British troops in front of the Turks. From our position at Rafa we could see a Turkish position at Khan Yunis and also a few enemy patrols about 1,000 yards away (too far to fire at them)."* [14]

The Brigade (consisting of the Lincs Yeomanry, the East Ridings and the 18th Squadron MGC) was deployed on the 1st March for another reconnaissance up to Karm ibn Musleh on the frontier. Lieutenant Frank Wood, whose Troop was in the vanguard wrote:

> *"How I remember the excitement and eagerness of all. El Musleh was supposed to be occupied by the Turks; in fact, our staff captain told me that our troops had never entered it as yet. This advanced guard was very interesting indeed, across a strange country, one had to find one's way by very poor maps, made years before under Lord Kitchener, and this was the real thing, no scheme. El Musleh was a disappointment to many, as it proved to be unoccupied… this was our first glimpse of Palestine and although it did not look very inviting, it certainly looked much better than the desert of the Sinai Peninsula."* [15]

Turkish patrols were again spotted during the day, but none could be engaged. George Lancaster recorded in his diary:

> *"was signaller to Major White* (OC 'B' Squadron) *when troop went in chase of Turkish patrol but could not get within rifle distance of them."* [16]

The regiment returned to camp by 8pm after a long hard day's riding.

On March 5th it became apparent that the Turks had withdrawn from the town of Khan Yunis (6 miles north of Rafa) and the ANZAC Mounted Division was ordered to occupy it. The 2nd Australian Light Horse Brigade, with the East Ridings in support, entered the town and secured it until the infantry could be brought up. Lieutenant Frank Wood recalled:

> "*We travelled over undulating country, partly grassed and partly sandy desert until we arrived on a hill 320 feet high and there in the valley below lay the village of Khan Yunus, surrounded by gardens in which grew olive, orange and almond trees with hedges of prickly pear*". [17]

There was the welcome opportunity to purchase chickens, oranges and eggs from the local population. Despite some ineffectual shelling by the Turks there were no casualties and at 7:30pm the regiment was withdrawn. It was another 12-hour day and a round trip march of 50 miles.

Back in camp the units of the 22nd Mounted Brigade were ordered to hand in all their rifles and ammunition, disrupting preparations. Like the rest of the 22nd Mounted Brigade, the East Ridings were equipped with Lee-Enfield Mk. III rifles sighted for Mk.VII (sharp-nosed) ammunition whereas the units of the ANZAC Mounted Division were equipped with rifles sighted for the older Mk.VI (blunt nose) ammunition.

To avoid potential supply problems the 22nd Mounted Brigade swapped rifles with the 3rd Australian Light Horse Brigade, who were leaving the division to join the new Imperial Mounted Division. The Regimental war diary notes that the rifles received in exchange were in very bad condition and a large percentage were unserviceable; some 200 rifles were in need of repair. The men also had their clothes fumigated.

With the frontline moving ever closer to Gaza (the main Turkish defensive position covering southern Palestine) the East Ridings moved up to Bir El Melalha, on the Mediterranean coast near Rafa, on 10th March. Here they mounted reconnaissance patrols as far east as the Wadi Ghuzze (which now formed the *de facto* frontline before Gaza) and provided cover for the working parties constructing the Sinai railway (the railhead reached as far as Khan Yunis by 24th March 1917). The Regimental transport finally caught up, arriving on 16th March.

Despite the obvious preparations for battle, outpost duties, reconnaissance patrols and the poor weather (frequent rain and sandstorms), the men still found time to indulge in some leisure activities. Once again there was ample opportunity for sea bathing and on the 21st March the brigade held the 'Rafa Spring Race Meeting' on an improvised racetrack that even included jumps. According to Lieutenant Frank Wood:

> *"The racecourse was made on a hollow plain on the Rafa battlefield, with a hill on each side to act as grandstands. This meeting was a huge success"*. [18]

The card featured such races as the 'Sinai Grand National', 'ANZAC Chase' and the 'Jerusalem Scurry'. Trophies were even ordered from Cairo!

The First Battle of Gaza

General Murray had set his sights on capturing the Turkish positions at Gaza, the key to the defence of Palestine, in preparation for his planned offensive in the autumn. The plan of attack, to be under the command of Lieutenant General Dobell, was agreed on 18th March and the forces required began to assemble at Deir El Belah, 10 miles south west of Gaza. It was to here that the East Ridings moved during the night of the 24th/25th March, arriving in camp at 6:30am. According to Acting Sergeant Wass Reader:

> *"At night we were ordered to have everything ready to move out at 2.00am and we slept in one blanket... Tomorrow is the big day when Gaza is to be attacked by the infantry while our division try to cut off the enemy in the rear. Left camp in the dark at 2.00am and marched about 12 miles out. The whole of the forces on this front are out today and we expect a big show."* [19]

The Turkish forces defending southern Palestine, commanded by the German General Kress von Kressenstein, numbered around 16,000 men, with about 4,000 of those in Gaza itself, supported by 7 batteries of artillery (including 1 German and

2 Austrian batteries). The Germans also provided aircraft which were more modern than those of the British, giving them air superiority. The key defensive position at Gaza was the ridge of Ali Muntar, just east of the town. Behind it there was a maze of thick cactus hedges as effective an obstacle as the barbed wire entanglements of the Western Front.

General Dobell planned to encircle Gaza to the north and east using the 'Desert Column', consisting of two mounted divisions (including the ANZAC Mounted Division) and the Imperial Camel Corps Brigade, cutting the garrison off from reinforcements, before attacking the Gaza defences with his infantry (53rd Infantry Division supported by a brigade from the 54th Division).

On the 25th March the Wadi Ghuzze was reconnoitred by the ANZAC Mounted Division and crossing points and potential water sources surveyed. The East Ridings were only involved in a supporting capacity, but this still meant leaving Deir El Belah at 7:30am, only an hour after they arrived. The regiment was held in reserve until 4:30pm and then had a spell manning the outpost line until relieved at 8:45pm, finally returning to camp by midnight. There was to be neither time for sleep nor for food though. Only 2 hours after arriving back at their camp, and after only having had barely enough time for a brew of tea and to feed the horses, at 2:00am (on the 26th March), the East Ridings and the rest of the ANZAC Mounted Division moved out for the attack on Gaza.

In spite of the pitch darkness and developing sea fog, which made navigation difficult, the division succeeded in crossing the Wadi Ghuzze about 4½ miles east of Deir El Belah on time and without incident, and proceeded to their allotted positions near Beit Durdis, east of Gaza. The thick fog enabled the cavalry screen to deploy largely unopposed and by 10:30am elements of the 2nd Australian Light Horse Brigade reached the Mediterranean coast to the north and Gaza was surrounded. Leonard May described the advance:

"*We marched all night making a wide detour. It was a night to remem-*

ber. *The General in command had us in a different formation. I think it was done to keep us awake as we kept dozing off and you would see men going off at a tangent. I remember the early morning, we were in section formation (fours) and I couldn't see the beginning or the end of horsemen, and one could see miles in the desert. We kept going until three or four in the afternoon and had got well past Gaza".* [20]

The fog had however slowed the progress of the infantry and supporting artillery somewhat and the infantry commander, General Dallas, decided to delay his attack until the fog lifted. At noon the infantry attack finally commenced but the 53rd Division met heavy resistance from the Turkish positions on the high ground in front of Gaza and progress was slow. General Chetwode, the cavalry commander, felt that the delay in launching the infantry attack and the slow progress being made would leave insufficient time to capture the town before nightfall, when the assault would have to be abandoned for a lack of water. He therefore ordered the ANZAC Mounted Division to mount a flanking attack from the north and east in support of the infantry.

Chetwode's orders were issued at 1pm but before the attack could be mounted the Imperial Mounted Division, who were positioned to the south, would have to move up and relieve the units of the ANZAC Mounted Division. This took time and consequently there was a considerable delay before the attack could begin; the ANZAC Mounted Division finally moved off at about 3:30pm, by which time the infantry had succeeded in reaching the top of the hill at Ali Muntar.

The East Ridings and the Lincolnshire Yeomanry left their forming up point 1½ miles east of Ali Muntar at around 3:30pm and advanced at the gallop through machine gun fire and shrapnel towards a hill on the outskirts of Gaza. Frank Wood wrote:

"our orders were 'attack', so we went in fine order, in line of troop columns at the canter. Oh, that ride, under heavy & what appeared to us well directed shell fire & over about two miles of rough plain, was as good as a fox hunt, quite a few came to grief, not so much through enemy shrapnel as through their horses falling". [21]

The East Ridings managed to get within a few hundred yards of the hill before being forced to dismount by thick cactus hedges. Leaving 'A' Squadron in reserve and one man for every four horses behind, the rest of the regiment carried out a dismounted attack under fire, capturing a Turkish redoubt along with 50 prisoners. According to Lieutenant Wood:

> *"we dismounted to attack the hill on which we could already see the Jackos (Turks) running, evidently our galloping advance had put the fear of something into them. As we advanced our RHA did some very good shooting, for their shrapnel was sweeping the ground only 30 yards in front of us. We took this hill, afterwards called Fryer's Hill after our Brigadier, at the same time as some of the infantry arrived on it – taking some 50 or 60 prisoners. A perfect hail of machine gun bullets greeted us on the ridge. It has always been a mystery to me why I did not lose more than one man at this time, when my troop was in front; we could not locate the enemy guns among the dense prickly pear hedges, nor could we advance, as there was a steep descent or a kind of cliff in front of us".* [22]

With their hill secured, the East Ridings sent out a patrol towards Ali Muntar which found that hill already in the possession of the infantry. The cost to the East Ridings of their first action was 1 OR killed (Private Robert Butler Throssel was killed by shrapnel), 2 wounded and 9 horses killed or wounded.

The entire Ali Muntar position had been secured and the ANZAC Mounted Division, including the East Ridings, was now in the suburbs of Gaza. To those on the ground it seemed that victory was theirs and this opinion was shared by the defenders. In Gaza the garrison commander destroyed his wireless and prepared to surrender. Outside the city the Turkish commander, General von Kressenstein, halted his reinforcements fearing it had already fallen.

Unfortunately, that was not how the British commanders saw things. Communications and coordination had been poor all day and now General Dobell believed that the infantry assault was getting bogged down and was in danger of failing, and he was not altogether sure of the location of the cavalry screen. Fearing that Gaza would not be taken before nightfall and knowing that mounted patrols were reporting Turkish reinforcements in the vicinity (as many as 10,000 men), he ordered a withdrawal at 6pm. The order came as a surprise to many, including the commanders of the cavalry divisions, since they felt the day had already been won. Bill Austin recalled:

> *"we had orders to retire. This we could not understand, as we thought we had done what we set out to do, but we retired in a north easterly direction for several hours, in fact until night fell."* [23]

The cavalry units withdrew back to their starting positions and Ali Muntar was evacuated, although the infantry remained in positions on the outskirts of Gaza. The East Ridings departed from their positions on Ali Muntar at 8pm, returning to their horses and making their way back to their starting point. At midnight they set off to march back to the camp at Deir El Belah, finally arriving at there at 8am, exhausted.

'B' Squadron, who had been out the longest, were able to water their horses first and feed them, but there was still to be no rest and barely any time for the men to snatch a meal. With dawn had come the realisation for Dobell that he had let Gaza slip through his fingers and he now made an attempt to renew the attack and finish the job.

He directed General Dallas to reoccupy Ali Muntar. The 53rd Division quickly sent out patrols to reconnoitre the positions given up the previous day and found them unoccupied, but the Turks had brought up reinforcements during the night and the British were soon driven off. More Turkish reinforcements arrived as the day progressed threatening the positions of the infantry and eventually Dallas was forced to withdraw, crossing back over the Wadi Ghuzze.

As a consequence of the attempted resumption of the attack the East Ridings were ordered back out of their camp after only an hour, advancing along the beach to Tel El Ajjul with the rest of the brigade, to take up outpost positions to the north east of the mouth of Wadi Ghuzze. The regiment withdrew to a new outpost line running from Sheik Rashid to the sea during the

THE FIRST BATTLE OF GAZA

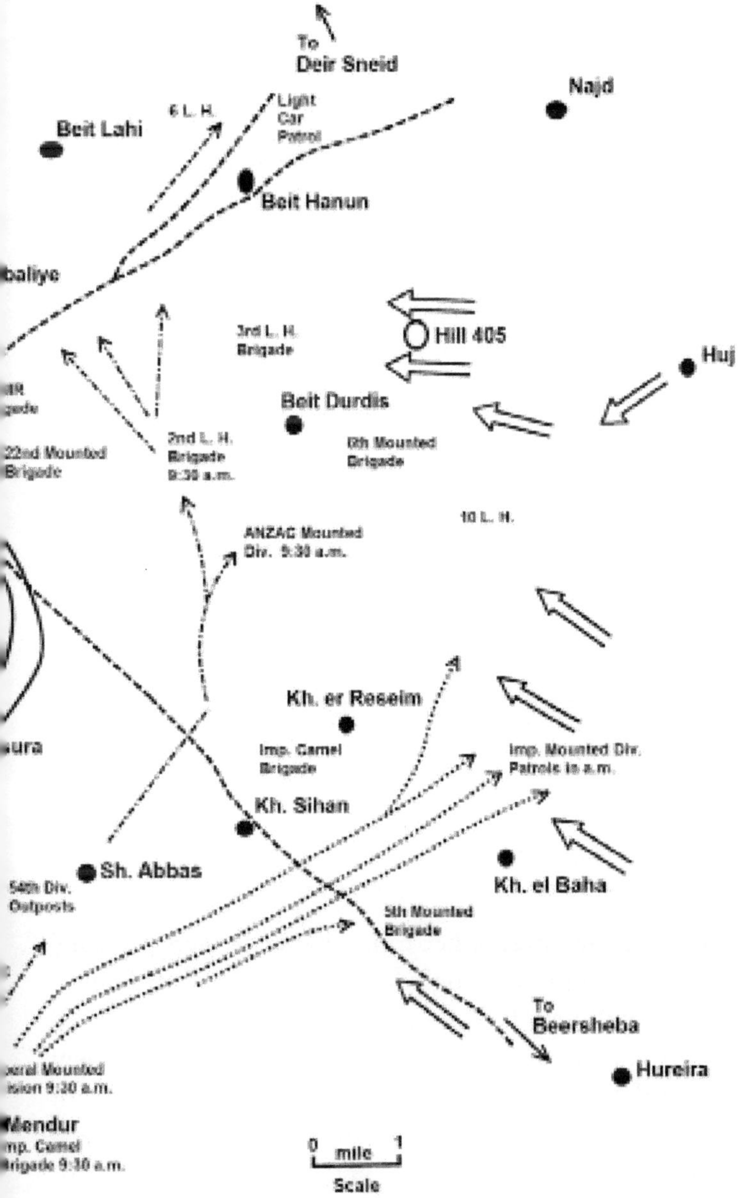

To
Deir Sneid
Najd
6 L. H.
Light
Car
Patrol
Beit Lahi
Beit Hanun
3rd L. H.
Brigade
Hill 405
Huj
Beit Durdis
2nd L. H.
Brigade
9:30 a.m.
22nd Mounted
Brigade
6th Mounted
Brigade
ANZAC Mounted
Div. 9:30 a.m.
10 L. H.
Kh. er Reseim
Imp. Camel
Brigade
Imp. Mounted Div.
Patrols in a.m.
Kh. Sihan
Sh. Abbas
54th Div.
Outposts
Kh. el Baha
5th Mounted
Brigade
To
Beersheba
Hureira
0 mile 1
Scale

H MARCH 1917

night of the 27th/28th March to cover the withdrawal of the 53rd Division. The men and horses were now totally exhausted having only managed about two hours sleep over the last 3 nights. Wass Reader wrote:

> "have been fighting nights and days now without a wink of sleep and have lived pretty nearly on water." [24]

In the morning the 22nd Mounted Brigade was sent out to reconnoitre the enemy positions from Gaza westward to the sea which aerial reconnaissance had reported evacuated. Orders were to avoid a serious engagement as there were no supporting troops available. 'B' Squadron of the East Ridings acted as advanced guard. Frank Wood wrote:

> "Away we went over the Wadi mouth towards Gaza, expecting every minute to meet heavy shell fire; but no, Jacko was again playing his game of wait & see. I pushed on over the good ground to within about 400 yards of Sampson's ridge, when the enemy got up out of their front line & ran back over the ridge – However, I had seen this trick played before, but had to wait for Wright's troop on my left, for they had been delayed by the soft sand dunes… the Turks came back to their front line trenches & opened a hot fire on us, which we could not return because of the blowing sand clogging our rifles. The Lincolns on my right had become heavily engaged and were falling back, leaving me in a very unsafe position with my right flank open. However, I hung to my position, keeping close observation of the enemy and getting all the information required, but was at last ordered to withdraw. This was very exciting, under hot fire from the Jackos, but once more I was very lucky and got away with only one horse killed and two wounded." [25]

The war diary records, rather more matter of factly, "enemy front line trenches found strongly held - reported accordingly". The order to withdraw back to the bivouac area was received about noon, but this was delayed when a British aircraft was seen to crash into the sea close by. It was piloted by 2nd Lieutenant George Dell-Clarke, of the Royal Flying Corps, who had been involved in a dog fight with an enemy aircraft near Gaza. His engine was hit, and he was slightly wounded and was forced to ditch in the sea. Private Sherwood and Lance Corporal Smales bravely swam out under fire to rescue him – an action for which they were both awarded the Distinguished Conduct Medal. Their citations read:

> *"For conspicuous gallantry and devotion to duty in swimming out to sea with a comrade under heavy rifle fire to assist an airman whose machine had fallen into the sea three hundred yards from the shore".* [26]

The East Ridings finally made it back to their bivouac at 4pm. Despite their exhaustion (the horses had done some 95 hours work with saddles off for only 6 hours in total) men and mounts were able to enjoy a dip in the sea and then, finally, get a full night's sleep.

After the battle

Despite the reverse General Murray felt encouraged that he had nearly captured Gaza and reported back to London positively, exaggerating the number of Turkish casualties and suggesting the battle had in fact been a British victory. The British government, believing that Murray was on the verge of a breakthrough, and keen for a morale boosting success, ordered him to resume his attack immediately, this time with the capture of Jerusalem as the ultimate aim (rather than waiting until the autumn as originally planned).

The Turks were equally as encouraged as, after a series of reverses in the Sinai, they had successfully held off a significant British attack and they resolved to reinforce the Gaza defences. The garrison was increased to 4 infantry divisions supported by a cavalry division and some 100 guns and 95 machine guns. They also constructed a line of fortified outposts and strong points (known as redoubts) running from Gaza all the way to Beersheba in order to prevent the Allied mounted divisions again outflanking Gaza.

The urgency of his new orders left General Murray with little option but to renew his attempt to take Gaza with a set-piece attack, reminiscent of those on the Western Front. His supply lines ran along the coast via the Sinai railway which now reached El Arish, only 8 miles from Gaza. The desert to the south was

THE REGIMENT SEA BATHING, DEIR EL BELAH, MARCH 1917
(ERYC)

THE 1/1ST EAST RIDING YEOMANRY LEAVING DEIR EL BELAH ON
THE EVE OF THE 2ND BATTLE OF GAZA, APRIL 1917
(ERYC)

barren and waterless and the logistics of moving and sustaining a large force there would require more preparations than he had the time for. That meant that Murray's forces could only realistically attack Gaza directly from the vicinity of the railhead. Of course the Turks were now fully alerted and knew he must come again and the availability of superior aircraft meant that the Turks had good aerial reconnaissance, not that the British were hard to find, camped out in the open in the area around Deir El Belah.

The new British plan called for 3 infantry divisions, again under General Dobell (the 52nd (Lowland), 53rd (Welsh) and 54th (East Anglian) Divisions) to mount a frontal attack, supported by a preliminary artillery bombardment lasting 2 days. The British also had 6 of the new tanks available (first used on the Western Front in 1916) and some 4,000 gas shells (gas had yet to be used in the Middle East). On the right flank the Imperial Mounted Division and the Imperial Camel Brigade of the Desert Column, under General Chetwode, would launch a diversionary dismounted attack aimed at pinning down the defenders of the redoubts and preventing them from coming to the aid of Gaza. The ANZAC Mounted Division, including the East Ridings, was to play only a subordinate role, being held in reserve, protecting the flanks of the attack but ready to exploit any breakthrough and to prevent Turkish reserves from reinforcing Gaza itself.

As Murray prepared for the attack the East Ridings remained at Deir El Belah, undertaking outpost duties, digging trenches, and providing patrols to protect working parties in the wadi preparing additional crossing points and developing additional water supplies. Training continued too, the regiment was able to complete its training on the Hotchkiss gun and the men received their first instruction on 'gas helmets' (as early gas masks were known) which would be needed if gas was used in the coming battle. On the night of the 16th/17th April the East Ridings and the rest of the ANZAC Mounted Division carried out a long night march to Shellal, at the extreme right of the line,

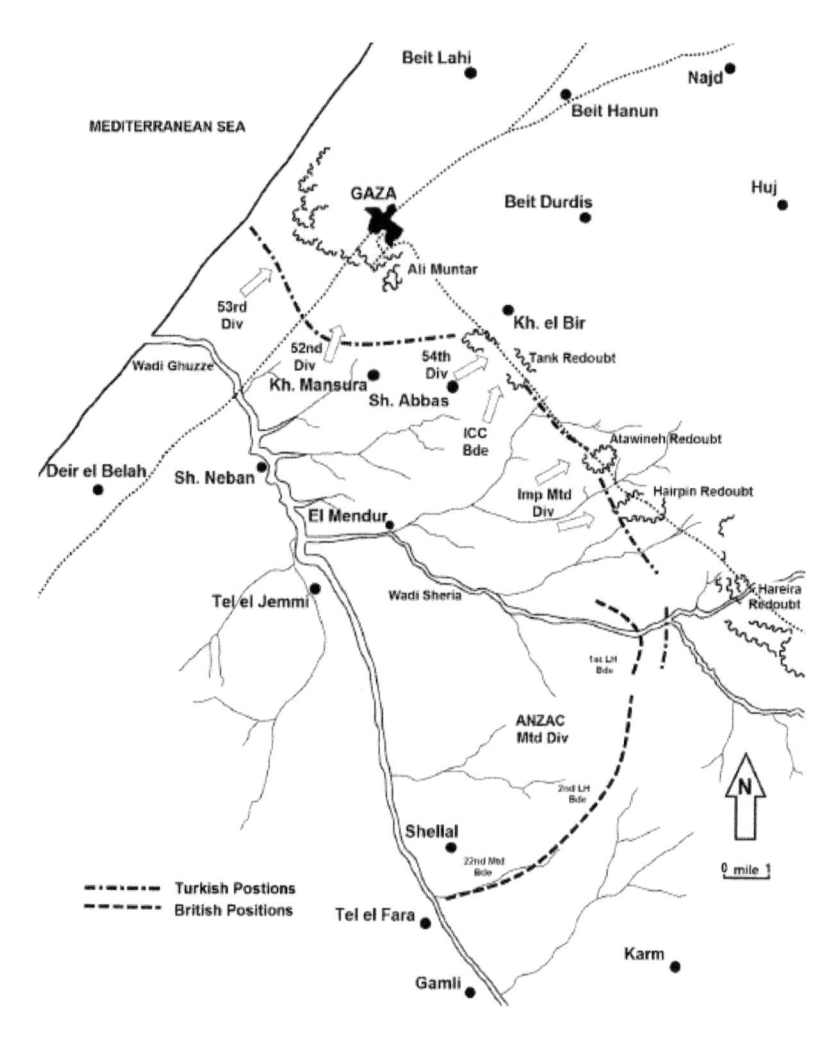

THE SECOND BATTLE OF GAZA, 17TH–19TH APRIL 1917

in order to protect the flank of the forthcoming attack, arriving there at 5:30am.

The Second Battle of Gaza

The renewed British offensive against Gaza began on the morning of 17th April 1917, with the opening of the artillery bombardment at 5:30am. General Dobell's artillery had been strengthened for the attack and he could count on 16 additional heavy guns, together with naval gunfire support from ships offshore. The bombardment was heavy compared to those of the preceding Sinai battles, but not when compared to those on the Western Front; there was insufficient artillery to adequately cover the frontage of the attack and consequently the guns were spread too thinly to achieve the desired concentration of fire at any point along the enemy's lines. Accordingly, the bombardment had only a limited effect, whilst serving as a warning to the Turks that an attack was imminent.

In addition, there were no guns allocated to counter-battery fire (i.e. to knock out the Turkish guns), which meant that the infantry, who advanced to their starting positions during the day, remained horribly exposed to Turkish artillery fire until the attack started. The infantry was held at their start point by the need to move up the heavy artillery, together with water and ammunition, in preparation for the next phase of the attack.

Having watered and fed the horses the East Ridings left camp at Shellal at 7am to act as escort to the artillery but were not engaged with the enemy. After a seven-hour march, they arrived back at the bivouac at Shellal at 2am on the 18th. The afternoon was spent patrolling, trying to establish the whereabouts of the enemy and then at 7:20pm the regiment moved out to Tel El Fara, taking up positions to protect the right flank for the following day's battle.

On the morning of 19th April, as the start time for the infantry assault approached, the guns concentrated on the Turkish positions around Ali Muntar. The barrage now including gas shells for the first time although they were generally ineffective, largely due to insufficient numbers of shells. At 7:15am the infantry attack commenced but it was a disaster. The advancing troops came under heavy artillery and machine gun fire from the intact and formidable Turkish defences, suffering heavy casualties and by noon the attack was faltering.

For the East Ridings there was little action during the morning, with only the sound of the artillery to the north indicating a battle. Then during the afternoon, the Turks attempted to reinforce Gaza with their 3rd Cavalry Division. At 2:15pm three troops of 'C' Squadron were dispatched to engage an enemy force seen advancing from the south and at 5:10pm another large enemy force, of approximately regimental strength, was spotted 4 miles in front of the lines, and 'B' Squadron was sent out to engage. Fire was exchanged and the Turkish cavalry advance was halted and there were no casualties reported.

However, by nightfall it became apparent to General Dobell that the attack had failed and orders to renew the attack the following day were cancelled. The East Ridings withdrew to a new outpost line at 10pm, digging in at Karim Abu Hiseia, back at the Wadi Ghuzze.

The Turks had defeated the second attempt to take Gaza, causing the British more than 6,000 casualties, compared to around 2,000 of their own.

Aftermath

It was General Dobell who paid the price for the failure to capture Gaza; General Murray sacked him as Commander of the Eastern Force on the 21st April, promoting General Chetwode (Commander of the Desert Column) in his place. In light of the casualties and loss of morale suffered by the British, and the likely strengthening of the Gaza defences by the Turks, it was apparent that it would be some time before any attack could be renewed and thus Murray's first priority was to secure the British position and reorganise and strengthen his exhausted and demoralised troops.

Accordingly, the British set about fortifying the line in front of Gaza, as far east as Shellal, with trenches and barbed wire. From there inland the line was more lightly held, consisting of outposts manned by one of the mounted divisions in rotation. Initially this was the ANZAC Mounted Division and consequently for the next month the East Ridings spent their days digging trenches, erecting barbed wire entanglements, manning outposts and mounting patrols in the Tel El Fara area.

On April 22nd one man was wounded in a clash between a 'B' Squadron observation post and a Turkish patrol, and the following day several patrols from 'A' Squadron were fired on by artillery and machine guns, although no casualties were sustained.

Morale was low, as noted by Wass Reader in his diary:

"I cannot quite make out how the position is here because we are putting down trenches and wire as though we were not going any further and expect to be attacked. The lads all look very weary and done up. Rumour was Dallas, Doble (sic) and Murray have been sent away as useless". [27]

On the 4th May a German squadron carried out an air raid on Deir El Belah. Five aircraft dropped thirty bombs, some of which hit the hospital, killing 6 and wounded 20 others. Amongst the wounded were Private Alvara Lofthouse and 2nd Lieutenant Gresham of the East Ridings. Private Lofthouse sadly died of his wounds soon after and Lieutenant Gresham succumbed a few days later on the 7th May.

Morale was probably not improved by the arrival of the remnants of a draft from the 3/1st East Ridings under Lieutenant Ullyot on the 9th May, the survivors of the sinking of the troopship *Arcadian* which cost the lives of 19 of their comrades. On the 16th May Acting Sergeant Reader confided in his diary that:

"I think the hot weather and the monotony of the outpost work is beginning to tell on the men." [28]

However, the regiment was finally relieved the following day by the Suffolk Regiment and moved into a bivouac area behind the front line at Tel El Fara allowing the men chance to have their clothes off for the first time in three weeks.

EAST RIDING YEOMANRY POSITIONS ON THE WADI GHUZZE,
MAY 1917
(ERYC)

Murray informed the government of his appraisal of the situation in early May, concluding that he needed at least two more infantry divisions and more artillery in order to take Gaza. This was eventually reluctantly agreed, but it would take some time for the reinforcements to reach Egypt. Despite this, and Murray's ongoing correspondence with London, the lack of activity led to mounting pressure on him to do something.

Somewhat fortuitously it was discovered that the Turks had a railway line still operating beyond Beersheba (to Asluj and Kossaima) and it was therefore decided to mount a large-scale raid to destroy it. The Imperial Mounted Division would make a diversionary attack against Gaza whilst the ANZAC Mounted Division and the Imperial Camel Corps Brigade would carry out the actual raid. This they did on the 23rd May with some success, destroying 15 miles of railway track and blowing up the bridge at Asluj.

In support of this operation the East Ridings acted as escort to the Divisional Ammunition Column, mounting a night march from Tel El Fara to a position just north of Khalasa, where they arrived at 4:45am. William 'Wass' Reader described the day:

"We stayed in one position all day except to go to water, which we were very lucky to find in the wadi"[29].

After an uneventful day without any contact with the enemy the regiment commenced their return march at 4:30pm, finally arriving back at Tel El Fara at 8:15pm after a round trip of 70 miles. George Lancaster noted, *"feeling very sore"*[30], whilst Sergeant Reader:

"…heard that the Australians had the day of their lives blowing up all they came across and burning villages galore. They destroyed 24 miles of railway lines including a mass of points and crossings".[31]

Patrolling continued, resulting in numerous skirmishes with the Turks, including one 'hairy' one on the 27th May which ran into an enemy force resulting in an *"exciting gallop out of fire"* according to the entry in Terry Ward's diary[32]. There were no casualties, but it was a lucky escape; several horses were shot. The

East Ridings and the rest of the brigade were finally withdrawn to Tel El Marakeb on the coast for a rest on the 28th May. Men and horses were exhausted and, after their long stint in the front line, everyone was 'lousy', Wass Reader was:

> *"becoming simply smothered with sand lice and the seams of my breeches are absolutely thick with eggs"* [33]

and so, the regiment had to be disinfected. Consequently, the following day the regiment was sent to Khan Yunis. Jimmy Seddon recalled:

> *"We collected at the rail side where a train, which had been adapted for the purpose, had been sent. It consisted of large trucks full of sacks. We rolled up our clothing in bundles which were then placed on the sacks. Then the trucks were sealed, and steam was driven in from the engine. While we were waiting for the tops to be cooked, we sat on our haunches naked as on our birthday chanting snatches from such Arab songs as we had acquired. Sad to say, the experiment was a failure and the creatures in the middle of the bundles had survived. At times the discomfort caused by these lice was anything but a joke and there was the danger of typhus".* [34]

After a week or so of light duties and training, including a training session using the 'gas helmets' (gas masks) with real Chlorine gas, the regiment moved inland to a new bivouac area at El Fukhari, between Rafa and Khan Yunis, on June 8th 1917.

Allenby

The success of the raid on Asluj was not enough to save Murray and on the 11th June he was sacked. Setbacks elsewhere meant that a successful offensive in Palestine was now seen as imperative, but ultimately the War Cabinet lacked confidence in Murray after his two failed attempts. General Sir Edmund Allenby, the successful Commander of the Third Army on the Western Front and renowned cavalry officer, was appointed to succeed him. Allenby was given orders to recommence the offensive into Palestine and to capture Jerusalem before Christmas.

He arrived in Egypt on the 27th June and assumed command of the Egyptian Expeditionary Force (EEF) the following day and immediately embarked on a 3-week inspection of his command, paying frequent visits to front line units and moved General Headquarters from Cairo forward to Um el Kelab, near Khan Yunis, to be nearer the front line. He re-established discipline and by his visible presence amongst the frontline troops encouraged feelings of confidence and boosted morale. He re-organised his force along more formal lines, and to take account of the reinforcements now beginning to arrive in Egypt from Salonika and elsewhere.

The Eastern Force and Desert Mounted Column were abolished and the EEF grouped into three corps: the XX (Twentieth) and XXI (Twenty-first) Corps, totalling seven infantry divisions, and the Desert Mounted Corps, which replaced the Desert Mounted Column. Each of the existing mounted divisions gave up one brigade and together with two additional yeomanry brigades from Salonika constituted a force of three mounted divisions of three brigades each, plus the Imperial Camel Corps brigade.

As a consequence of this reorganisation, the East Ridings and the rest of 22nd Mounted Brigade were transferred from the ANZAC Mounted Division to the new Yeomanry Mounted Division. Besides the change in their parent division this also entailed all the regiment's rifles having to be handed in again, reverting back to Lee-Enfield Mk. III rifles sighted for Mk. VII (sharp-nosed) ammunition for commonality with their new division.

Prior to Allenby's appointment, General Chetwode had prepared a paper setting out his proposals for the continuation of the campaign. Chetwode realised that further frontal assaults on Gaza would be costly and potentially futile. However, to the east there was a gap between the end of the Gaza defences at Hareira and those at Beersheba of about 4½ miles, which could be exploited in an outflanking manoeuvre. The Turks assumed that the lack of water in this area would limit the extent of British operations and consequently only one division was stationed there.

General Chetwode proposed that a forward depot be established in the vicinity of Beersheba which would permit an attack against this weaker flank. A breakthrough achieved there would outflank the Gaza defences permitting them to be 'rolled up' and, if a mounted force could advance north west towards the coast, the defenders would be cut off from any reinforcements and their supply lines (essentially a similar plan to that of the first battle, albeit on a larger scale).

Alternatively, if a general breakthrough could not be achieved, the Beersheba attack would draw the Turkish reserves away from Gaza, weakening the defences there, thus making an attack against the city more likely to succeed. The raid on the railway at Asluj had demonstrated that it was possible to operate a large mounted force in the area, albeit for a limited time. It would therefore be vital to capture Beersheba and its wells and water supplies quickly, during the first day of the attack, as stockpiled and local supplies of water would only be sufficient for about 24 hours.

Chetwode's plan was for two divisions of XX Corps (60th (London) and 74th (Yeomanry) Infantry Divisions) to attack Beersheba from the south west while two of the mounted divisions of the Desert Mounted Corps (The ANZAC and Australian Mounted Divisions) attempted to encircle the town to the south and east. The gap between XX Corps attacking Beersheba and XXI Corps to the West facing Gaza would be filled by the Yeomanry Mounted Division, who would act as a reserve ready to continue the advance should a breakthrough be achieved. Diversionary attacks would be launched by XXI Corps against Gaza itself in order to persuade the Turks that the main attack would once again be against the city.

On his arrival Allenby accepted the basis of this plan and immediately set about implementing it. Assembling a force of sufficient size in the Beersheba area would require a significant logistical effort to move and support the men, horses and supplies (the mounted units would have to cover some 70 miles to reach their start points, the infantry 20 miles). What local water sources were available would have to be developed and expanded, and the routes across the desert would have to be improved and marked on the maps. Detailed reconnaissance of the enemy positions south and west of Beersheba would have to be carried out as Allenby wanted his commanders to gain first-hand knowledge of the terrain over which they were to lead their men.

Allenby's Preparations

In preparation for the planned offensive the railway running from Kantara on the canal to the railhead at Deir El Belah, 8 miles from Gaza, was to be doubled (the new doubled track had reached El Arish by the time the attack was launched) and a new branch line laid from Rafa to Shellal, on the Wadi Ghuzze. This would enable the large numbers of men, animals and all manner of supplies, stores and ammunition to be moved over to the right flank. There was also a light railway constructed from the railhead at Deir El Belah, eastwards along the bank of the Wadi Ghuzze. Supplies for XXI Corps, who would remain in front of Gaza, were moved from Kantara to Deir el Belah by sea to ease the burden on the railway.

There was, however, still the question of getting the supplies from the beach and railheads to the front line troops. XXI Corps gave all their transport to support XX Corps and the Desert Mounted Corps. In addition to the extensive use of camels (some 30,000 for transport) and several caterpillar tractors, hundreds of miles of wire netting roads were laid on the sand allowing the more extensive use of wheeled vehicles.

Water supplies were enhanced as old or destroyed wells were repaired and new wells and bore holes dug. At Shellal a number of springs in the Wadi Ghuzze were developed by the engineers that yielded nearly 300,000 gallons a day and a damn was constructed to create a reservoir capable of holding 500,000 gallons. The existing Sinai water pipeline was extended, and branches run out to several areas further inland.

Whilst the logistic arrangements were put into place the training of the army commenced. General Allenby had restored the morale of the men through his no nonsense approach, but they still needed a rigorous training programme to hone their battle skills and improve their fitness levels. There was also water abstinence training (the men were restricted to half a gallon a man per day for all purposes) to prepare them for the arid ground over which the offensive was to take place.

Consequently, throughout the remainder of June and into August the East Ridings were engaged in training at El Fukhari, concentrating on musketry and 'bombing' (grenade throwing) with more gas training, sword and bayonet drills and rehearsing both mounted and dismounted attacks. There were inspections by General Chauvel, at the time the Commander of the Desert Column, and General Chaytor commander of the ANZAC Mounted Division. General Chaytor inspected the regiment's horses and took the opportunity to say goodbye to the regiment as they were formally transferred to the new Yeomanry Mounted Division on 6th July.

Life was monotonous and rough; conditions were similar to those of the Western Desert the year before; intolerable heat, dust and flies and this time the men were living in bivouacs rather than tents. To compensate there were plentiful rations and the training routine was punctuated with regular 'bathing parades' where the men and horses were able to swim in the sea. Some lucky men were sent to a rest camp at Khan Yunis for a week and there were the usual regimental sports (including a rugby union match which resulted in a 3 – 0 defeat to the Staffs Yeomanry) and a brigade horse show and sports meeting on the 16th August. Several long mounted route marches were carried out, each lasting many hours, in preparation for the move into the area earmarked for the mounted attack.

It was during August that a number of cases of Bilharzia were reported in the regiment. Bilharzia, (also known as Schistosomiasis) is caused by parasitic worms (trematodes or 'flukes') and although easily treatable, even in 1917, it is a chronic illness that can damage the internal organs. Infection occurs by swimming or washing in infected water, allowing the parasitic larvae to enter the body through the skin. The regiment's first positive case was reported in January 1917, but the majority were diagnosed after the beginning of June 1917.

The NCOs and men of 'C' Squadron who were stationed at Gharack South were tested on the 14th, 15th, 16th and 17th August resulting in 15 out of 59 men testing positive. This brought the total infected in the regiment to 40: all at one time with 'C' Squadron at Gharack South (with one exception). The majority were evacuated to hospital. It was concluded that the infection was caused by the fact that there were no horse troughs erected at Gharack South for several weeks and the NCOs and men had to water their horses from buckets, direct from the canal in the camp.

Although readily treatable the parasites can survive in the human body for many years; the Hull Daily Mail was reporting in December 1925 that there were still yeomen suffering from the effects of the disease.

On August 18th the East Ridings returned to the front line with the rest of the 22nd Mounted Brigade at El Shauth, near Tel El Fara. The East Ridings were responsible for mounting patrols day and night and with manning observation posts along their section of the front, in order to dominate the area and prevent any Turkish interference with the preparations going on behind the lines.

To permit the officers to reconnoitre the area in which the forthcoming operations were to take place, particularly with regards sources of water, a number of raids and large reconnaissance patrols were mounted. Throughout this time clashes with the enemy occurred on a daily basis as their patrols were also operating in the area.

During the night of 26th/27th August a 'C' Squadron patrol of a dozen men, led by Captain Robinson, were surprised by a Turkish ambush. Captain Robinson saw the situation unfolding and dashed forward to warn his men. The Turks waited until the leading men got within 100 yards and opened fire and one horse was shot. Captain Robinson plucked the unhorsed trooper and carried him away under intense fire, an action for which he was subsequently awarded the Military Cross.

Intelligence gathered during these patrols indicated that a small force of Turkish cavalry would come out of their lines every morning to water their horses from a well in no-man's-land, in the vicinity of El Buggar.

It was decided to attempt to surprise and capture them and so on the 29th August the East Ridings mounted an operation with this objective. 'A' and 'C' Squadrons left camp at 8pm on the night of the 29th, followed at midnight by the rest of the regiment in support. The two lead Squadrons would carry out a pincer movement, each marching some 10 miles around to the north and south. For the plan to work the East Ridings would have to approach almost to the enemy positions and remain undetected. 'A' Squadron, under Captain Pearson, reached their allocated positions during the night and concealed themselves.

Unfortunately, 'C' Squadron, under Captain Robinson, was not able to find suitable cover and was spotted at first light by the enemy and the alarm was raised, allowing the enemy force (approximately 2 Troops of cavalry) to escape. Captain Pearson and his men immediately advanced at the gallop and opened rifle fire on the enemy, wounding the horse of one man, who was captured, the sole result of the operation apart from two 'A' Squadron horses which were wounded in the exchange of fire. No other casualties were sustained.

Two days later a major operation was mounted to reconnoitre the area around Khalasa. The Staffordshire Yeomanry were to carry out patrols in the area to "round up any Arabs detected committing any hostile acts or found carrying arms". The East Ridings would be responsible for reconnoitring the water supplies in the area and the Lincolnshire Yeomanry would provide protection for the officers of the ANZAC and Australian Mounted Divisions who were to reconnoitre the area in preparation for their divisions' role in the coming battle.

The regiment left camp with a special party of Royal Engineers attached at 1pm on the 31st and bivouacked overnight south of Abu Ghalyom. The following morning the regiment marched on to Khalasa and then sent out four patrols on water reconnaissance to check on the status of various wells in the area. Whilst the patrols were out checking the wells the remainder of the regiment moved on to Asluj where there was a skirmish with a group of Bedouin. The regiment then withdrew back to Khalasa where all the patrols reported in. The return march commenced at 2pm on the 1st September and following another night bivouac, the brigade returned to camp at 8am on the 2nd. It had been a long, stern test across harsh, largely waterless country in the heat but good preparation for the operations to come. Bill Austin remembered that the march was:

> *"our longest one... to a place called Kilassa (sic), miles south of our positions and to the east and north of Beersheba, and we went nearly up to the Dead Sea. That jaunt was our longest and last, and we had a few alarms and patrols and engagements with other Turkish patrols, but the most serious was to come later".* [35]

Although no casualties were suffered amongst the men, a number of horses had to be destroyed, primarily due to exhaustion.

Another large-scale reconnaissance in force was carried out by the Yeomanry Mounted Division south of Beersheba on September 12th. The East Ridings deployed during the morning, occupying a line of outposts to cover the various parties of officers and engineers reconnoitring the ground and also provided escorts to two batteries of the Leicestershire Royal Horse Artillery and a patrol of Royal Engineers, tasked with checking a suspected spring.

A number of the regiment's patrols came under fire from Turkish trenches and the regiment's positions came under Turkish shell fire intermittently all day. The shelling forced the water patrol to be abandoned but there were no casualties. A more serious situation arose at 4:30pm when an 'A' Squadron outpost, held by a Troop under Lieutenant Bailey, came under attack by a force of Turkish infantry approximately 60 strong, supported by artillery fire. Lieutenant Bailey wrote in a letter to his sister:

"I took my troop to a forward post, feeling far from secure. But having made my dispositions, which consisted chiefly in lying very doggo and packing the horses in little pockets of ground, wishing to resist the temptation of being an extra sentry (i.e. one more head or hat to be seen) I pulled out the paper (a copy of the Times Literary Supplement) *for a long, pleasant looking discourse on pictures. I hadn't done the first paragraph when the sentry pointed out that the Beersheba's* (sic) *were climbing down from their trenches and coming to look for me. Those who didn't come turned out to see the fun, like the populace on the city wall in olden days, cheering their champions below, as no doubt these did and what was much more serious than the champions, their shrapnel and explosive. We ran a little battle on our own for half an hour and only had one man hit in the calf* (the Troop sergeant), *and my Bob rather lame, whether from stony ground or shell shock I don't know. Not being able to return their hate, except with our rifles, we dodged about, retiring from hill to hill and cursing the 'stony wilderness' till Smith came to help".* [36]

This was another 'A' Squadron troop dispatched by Captain Pearson to help and the attack was eventually repulsed. The regiment withdrew at sundown, around 6:15pm (*"supper time in Beersheba, no doubt"* thought Lieutenant Bailey[37]), finally returning to camp at 1am on September 13th.

These operations were important but were hard on men and horses, as noted by Lieutenant Bailey, and it was clear that for the forthcoming attack the mounted units must be in top condition.

Therefore a few days later, on the 18th September, the 22nd Mounted Brigade was withdrawn back to Tel El Marakeb for a period of rest and recuperation and inevitably, yet more training. Once again, for the lucky ones at least, there was the chance of a trip to a rest camp, this time at Port Said on the Suez Canal.

Beersheba

The completion of the rail link and water pipe from Tel el Fara to Karm marked the end of the logistic preparations and orders for the coming battle were issued. The troops earmarked for the attack began to move unobtrusively by night to their concentration areas. Their old camps were left intact with small parties remaining behind to set fires and lights in the tents at night to deceive enemy aerial reconnaissance and convince the Turks that the main gathering of British forces remained opposite Gaza.

This deception was aided by the Turks' own attack on El Buggar ridge which diverted their attention from elsewhere for a few crucial days. As a result, General Allenby was able to move some 40,000 men, horses and supplies over to the area of Beersheba undetected.

The East Ridings left their camp at Tel El Marakeb on the morning of October 28th, marching to Shellal whence they arrived at 4pm. The regiment endured a wet day at Shellal before moving out to occupy an outpost line during the night of the 30th. Sergeant 'Wass' Reader noted:

> *"There must be at least ten thousand troops here and big guns etc. are moving past all the night. It is their wish to try to break the Turkish lines in the middle which is just here".*[38]

The following morning, as the attack on Beersheba began, the regiment was up and ready to move by 9am, standing by on 30 minutes notice. They remained stood-to all day. According to Reader:

> *"There was a very heavy barrage fire for about fifteen minutes at 05.30 this morning in the direction of Gaza. Convoys miles long of motor ambulances and lorries have been passing here on the main road all day long. We were ready to march out at a few minutes' notice at 09.00 and are now stood by awaiting orders. Things seem to be very quiet and there is nothing to show the big attack at Beersheba is going on".*[39]

The attack on Beersheba by XX Corps began at 5:55am on 31st October with an artillery barrage. The infantry commenced their attack at 8:30am with the capture of several Turkish outposts, clearing the way for the main attack by four infantry brigades of the 60th and 74th Divisions, which began at 12:15pm.

The infantry quickly reached their initial objectives but now halted to await the attack of the mounted units. This attack was held up however, as the ANZAC Mounted Division struggled to capture the strongly held positions on Tel el Saba, a 1,000 ft hill east of Beersheba. These were not secured until 3pm and by then it seemed that there might not be enough time left for the planned combined infantry and cavalry attack to capture Beersheba itself before nightfall.

General Chauvel considered calling off the attack, particularly since the horses had not been watered for nearly 24 hours, but Allenby ordered him to proceed and as reports began to come in that the Turks were withdrawing, Chauvel saw his opportunity. Orders were given to General Grant's 4th Australian Light Horse Brigade to attack and take the town from the east.

The Light Horse regiments began their advance at 4:30pm. After advancing 1½ miles the first line charged. The Turks opened fire with their artillery, but the shrapnel had limited effect against the dispersed horsemen and when machine gun fire was opened from the left it was silenced by a battery of artillery. Despite rifle fire from the enemy trenches (largely ineffective because the defenders struggled to compensate for the speed of the horsemen and fired over their heads) the Australians reached the trenches jumping them and dismounting behind the enemy positions.

The Australians turned, drew their bayonets and engaged the Turks who were so demoralised that they quickly surrendered, the whole position being in the hands of the Australians in only 10 minutes. The following units continued the advance into Beersheba and the town was in British hands, with 15 of the 17 wells intact, by nightfall. In addition, two reservoirs containing 90,000 gallons each were captured intact. Fortuitously, due to the preceding day's rain, there were pools of standing water which allowed the horses to be watered quickly. Thirty-eight Turkish officers and 700 men were captured along with 4 field guns for a cost of 171 men killed.

Although Beersheba had been taken with its vital water supplies largely intact, the delay in taking the town prevented the advance being continued into the hills beyond. The Turks were therefore able withdraw to the north and form new defensive positions at Khulweilfe, el-Jammama and Huj, which all contained wells the British had hoped to capture on the first day.

Denied access to these additional water sources the British would need time to prepare adequate water supplies at Beersheba to continue the advance. Engineers were quickly set to work to expand the water sources and by 4th November the water supply at Beersheba had reached 390,000 gallons a day, enough for the next phase of operations, although the mounted divisions would still only be able to operate away from Beersheba for a day at a time until the supplies to the north were captured.

Whilst the engineers worked to improve the water supply numerous attempts were made over the next 4 days to capture the Khuweilfe position and although gains were made, the position could not be taken. Due to the shortage of water, each night the attacking mounted brigade was relieved in order to water its horses at Beersheba and another brigade resumed the assault.

Although the Khuweilfe position could not be captured the attacks served to pull in the Turkish reserves, which was important as the attack on Gaza itself was launched on the 2nd November. The infantry of the 54th (East Anglian) Division, with substantial support in the form of artillery, six tanks and the Imperial Service Cavalry Brigade (made up of Indian cavalry units), attacked the Turkish positions between Gaza and the sea before dawn on the 2nd, advancing about 2 miles, but a stubborn Turkish defence ultimately prevented a breakthrough being achieved.

Whilst these actions were in progress the East Ridings remained in reserve around Shellal. On the 31st October a Troop under 2nd Lieutenant Wright was despatched to escort some 250 Turkish prisoners to XX Corps at Karm and again another 1,300 were escorted to the rear on the 2nd November. Private Jimmy Seddon remembered that:

> *"we rode through the night and arrived at our destination in the small hours of the morning. The prisoners were in a large compound surrounded by barbed wire. There were hundreds of them, but they marched along as docile as sheep. We rode alongside of them with drawn*

A GROUP OF TURKISH PRISONERS, NOVEMBER 1917
(Author's collection)

THE EAST RIDINGS RESTING AT HATTEH AFTER DRAWING RATIONS, ENROUTE TO MEJDEL, 11TH **NOVEMBER 1917**
(ERYC)

swords at the slope...." [40]

The Turks were in a poor condition. During one rest stop a Turkish Officer offered Private Seddon his gold ring in exchange for a drink:

"I did not want is ring, but I handed him the (water) bottle with the intention of letting him have a reasonable swig. He would have drunk the lot, although some of his men were beseeching him to give them a drop and I had to give him a rap on the head with the flat of my sword to get my bottle back. I gave some of the men a sip, but one water bottle does not go far. The poor blighters must have been a long time without a drink". [41]

In fact, as the column approached their destination the Turkish prisoners spotted the horse troughs and, according to Private Seddon's account:

"there was no holding them back. They made a dash for the water and nothing but bullets would have stopped them whether the water was fit to drink or not." [42]

The East Ridings then took up outpost positions around Goz El Geleib, near Karm, on the 4th. Although they reported no enemy activity to their immediate front large numbers of enemy cavalry and infantry could be observed moving between Sheria and Abu Hareira. Due to the lack of wells in the area the horses had to be taken the 18 miles back to Shellal for water.

The regiment was withdrawn from their outposts on the 5th and moved via Karm to Beersheba where they were able to water their horses, which took 4 hours. This delay meant that although they prepared their bivouacs there was no time for sleep as about an hour after finishing watering they were ordered to the divisional rendezvous at midnight. Before them lay a night march as the division moved across to the right flank for the next phase of operations.

Breakthrough

With his water supplies consolidated Allenby could renew his attempts to break the Turkish line and at dawn on 6th November

XX Corps (the 10th, 60th and 74th Divisions) attacked on a broad front near Sheria, in the centre of the Turkish line. The initial objectives were reached by 1pm and, although the 74th Division could only make slow progress on the right, the 10th and 60th Divisions were through the Turkish positions by 2.30 pm, with the 60th Division capturing the railway station at Sheria.

The following morning XXI Corps launched the main attack on Gaza, the 52nd Division attacking from the positions previously taken by 54th Division in the sand dunes to the east, and from the west the 75th Division advanced against the positions on Ali Muntar, the key high ground that had been fiercely fought over during the First Battle of Gaza. On this occasion however all the objectives were taken with relative ease and the Imperial Service Cavalry Brigade entered Gaza at 9am.

In the centre the XX Corps attack continued, the 10th Division capturing the Hareira Redoubt and the 60th Division taking Tel el Sheria itself. By the evening of the 7th November the whole front was crumbling and the German commander of the Turks, von Falkenhayn, realised that the Turkish position was untenable and at risk of being cut off by the mounted forces (as was Allenby's plan) and had ordered his forces to withdraw. This was skilfully done, and the British did not realize the Turks had retired until they entered the deserted Turkish positions on the 8th November.

On the right a renewed attack against the Khuweilfe position by the infantry of the 53rd Division and the Imperial Camel Corps Brigade also commenced on the 6th November, although again this initially made limited progress. To protect the flank of this attack the East Ridings dug in just north of El Muweile and spent a grim two days under constant artillery and sniper fire (in his diary Private George Lancaster recorded, with a certain amount of understatement, *"our dugout is not very healthy owing to snipers and shrapnel."*[43]) Remarkably only 2 ORs and 3 horses were wounded.

The harsh nature of the terrain was once more illustrated here; the horses again had to be led back behind the lines some considerable distance for water, in this instance back to Beersheba. The watering party departed at 7pm, completed watering the horses by 4am and returned to the regiment's lines by noon the following day. Drinking water for the men was also scarce and orders were given to eat out of the emergency rations.

Pursuit

Allenby's aim from the outset had been the destruction of the Turkish Army in southern Palestine and his plan now called for the Desert Mounted Corps to exploit the breakthrough in classic cavalry fashion and strike north-west from Beersheba, through the villages of al-Jammama and Huj, to the coast in the hope of cutting off the retreating Turks.

The ANZAC Mounted Division was to advance on the right against al-Jammama whilst the Australian Mounted Division and 60th Division were to advance towards Huj in the centre. The Yeomanry Mounted Division was to protect the right flank.

The 60th Division advanced northwards from Tel el Sheria but encountered a strong Turkish rearguard which held up the advance until the evening of the 7th. The Australian 4th Light Horse Brigade attempted a mounted charge, but the men were forced to dismount and take cover by the weight of fire from the enemy positions.

The advance on Huj resumed the next morning (8th November) and another strong rear guard of artillery and machine-guns was encountered. This time a small contingent from the British 5th Mounted Brigade (attached to the ANZAC Mounted Division) made a true cavalry charge with swords (the Australian Light Horsemen did not have swords and had to rely on their bayonets in the charge). These 200 men from 1/1st Warwickshire Yeomanry and 1/1st Worcestershire Yeomanry suffered heavy casualties but managed to reach the guns and cut down the mainly German and Austrian gunners.

Overcoming this position permitted Huj to be taken later that day but the majority of the Turkish forces had managed to escape the trap. The remainder the of the ANZAC Mounted

Division, advancing towards al-Jammama, had less success and did not manage to capture their objective until 9th November.

Following the news that the Turks were apparently withdrawing the 22nd Mounted Brigade was ordered to carry out a reconnaissance to establish the situation in front of the Khuweilfe position and consequently the East Ridings left their outposts at Kh. El Muweile, collected their horses and at 6:30am on the 8th November, moved out as advanced guard to the brigade. They found the area clear, the Turks apparently having already withdrawn. Sergeant William 'Wass' Reader wrote:

> *"We left our trenches this morning and went further north (to the front) on our horses. The Turks must have cleared in a big hurry for we found dozens of his wounded also a complete hospital packed ready for moving and large numbers of big heaps of shells. We are doing a flank guard today whilst the 8th Brigade make a reconnaissance and they are being heavily shelled".* [44]

The regiment was then ordered on to Sheira, arriving there at 2am on the 9th whence they proceeded to water their horses for the first time in 50 hours (their last drink being at Beersheba on the night of the 6th). Tel El Sheria had only been captured the previous day and Private Terry Ward noted:

> *"Trekked to Sheria at sunset to water. Finished watering 3am. Viaduct over wadi has been destroyed. Wadi strewn with dead men and horses. Smell terrible".* [45]

Once the horses were watered the regiment continued on to Huj, the 22nd Mounted Brigade and the rest of the Yeomanry Mounted Division now having been ordered to rejoin the Desert Mounted Corps.

After spending the night of 9th/10th November at Huj the regiment set out after the Australian Mounted Division (who had left the night before) and marched to Tel El Nejile where they arrived at 9am and were able to water their horses again. Terry Ward noted that he was able to have his first 'wash' for a week although there was only three quarters of a bucket of water for a troop of 20-30 men. There was little food, the rations not having kept up with the pace of the advance, but the war diary notes that the short ration was supplemented by supplies abandoned by the retreating Turks: the area across which the regiment had marched was strewn with abandoned equipment and dead horses and men.

With the hot *Khamsin* blowing, making the conditions difficult, the regiment continued onwards, finally reaching Mejdel, near the Mediterranean coast, at 8:30pm on the evening of the 11th November.

Here the regiment was able to water again, the war diary noting that "horses extremely thirsty drunk freely". Likewise, George Lancaster recorded in his diary that they had:

> *"terrible sufferings in search of water – was just about done – drank gallons and so did Jimmy* (his horse) *– he is awfully thin".* [46]

The men were able to draw two days rations and Private Ward noted that they were able to get a *"good supply of Jaffa oranges"*[47].

The following morning the regiment marched forward to Esdud. Again the horses were able to be watered, this time from pools in the Wadi Sukerier, which were rather boggy and which resulted in the loss of two horses, including that of Terry Ward:

> *"my horse floundered in mud, sank and was drowned. I lost all my kit – transferred to next horse. Got a nasty ducking in slimy mud and then rode bareback – cold ride!"* [48]

El Mughar Ridge

The commander of the Turks, Erich von Falkenhayn, now attempted to rally his forces and establish a new defensive line in order to defend the Jaffa to Jerusalem railway line. By the evening of the 11th November he had managed to establish a 20-mile-long line from the coast inland, centred on the vital station at Wadi Sara, known to the British as Junction Station. Endeavouring to catch the British unawares, Von Falkenhayn ordered a counterattack by 4 Turkish Divisions against the right flank of the British advance, in an attempt to outflank and surround the forward units. The Turkish units advanced against the

MEDITERRANEAN SEA

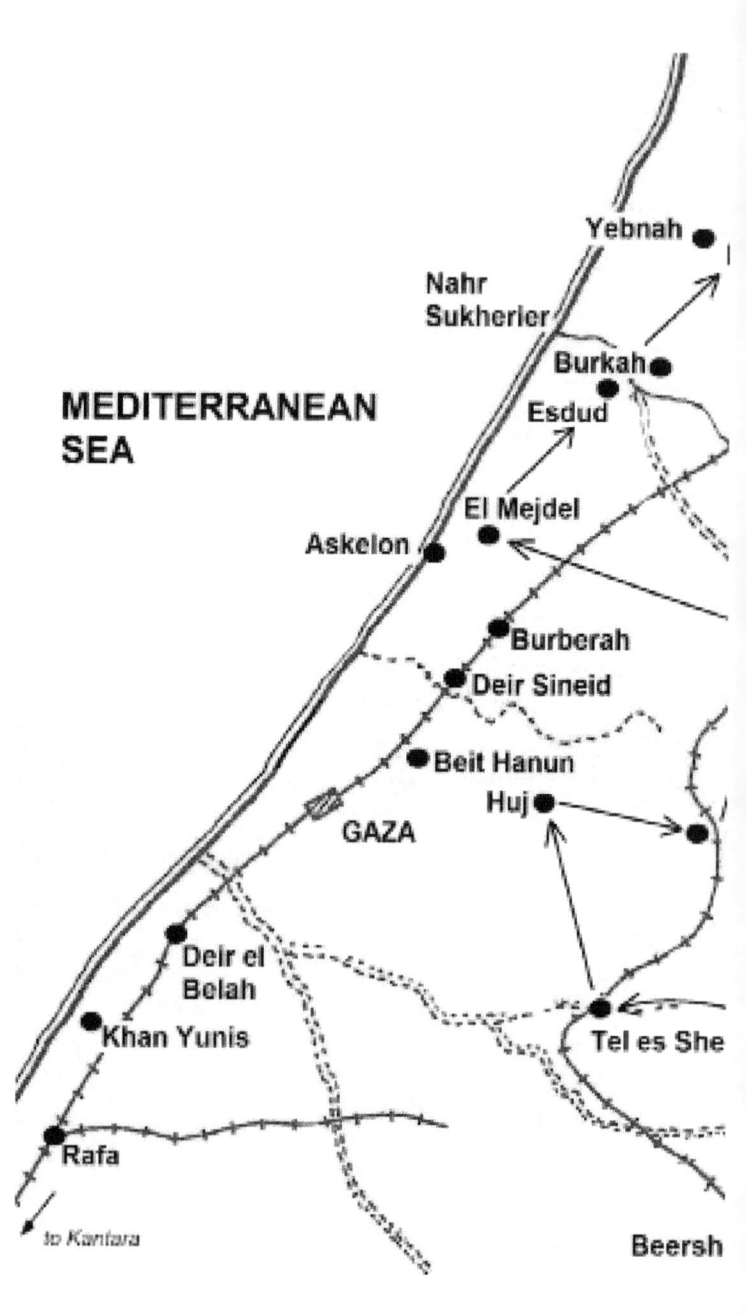

- Yebnah
- Nahr Sukherier
- Burkah
- Esdud
- El Mejdel
- Askelon
- Burberah
- Deir Sineid
- Beit Hanun
- GAZA
- Huj
- Deir el Belah
- Khan Yunis
- Tel es She
- Rafa
- to Kantara
- Beersh

ADVANCE OF THE EAST RIDING YEOMANRY,

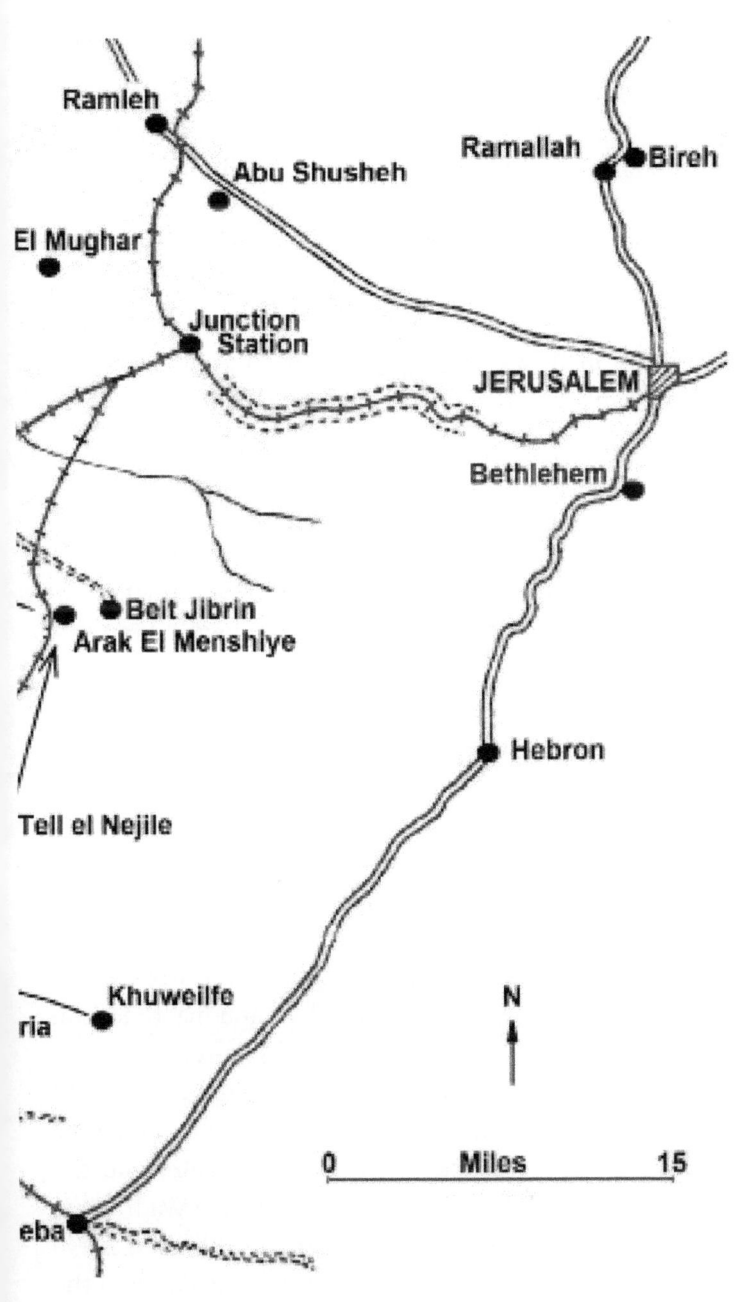

6TH–12TH NOVEMBER 1917

Australian Mounted Division and in fierce fighting the Turks managed to gain some ground until the dogged defence of the Australians finally halted the attack.

Meanwhile, General Allenby was planning his next move. East of Junction Station the Turkish line ran almost alongside the railway, but passed through the Judean Hills, country not particularly suited to cavalry operations. West of Junction Station the line ran westwards along a ridge to the villages of El Mughar and Katrah, on either side of the Wadi Janus, and then turned north.

The obvious plan was therefore to attempt to turn the Turkish right flank by the coast where the Desert Mounted Corps could operate to best effect. The Yeomanry and ANZAC Mounted Divisions would attack towards El Mughar on the left flank, with Yibna as their first objective and Akir the second. Once Junction Station was captured they were to swing north to occupy Ramleh and Ludd and reconnoitre towards Jaffa.

The Australian Mounted Division (reinforced with 2 mounted brigades from the other divisions) would hold the right flank and advance north toward the station whilst the infantry of XXI Corps (52nd and 75th Divisions) would attack along the line of the main road from Gaza to Junction Station.

The British advance began at 7am on 13th November but by around 10am, despite having taken the Turkish forward outposts, the advance became bogged down in the face of strong resistance from the main Turkish defensive positions. The 52nd Division, attacking Katrah and El Mughar, was having the hardest time of it, becoming pinned down by artillery and machine-gun fire in the Wadi Janus 600 yards from their objective.

The 6th Mounted Brigade was therefore ordered to attack El Mughar ridge in support of a renewed attack by the infantry. At about 3pm the Royal Buckinghamshire Yeomanry and the Queen's Own Dorset Yeomanry advanced from the Wadi Janus. The column had to cover 3,000 yards, trotting for the first 2,000 yards and then breaking into a gallop only as it the climbed the ridge. Despite the enemy fire the yeomen took the crest of the ridge, but the uphill charge had taken its toll on the horses and they were completely exhausted, preventing the pursuit of the fleeing Turks. The cost was heavy, 16 men killed, 114 wounded and 265 horses killed. The defenders of the village of El Mughar itself were dislodged a little later by two dismounted squadrons of the Berkshire Yeomanry and Katrah was also subsequently captured by elements of the 52nd Division.

The Charge of Wenlock's Horse

The Yeomanry Mounted Division's advance began with the capture of Yibna by the 8th Mounted Brigade. The village was secured by noon and then they continued on towards the villages of El Kubeibe and Zernuka. The 6th Mounted Brigade followed them into Yibna before being directed to attack El Mughar and Katrah and mounting the charge described above. The remaining brigade of the division, the 22nd Mounted Brigade, was to advance on the left flank of the 6th Mounted Brigade and once the ridge was secured press on towards Akir, which lay beyond El Mughar.

The 22nd Mounted Brigade commenced its advance about 30 minutes after the 6th Mounted Brigade. The Brigade cantered down the slope onto the plain in open order, 'A' Squadron of the East Ridings in the lead with 'B' Squadron behind and to the left. On the right was a Squadron of the Staffordshire Yeomanry, with the Lincolnshire Yeomanry bringing up the rear. Major Robinson, commanding 'A' Squadron ERY, left a written account of the action:

> *"Just before dropping into the Wadi Janus I look round, the 6th Mounted Brigade was spread out galloping in on my right front in open order. I then looked back, and my own brigade was cantering down the slope behind in similar lines. Every bit and button shining, and swords drawn, all horses in hand and beginning to lather, shells dropping, and the men cheerful and ready to go all out."* [49]

The regiment paused in the Wadi Janus and then set off all out for the ridge. Jimmy Seddon described the charge:

> *"we received the order to draw swords and the horses were urged forward*

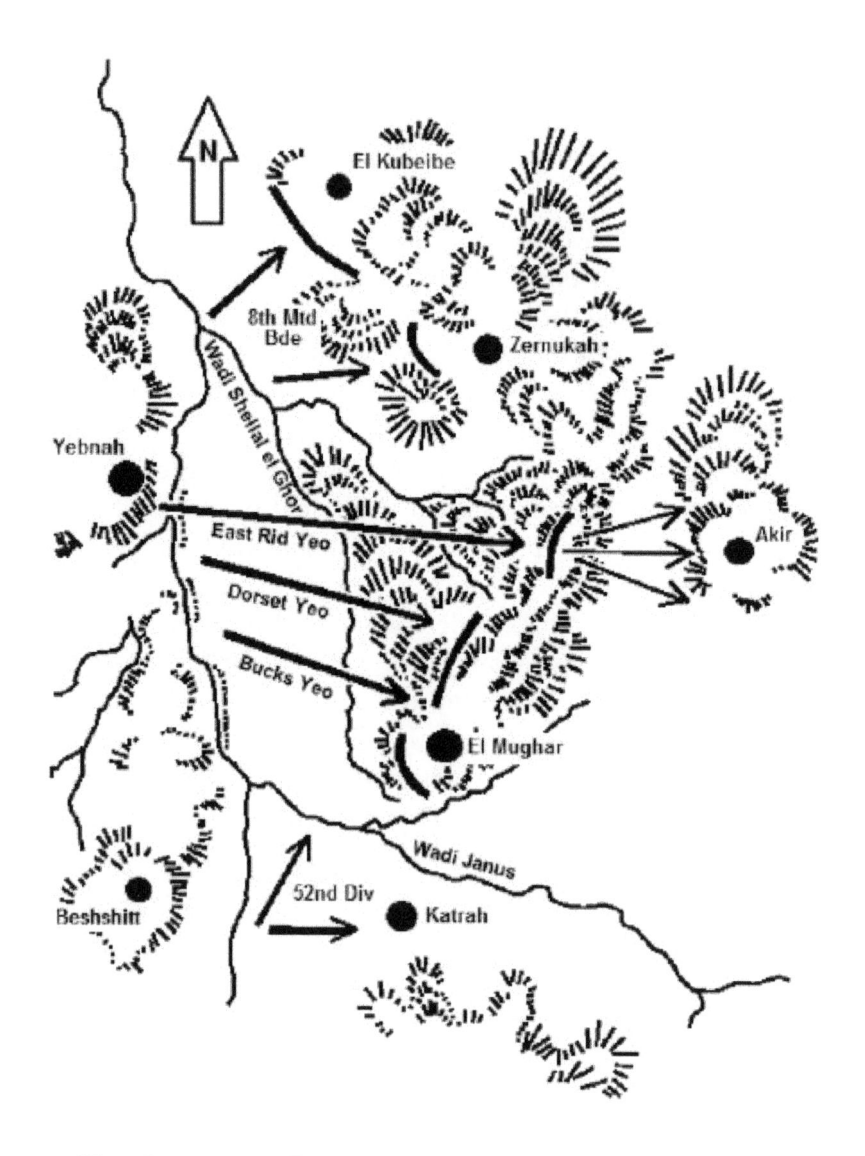

THE CHARGES AT EL MUGHAR RIDGE, 13ᵀᴴ NOVEMBER 1917

for us to charge machine gun positions over a ridge. The top of the ridge was a mass of exploding shells and the impression I got was that not many could get through this barrage…" [50]

Private Terry Ward thought it an:

"exciting gallop against artillery and machine gun barrage in exposed area". [51]

The leading Squadrons reached the crest at about 4:15pm. Major Robinson recalled:

"As we came up the ridge I saw what we had previously suspected; that the point we were to attack was a false crest and there was a machine gun emplacement covering it. Although the men were by then going all out I managed to control half the squadron and lead them to the real crest, killing what Turks we could on the way, captured the machine guns, and went into action dismounted, doing good execution with our rifles and Hotchkiss guns that had kept up well." [52]

The East Ridings quickly established good defensive positions amongst the rocks: Major Robinson's 'A' Squadron joined by 'B' Squadron (under Captain Sykes) and the Staffs Yeomanry Squadron (under a Captain Sidebottom). From their positions on the crest they could clearly see the valley below crawling with Turks, fleeing towards the village of Akir (or Aqir) and another 'European-looking' village beyond with red tiled roofs not shown on their maps (known as Ekron or New Akir/Aqir). Major Robinson, who could not find Lieutenant Colonel Moore the acting CO, held a quick conference with the commanders of 'B' Squadron and the Staffs Yeomanry Squadron and decided, as the senior officer present, that:

"now was the chance to both kill Turks and capture Old Aqir and the ridge beyond, which obviously was the jumping off ground to capture New Aqir. I remember pointing out to Captains Sidebottom and Sykes that it was against our orders (they had been ordered only to take El Mughar Ridge and no further), *but we must go after putting up all our Hotchkiss Guns and sufficient men to hold the present position".* [53]

Major Robinson would lead the charge on Akir himself, whilst 'B' Squadron and the Staffs Yeomanry Squadron would

The East Riding Yeomanry sheltering in the Wadi Janus just prior to the charge on El Mughar Ridge, captured, 13th November 1917
(ERYC)

attempt to encircle the village to the north-east and north respectively. Unfortunately, the majority of 'A' Squadron had remained on the false crest, so Robinson had barely half his Squadron available. After detailing sufficient men under Corporal Appleby to hold the positions on the ridge he was left with only a tiny force:

> "*I collected about fifteen men and we slid in single file down a water course, spread out when the going was better and raced amongst the Turks, killing some, and so through the cemetery into Old Aqir, a village with only donkey paths where we went in single file, shouting and I using a revolver when I could, driving the Turks out before us we went across the square, out the other side and dismounted behind a ridge.*" [54]

Private Bill Austin remembered:

> "*we eventually drove them out* (of Akir) *with a cavalry charge. Not as celebrated as the Six Hundred but as exciting for us and we got them out and took a lot of prisoners*". [55]

Once through the village the yeomen dismounted on the far side in order to engage a large column of the enemy which could be seen withdrawing to the north. Major Robinson wrote:

> "*Here the men were able to use their rifles with wonderful effect as there was a solid column of Turks retiring across our front at under a thousand yards, and we could see them falling.*" [56]

The enemy column was being directed by an officer conspicuously mounted on a white horse who, despite being repeatedly shot at, escaped unscathed. It was subsequently discovered that the column was in fact the headquarters of the Turkish XXII Corps and the officer the Corps Commander. Had he been killed or captured the outcome of the battle may have been very different.

Major Robinson could now take stock of his situation. The rest of the regiment and the Brigade had not advanced down from the ridge leaving his tiny force exposed. Despite having four signallers and a heliograph with him, Major Robinson was unable to establish contact with either the Regiment or Brigade Headquarters. On his right he could see that 'C' Squadron under Major Lyon had moved around to the south but had been

THE EAST RIDING YEOMANRY ENTERING NEW AKIR,
14TH NOVEMBER 1917
(ERYC)

THE EAST RIDING YEOMANRY WATERING THEIR HORSES NEAR ABU
SHUSHEH, 15TH NOVEMBER 1917
(ERYC)

halted on the approach to New Akir by heavy enemy fire from the Corps Headquarters rearguard. It was clear that no support would be forthcoming, and with the light fading Major Robinson decided he could not remain in Akir and must withdraw.

After watering his horses at the village well the small party fell back to re-join the rest of the regiment on El Mughar ridge. Major Robinson subsequently felt that had the orders to take Akir been known to the officers on the front line, the village could have been taken and the railway to the north cut and the divisional objectives taken. This was not to be however, and the regiment dug in on the ridge for the night.

Overall the attack on El Mughar Ridge had been a success, the Turkish XXII Corps had been routed with 1000 prisoners taken (71 by the East Ridings) and some 400 killed. British casualties were around 600. The East Ridings suffered 1 OR killed and 13 wounded. Amongst those injured was Private Arthur Best, from Beverley, who subsequently died of his wounds. Major Lyon later wrote to his parents:

> *"The action in which your son was wounded was the taking of Akir on the 13th November. The infantry had been held up all day by the Turks holding a ridge, which covered the village, and in the afternoon the yeomanry division was ordered to gallop the position. This was carried out most successfully, and resulted in capturing over 1000 prisoners. The yeomanry were pursuing the Turks still further and whilst my squadron were galloping in line we came under heavy machine gun and rifle fire, and it was then your son was hit through the stomach. He was able to ride back to the dressing station and went off in the ambulance the same evening. He got to the Casualty Clearing Station at Deir Senaid where he died the next day."* [57]

Junction Station

Junction Station was occupied by units of the 75th Division without opposition during the morning of the 14th November, cutting the Jaffa to Jerusalem railway and capturing two locomotives and 60 wagons which were in the station. Junction Station was a crucial logistical centre, where branch lines running to El Tineh and towards Beersheba and Gaza met the main Jaffa–Jerusalem line. There was also a water pumping station offering large quantities of easily accessible water which was found intact and functioning. The capture of the station effectively split the Turkish forces in two; the Turkish 8th Army along the coastal plain who were withdrawing northwards whilst the 7th Army withdrew eastwards into the Judean Hills toward Jerusalem.

The Australian Mounted Division occupied El Tinah where there was a good water supply but without pumps it would take all day to water the division. The ANZAC Mounted Division was ordered to advance towards Ramleh and Ludd and cut the road linking Jaffa and Jerusalem whilst the Yeomanry Mounted Division was to advance northwards and cut the railway north of Junction Station. The East Ridings advanced to Akir only to find that the Turks had withdrawn during the night and entered unopposed and watered their horses from the village well. The regiment was then ordered onto Naane. Along the route of the advance the regiment entered the previously unknown village seen the day before, known as New Akir. It made a big impression on many of the men. According to Terry Ward:

> "(we) *came across the prettiest village I have yet seen out here. People are evidently Jewish refugees and quite European and clean in their ways*". [58]

Jimmy Seddon noted the rather unusual appearance of the villagers, noticing that:

> "*some of these were wearing straw boaters and their clothes looked like Victorian style*". [59]

The villagers were welcoming and sold the men Jaffa oranges, figs, a dark rye bread and wine (not obtainable from the Muslim Arab population). This was very welcome to men on short rations, although the wine was perhaps not that advisable under the circumstances; Jimmy Seddon remembered that he:

> "*had a fair share of the wine and was beginning to take a more cheerful view of life when suddenly the Turks, who had apparently regrouped, began to shell the place. In spite of this I could not refrain from laughing when I saw the inhabitants disappear under any cover available, straw*

boaters and all. We mounted smartly and galloped out of range." [60]

This village was one of the earliest model Jewish settlements funded by Edmond de Rothschild of the Rothschild banking family.

The regiment moved off towards Naane, occupying the high ground north of the village, which was again found to be unoccupied, and cutting the railway line along which Turkish trains, escaping from Jerusalem, had been passing earlier in the day. The Turkish artillery fire that had begun earlier continued in earnest and the regiment's positions had to be held all day through artillery, machine gun and sniper fire before they were withdrawn at 6pm. George Lancaster recorded in his diary they *"got it very hot from shrapnel"*[61] and Terry Ward thought it was the *"hottest spot we have had yet for shrapnel"*[62].

The heavy fire and exposed positions brought many casualties, with 2 Officers wounded (Major Lyon and Lieutenant Bailey) and 2 ORs killed and 14 wounded. Lieutenant Bailey (a House of Commons Clerk) subsequently died from his wounds in Cairo, 1st December 1917

The next day (15th) the 75th Division and the Australian Mounted Division continued the advance eastwards towards Latrun, where the Jaffa to Jerusalem road enters the Judean Hills, whilst the Yeomanry and ANZAC Mounted Divisions were to continue their advance northwards towards Ramleh and Ludd. The Yeomanry Mounted Division was ordered to attack a Turkish rearguard at Abu Shusheh on the right flank of the advance on Ramleh. This rearguard position was charged and overwhelmed by the 6th Mounted Brigade in a charge described as even more daring than that at Mughar Ridge, owing to the rocky nature of the ground over which it was conducted.

The East Ridings were however in divisional reserve and saw no action, taking over the outpost line from the 6th Mounted Brigade during the afternoon, being themselves relieved by the Imperial Camel Corps at 8pm when they returned to Naane to bivouac for the night.

The following morning the regiment moved out to reconnoitre towards Latrun and Amwas which was found strongly held by the Turks with artillery and machine guns. The East Ridings took up positions opposite Amwas where they were shelled, suffering more casualties; 1 Officer wounded and 1 OR killed (Private Ellis Henwood Best), 1 missing and 4 wounded. They were withdrawn by mid-afternoon and marched to Ramleh. Elsewhere Jaffa was occupied without opposition by the New Zealand Mounted Rifles Brigade and Latrun was taken by the 75th Division.

INTO THE JUDEAN HILLS

After 17 days, an advance of some 60 miles from Beersheba (as the crow flies at least: the units of the Desert Mounted Corps had in fact covered over 150 miles) with virtually no rest and little food, General Allenby had intended a pause in the offensive to allow the supply lines chance to catch up.

Instead, he decided to capitalise on his success and attempt to take Jerusalem before the Turks could become too well entrenched in the Judean Hills, which provided excellent opportunities for strong defensive positions. Allenby's plan was to encircle the ancient city and force the Turks to withdraw in order to avoid unnecessary fighting and consequent damage in the Holy City.

The attack was to be carried out by two divisions of the Desert Mounted Corps (the Australian and Yeomanry Mounted Divisions) and two infantry divisions from XXI Corps (75th and 52nd Divisions). The attack was to be launched eastwards from Latrun in the same direction as the Jaffa to Jerusalem road. The 75th Division was to advance along the good main road but on their left the 52nd Division would have to march along various minor roads and tracks to the north. Beyond them further to the north the Yeomanry Mounted Division was to advance north eastwards along the old Roman road from Ludd to Ramallah and onward to Bireh in order to cut the Nablus road heading north out of Jerusalem. At the same time the 53rd (Welsh) Division was to advance northwards along the Beersheba to Jerusalem road to take Hebron and Bethlehem before moving eastwards to secure the road from Jerusalem to Jericho.

The East Ridings marched to Ludd on the morning of the 17th November and watered their horses. Most of the regiment took up bivouac positions but in preparation for the coming attack 2 Troops of 'A' Squadron under Lieutenant Stephenson (No. 2 and 4 Troops) were sent out to reconnoitre to, in the words of the war diary, "ascertain enemy dispositions and search for buried ammunition". The men were unable to reach their objective; however, according to Terry Ward the men:

> "*rode straight into heavy rifle and machine gun fire. (We) had to retire rapidly. 3 horses hit but luckily no men. The man on my right had his horse shot. I waited for him to jump up behind me but before doing so he got out his rifle and shot his horse through the head – saying "those buggers are not having my 'Tommy'"*. [63]

The regiment then returned to bivouac at Ludd.

On the 18th November the Australian Mounted Division secured the heights on either side of the main Jaffa to Jerusalem road at Amwas (and was subsequently withdrawn and sent to a rest camp) opening the way for the advance of the 75th Division, who entered Amwas the following morning having found it now unoccupied. The Yeomanry Mounted Division began its advance towards Bireh, but the rocky and steep terrain was hard going for the horses and only slow progress could be made. The 8th Mounted Brigade struggled to within 2 miles of Beit Ur el Tahta that night, while the East Ridings and the 22nd Mounted Brigade reached Shilta having had to lead their horses most of the way due to the rough going. No supplies were brought up and consequently there was no forage or rations.

The 19th November 1917 would turn out to be a trying day. As the mounted men struggled through the hills towards Jerusalem the winter rains began. The narrow roads were difficult enough for transport and artillery, but the rains turned them into sticky and heavy muddy tracks that were virtually impassable. The change in the weather also meant that the temperature, which had been hot during the day but more pleasant at night,

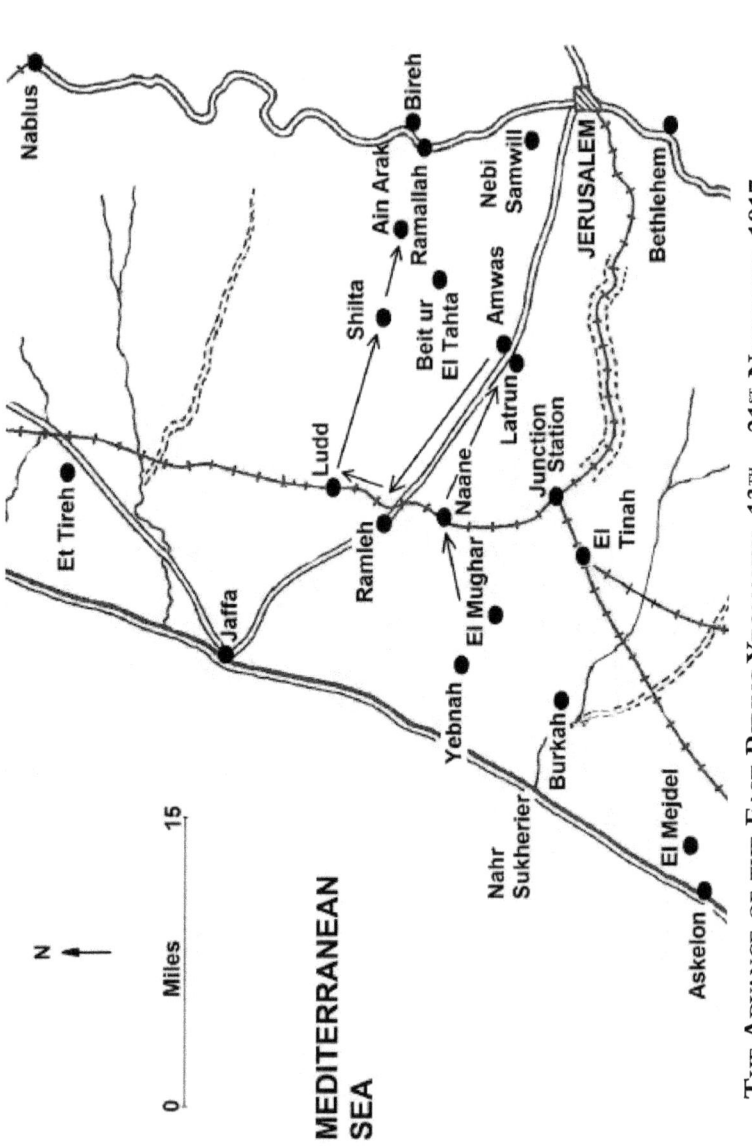

The Advance of the East Riding Yeomanry, 13th – 21st November 1917

dropped rapidly, becoming bitterly cold; particularly trying as the men were dressed in summer uniforms. During the day the East Ridings marched on towards the village of Ain Arak, again having to lead the horses all the way due to the terrain.

They were prevented from reaching the village by a shelling from Turkish position encountered at dusk and were forced to bivouac in a wadi. It rained heavily all night, and everyone got drenched (apart it seems, from Harold Lyon who lay on top of a stone wall covered with his ground sheet). Once again there were no rations or forage as the supply line continued to struggle.

The following morning the regiment resumed their advance on Ain Arak. The Turks had evidently withdrawn from the area overnight but nevertheless progress was painfully slow. Once again, the terrible terrain and poor weather meant that the horses had to be led. The men and horses, cold, wet and hungry were reaching the end of their tethers. Jimmy Seddon remembered that during the march:

> "*one of the youngest chaps in the regiment who was walking near me said to me "You must be tough!" There were tears on his cheeks and he looked like a young boy as he was under average height. I told him that what we could not avoid must be endured and that if we gave way it would only make worse of it and I tried to cheer him on. He admitted that he was about at the end of his tether and he was not alone as I heard of others who were at breaking point".* [64]

The regiment arrived at Ain Arak and found it abandoned. 'B' and 'C' Squadrons took up outpost positions, everybody enduring another night of heavy rain. No rations reached the regiment for the third day in a row and the men were ordered to eat their emergency supplies. The wet weather meant that some found them to have turned mouldy. There was little forage available in the village although some figs and a small quantity of tibben (hay or chopped straw) for the horses were found. Terry Ward noted in his diary:

> "*Miserable night. Everything and everybody drenched and hungry. Still no forage or rations".* [65]

The East Riding Yeomanry in the Judean Hills, November 1917
(Author's collection)

To the south the 75th Division was able to advance 10 miles along the road from Amwas, almost to the village of Saris. The terrain was becoming much more difficult as the road ran through narrow valleys and around hills that provided excellent defensive positions overlooking the road. There were other routes through the hills, but these consisted of a labyrinth of unmapped tracks and paths, little more than donkey tracks, which all made movement by infantry, dismounted cavalry, and artillery very difficult. The advance was consequently slow, and Saris was eventually reached on the afternoon of the 21st.

The 52nd (Lowland) Division, advancing along a track north of the main road reached Beit Likia on 19th November but its advance stalled when it encountered strong Turkish positions at Kustal and Beit Dukka. The division was unable to resume until the 21st when the 75th Division ousted the Turks under the cover of the early morning mist.

The Battle of Nebi Samwil

The 6th Mounted Brigade had now joined the two other Brigades of the Yeomanry Mounted Division and on the morning of the 21st November all three brigades attempted force their way to Bireh in a concerted attack. Facing them were elements of two Turkish infantry divisions, supported by artillery, occupying strong positions on the Zeitun Ridge.

The 6th and 8th Mounted Brigades attempted to take the ridge by a direct assault whilst the 22nd Mounted Brigade, on the left of the line, endeavoured to outflank the Turkish positions to the north. The 6th and 8th Brigades made several attempts to take the ridge but a combination of the bad weather, difficult ground and the poor condition of the men meant that although they were able to take a portion of the ridge, they were soon pushed off by strong Turkish counterattacks.

In the north the East Ridings approached Ramallah as part of the flanking attack, and finding it too strongly defended by the Turks, again supported by artillery, they took up positions in front of the village. Their positions were in direct sight of the Turks who proceeded to shell the regiment heavily all day, wounding 1 OR. A shell fragment passed through the helmet of the CO, Lieutenant Colonel Guy Wilson but he was unwounded.

'B' and 'C' Squadrons were ordered to advance on the left of the line but, as the war diary records, they were "unable to reach objective owing to exhaustion of men" and the regiment returned to their outpost positions for the night. There was a small measure of good news when rations finally arrived. Harold Lyon wrote:

> "*After more than four days, during which time we had only our emergency rations… there was some excitement when a pack horse bearing half a day's fresh rations arrived and we wondered how long these would have to last.*" [66]

The strengthening Turkish resistance and determined counterattacks, combined with the poor state of the British units in the front line, presented a serious situation and it was decided to withdraw the Yeomanry Mounted Division to less exposed positions. The orders to withdraw reached the East Ridings at midnight and at 2:30am on the 22nd they commenced a march back to Beit Ur El Tahta.

To the south the 75th and 52nd Divisions made steady progress towards Jerusalem despite strong resistance from the Turks. However, once the deteriorating situation of the Yeomanry Mounted Division became apparent, the 75th Division was ordered to change direction and move northeast to join up with the yeomen and to take Bireh. This necessitated the division cutting across the front of the 52nd Division (and clearing the Turkish positions that had been holding up the advance of that division) but it soon found its progress blocked by strong Turkish positions on the commanding hill of Nebi Samwil, the traditional location of the tomb of the Prophet Samuel. This hill dominates the approaches to Jerusalem and was taken by the 75th Division that evening after fierce fighting, but once again the British advance had been frustrated.

Following a long and weary march of nine hours (for five

hours of which the horses had to be led) the East Ridings reached Beit Ur El Tahta where they were finally able to draw adequate rations and forage for the horses ("*a rare feast*" according to George Lancaster) after having endured 5 days with only a half day's ration and virtually no food at all for the horses. The men were finally able to rest and get a full night's sleep, followed by a day's rest. There was plenty of food and having received mail there was time for writing letters home.

The rest was sorely needed, the three weeks since the breakthrough had been tough on both men and horses. The war diary records that between the 1st and the 23rd November the regiment lost 95 horses; 6 killed, 8 died, 14 missing and 29 that had to be destroyed, the remaining 38 being wounded and deemed unfit for service. The toll on the men was just as high; the Yeomanry Mounted Division was by now reduced to only about 1,200 men, of which only 800 would be in the front line, equivalent in strength to around two regiments, compared to the establishment of nine regiments in three brigades (approximately 5,400 men).

The Turks Counterattack

The difficult weather conditions, harsh terrain and the strain of 3 weeks of constant campaigning meant that by the 24th November it was abundantly clear that the attempt to capture Jerusalem could not continue. Fortuitously the logistical problems of supplying the whole of Allenby's force for the advance from Beersheba meant that General Chetwode's XX Corps (which had taken Beersheba) had been left behind during the pursuit, closer to the lines of communication, whence it could be supplied directly from the Sinai railway. As a consequence, these units had enjoyed 10 days of rest and had been reorganised and refitted, including being supplied with more appropriate winter clothing. General Allenby therefore ordered the fresh XX Corps to relieve the exhausted and weakened divisions of XXI Corps and the Desert Mounted Corps.

These fresh units had actually begun arriving at Latrun from

THE 1/1ST EAST RIDING YEOMANRY, BEIT UR EL TAHTA,
22ND NOVEMBER 1917
(ERYC)

AN 'A' SQUADRON OUTPOST IN THE HILLS IN FRONT OF
BEIT UR EL FOKA, 26TH NOVEMBER 1917
(ERYC)

Huj and Karm on the 23rd November and over the next few days would begin to move up and take over responsibility for the line from the weary men of XXI Corps.

This rotation of units inevitably meant a pause in the advance against Jerusalem and so in order to divert Turkish attention and prevent any reserves being sent to aid the defence of the Holy City, a brigade of the 54th (East Anglian) Division and the New Zealand Mounted Rifles Brigade of the ANZAC Mounted Division were ordered to mount a diversionary attack along the coast. The attack began on the 24th with an attempt to cross the Nahr el Auja north of Jaffa. The New Zealanders and infantry successfully forced crossings of the river and established two bridgeheads on the northern bank, but Turkish counterattacks the following day were too strong, and they were forced back across the river.

The poor condition of the roads and tracks (which were already causing severe logistical problems) meant that it was impossible for the moment to get an infantry division to relieve the Yeomanry Mounted Division and so they would have to continue to hold the line. Without adequate forage and given the unforgiving terrain it was felt that the division's horses were more of a hindrance to mobility than a help and therefore the division would be dismounted.

This decision would further deplete the strength of the division, as a quarter of the men had to be left behind to look after the horses. Major Moore, commanding the East Ridings' horse party, with an officer from each Squadron and sufficient men to provide one man to every four horses, trekked the animals back to Ludd. Bill Austin recalled:

> "*Owing to the nature of the country we had to send our horses down to lower ground and start climbing like mountaineers, it certainly didn't go down well but it was useless to try and drag horses up and down those rocky hillsides, besides they were well ready for another rest. The past month must have been hellish for them.*" [67]

Harold Lyon joked in his post war lectures, "*our horses were sent back to Ramleh and we became the East 'Walkings'.*"[68] That left only 13 officers and 166 ORs and 38 pack horses for the dismounted party (little more than an infantry company), who marched out on the 24th to take over the outpost line at Beit Ur El Foka, arriving there at 3pm. The next two days were relatively quiet, but on the 26th the regiment's positions began to come under long range sniper and machine gun fire wounding 2 ORs.

The pause in the British offensive had not gone un-noticed by the Turks and von Falkenhayn now attempted to take advantage of the situation. He planned a series of counterattacks against the British both in the Judean Hills (against Nebi Samwil and the Zeitun plateau) and also the thinly spread units on the coastal plain. The counterattacks, which were to utilise the 'storm' tactics developed by the Germans on the Eastern Front for the first time in the Middle East, began on the 27th November.

The Turkish counterattack against the Yeomanry Mounted Division struck on the morning of the 27th November when a large Turkish force of approximately battalion strength, supported by artillery and machine guns, attacked an outpost at the western end of the Zeitun ridge, held by 3 officers and sixty men of the 6th Mounted Brigade. Heavy fighting ensued and although reduced to only 28 men the post managed to hold out until nightfall. Two Troops (about 50 men) were sent to reinforce them but despite their dogged resistance the post was abandoned the following morning.

For the East Riding's, on the left of the 6th Mounted Brigade, the situation remained as it had been the previous day, troubled only by sniper and machine gun fire. George Lancaster recorded in his diary, "*plenty of activity, but Johnny did not attack although we were very weak*"[69].

On the Yeomanry Division's left flank another Turkish force discovered a 5-mile gap between the Yeomanry Division and the 54th Division at Shilta and stumbled onto a supply section of the Lincolnshire Yeomanry, capturing it and advancing to within 500 yards of the Brigade HQ. Thankfully the 7th Mounted Brigade had been ordered to assist and marched through the night, arriving at Beir Ur el Tahta at 5am on the 28th November just in time to break up the attack and plug the gap. A brigade from the 52nd Division (who had been in the process of being relieved) was also sent to assist the 7th Mounted Brigade cover the yeomanry's exposed left flank. The infantry successfully attacked and drove back the Turks, plugging the gap, but were unable to dislodge a larger force located at Suffa.

The 6th Mounted Brigade launched a counterattack to regain the ground lost and the Staffordshire Yeomanry were ordered to mount a 'demonstration' in support. The East Ridings took over the line from the Staffs during the night and the attack commenced at dawn. Heavy fighting ensued but the 6th Mounted Brigade and the Staffs were forced to retire to their starting positions.

Elsewhere there was heavy fighting as the Turks attempted to recapture Beit Ur Et Tahta and Beit Ur El Foka. There was no fighting on the East Ridings' front, but large numbers of Turks were seen heading in the direction of Beit Ur Et Tahta. The positions of the 22nd Mounted Brigade were in danger of being cut off; Bill Austin wrote:

> *"the enemy were on three sides of us and there was a practically unclimbable hill behind us, we had no rations and things looked rather black for us".* [70]

The Brigade was therefore ordered to withdraw. It was a difficult proposition. Jimmy Seddon recalled his experience:

> *"Late in the afternoon it was decided to retire to another position further back. I was sent to tell 'A' Squadron to withdraw from a ridge on our left. They were scattered about among the rocks and during the same afternoon SM Wilson stopped a bullet with his behind. I saw them helping him out. After delivering the message I returned to the spot I had started from. It was like Aberdeen on a flag day – not a soul in sight. What was more to the point was that I soon realised that I was being fired at. I ran for it in the only direction our men could have taken… the next thing I saw was the main body of the regiment scaling a steep slope on the side of the ridge further on in front of me. It was so steep that the pack horses, which they were trying to take with them, fell back into the valley and were running about loose".* [71]

Temporarily transferred to the command of the 6th Mounted Brigade the East Ridings and Staffordshire Yeomanry took up positions overlooking Beit Ur El Foka, which had had to be abandoned after the Turks managed to get around to the south of the village.

During the evening reinforcements arrived in the shape of the 11th Light Horse Regiment of the 4th Light Horse Brigade (from the Australian Mounted Division which had been held in reserve at Mejdel). The 4th Light Horse Brigade had arrived at Beit Ur El Tahta, the 11th Light Horse Regiment being pushed forward with two machine guns to hold Wadi Zeit south west of Beit Ur el Foqa and block the Turks pursuing the Yeomanry Mounted Division.

The East Ridings held their outpost line throughout the 29th coming under sniper and machine gun fire although not suffering any casualties. They were relieved at 10pm by a company of the Highland Light Infantry from the 52nd Infantry Division, Jimmy Seddon remembering:

> *"I was on listening post and during my spell on watch it was bright moonlight and I could see the white rocks on the opposite side of the narrow valley and the shadows in between them. Also I could hear the Turks talking and the clatter of stones as they were erecting barricades similar to what we had made. If I had known their language I could have heard what they were saying. Suddenly I heard with surprise a voice behind me saying "Come in Jimmy, we've been relieved". We had been holding the line while the main body of infantry came up. On our sector these were Scotchmen. Apparently, the enemy were also aware of their arrival because suddenly hell was let loose as they let go with everything they had got from shells to rifle fire. It was quite spooky as the noises echoed through the hills. Our side gave them a suitable reply."* [72]

The regiment withdrew back behind Beit Ur El Tahta before marching to Beit Sirra where they were able to draw rations. After a short halt the regiment set off for Annabeh where they were to be reunited with their horses, but their ordeal was not quite over. Jimmy Seddon again:

> *"We immediately began our march back behind the front line, but it*

was dawn soon after we started and we were raising a cloud of dust which drew Turks shell fire. As we were passing the Scotch troops at the time, they did not like it either and used some bad language to express it. We were very thirsty and as the day wore on the tongues of some of the men were so dry and swollen that they could scarcely speak. We were a grim and silent lot. However, we were now out of range of the guns and on our way to water. At the first opportunity there was a foot inspection at the roadside. A lot were in a sorry state and some feet were actually bleeding. Quite a number of boots had been badly worn down by walking on the rocky surfaces".* [73]

Despite the shelling there were no casualties and the regiment arrived at Annabeh around 5pm and bivouacked. Harold Lyon noted in his diary, *"drew rations, had tea and got down to it"*[74].

After a night's rest the regiment was roused at 6am on 1st December. The horse party arrived from Ludd at 10:30am and an hour later the regiment marched back to Ras Deiran. Harold Lyon noted that on the way they passed "miles of vineyards" where they were able to water the horses and have 'shower baths' at a wine press. According to Jimmy Seddon:

"at last we arrived at enough water for a wash and a shave. As we had not shaved for weeks we had an appreciable growth of beard and it would have been quite a problem if a few had not happened to have scissors. We took it in turns to use them". [75]

Harold Lyon noted in his diary that this was his first shave since 23rd November. In fact, both the men and horses were in a terrible state. Jimmy Seddon remembered:

"For a long time we had insufficient rest and food. Some had holes in their tunics due to the fact that during the brief halts when we were on the march they had laid down, lit a cigarette, and involuntarily dozed off for a few minutes. In the meantime, the cigarette fell on the tunic and burnt a hole in it… we had been reduced by war conditions to the state of poverty-stricken tramps". [76]

The horses had been pushed to the limit of their endurance having remained saddled for days at a time, many so worn down that their saddles could no longer be made tight. Many were ill with diarrhoea and sand colic, and lame too; their unshod feet (shoes and nails having been used up) cracked and broken as a result of the hard going over the rocky terrain. But now water and food were plentiful and there was plenty of bread and oranges, as well as almonds, that could be purchased from the locals.

The regiment rested here for a few days and the process of bringing the regiment back up to strength began; Captain G. H. Woodhouse, Captain C. G. Lloyd and 11 ORs joined the regiment from the 3/1st East Ridings in England on the 3rd December, followed by another 48 ORs on the 6th.

After Jerusalem

The Yeomanry Mounted Division was officially relieved by the 74th (Yeomanry) Division on the 29th November. On the 1st December the Turks launched another series of counterattacks against Nebi Samwil and along the front at Beit Ur el Tahta. However, after more fierce fighting the British managed to repulse the Turks. Despite these attacks the relief of the exhausted divisions was completed by the 2nd and for a few days the fighting subsided as both sides reorganised and solidified their lines.

Then on the 8th December General Allenby launched his next assault on Jerusalem. Previously Allenby had attempted to outflank the city to the north using a "left hook", but the unforgiving terrain had prevented any rapid movements and the attack had stalled. Chetwode, to whom command of the assault was once again delegated, adopted a different plan for this attack. He would advance from the area of Nebi Samwil, passing to the west of Jerusalem and attempt to cut the Nablus road much closer to the city. This would involve attacking the main Turkish defences but would allow the artillery to be brought up along the Jaffa Road.

The assault began before dawn and despite the poor weather the main defences had been captured by daybreak with less resistance than expected; the Turks, exhausted and demoralised after their losses in the Judean Hills, fell back, there being a certain amount of panic. It became apparent that their position was untenable and the order to evacuate was given. Jerusalem surrendered without a fight on the 9th December. Allenby had delivered on his promise.

On the 11th December, as General Allenby made formal entrance to Jerusalem (famously passing through the Jaffa gate on foot rather than on horseback or by motorcar to show his respects), the East Ridings marched to Esdud where they bivouacked for the night before continuing on to Mejdel the following day. Here, on the 13th December, another 23 ORs joined from England.

The weather remained very wet and there was little activity apart from routine rest camp activities, such as Regimental parades and fatigue duties, until the 19th when the entire division paraded for General Allenby. The General presented a number of awards to members of the regiment for gallantry in action during the recent operations. The divisional commander later signalled: "The Commander-in-Chief expressed himself as highly satisfied with the parade today. The divisional commander wishes express his to thanks to all ranks for their efforts to make the parade the success it was."

The regiment remained at Mejdel over the Christmas period, but the winter rains continued, and it was a wet, cold and miserable time, although the men made the best of it. In his diary entry for Christmas Day George Lancaster wrote:

> *"Terrible day – very wet & cold. Numerous thunderstorms during night. Good dinner of turkey & vegetables – extra plum pudding. Hot rum & milk & beer, cigar & cigarettes."*[77]

Likewise, Terry Ward noted in his diary:

> *"dinner of Turkey, mashed potatoes, peas, carrots, stuffing etc. and rum sauce over pudding. Orange jelly, blancmange, mince pies, jam tarts and cake for tea. Rum grog at 8pm. Very wet day."* [78]

Jimmy Seddon wrote:

> *"On Christmas Eve it blew a gale and flattened some of the tents. It also commenced to rain and poured down all Christmas morning. Volunteers were asked for to take the horses to water. I joined them but*

it was almost a useless journey. Several times the horses turned their behind to the cold wind and rain and it was hard work driving them to the watering place. When we got there nearly all of them refused to drink. We had Christmas dinner under unpleasant conditions, but we did manage to have a concert in the evening round a camp fire after it had ceased raining. Beer was brought round in cookhouse dixies and we dipped our enamel mugs in them. Then they produced a mixture of hot water, ideal milk and rum all in the dixies again. I repeated the motion with my pint mug but found that this elixir was more potent than I anticipated, especially after a fair portion of beer and I became hilarious. Later I discovered that I was not alone in that respect. We had made whoopee after a tough and depressing time in the front line." [79]

A further draft of 1 Officer and 86 ORs plus 65 remounts arrived on the 28th December bringing the regiment strength up to 17 Officers and 416 ORs. Lieutenant Frank Wood returned to the regiment after a spell in hospital and noted:

"I was quite pleased to join the regiment at Mejdel on December 29th, but how it had changed through casualties and sickness. Only about seven men of my old troop remained and five horses". [80]

Chapter 5: The Western Front, 1918-1919

The winter rains that lashed Palestine at the end of 1917 played havoc with the British supply lines. Rough seas prevented supplies being landed on the coast and the tracks of the Sinai railway were frequently washed away by the rains and flash floods. In addition, the units of the Desert Mounted Corps, in particular the horses, needed large quantities of food and water in order to rebuild their strength and fitness.

To reduce the burden on the stretched supply lines the mounted units were ordered further to the rear to be nearer the supply centres. Consequently, once the rains had abated, the East Ridings marched back via Gaza to Deir El Belah, arriving there on the 3rd January 1918. Frank Wood thought:

> *"How interesting it was to see the scene of our first big action and to view the battered Turkish positions. Gaza was a filthy place under the Turks, none of our dead had been buried and there they lay just in the place they fell; some as long ago as March 26th. The following morning we trekked to Deir El Belah and made our bivouac camp between the lake and the sea. We had a complete rest and then started training under our new commander Brigadier General Fitzgerald, who was a very clever and capable soldier.*[1]

As Lieutenant Wood states, initially there was little training, the emphasis being on getting plenty of rest and as the warm sunshine returned men and horses quickly began to pick up and as they did, so the training programme commenced. Lieutenant Stephenson built a firing range and in addition to rifle practice there were the usual schemes and bayonet drills.

Training continued at Deir El Belah throughout January and early February until on the 18th the regiment marched to a new camp near Gaza.

Besides the training and physical exercise programmes there were also concert parties, boxing, rugby and football competitions (the East Ridings beat the Staffs 5-1) and, as befitting a cavalry formation, a number of race meetings were held. These culminated at the beginning of March with the 22nd Mounted Brigade organising a race meeting for the whole of the Yeomanry Mounted Division. It was quite an affair, with a full racecourse laid out at Gaza. There were a number of experienced race officials, jockeys and trainers amongst the division as well as bookmakers, official or otherwise. Corporal William 'Wass' Reader (no longer acting Sergeant) wrote in his diary:

> *"The great day of our Brigade races. My hand is improving nicely and the doctor has placed me on light duty today so that I can leave camp to see the races. Very kind of him don't you think! The arrangements and the course for the races were just like any big English meeting with printed programme and everything complete. I had three bets and won one but I finished up 5 Shillings in pocket so didn't do so badly. Nearly everybody got hopelessly drunk; especially a big number of Australians who came and it really was a most successful day".* [2]

There were seven races: four on the flat and three over fences, with the "Palestine Grand National" and the "Gaza Hunt Cup" being the jewels in the crown, complete with trophies and prize money for the winners. However, this relaxed and enjoyable time could not continue; now the men and horses were fit again there was a war to return to.

General Allenby had already begun preparing for the resumption of the offensive against the Turks with the capture of Jericho on the 21st February, which secured his right flank. Allenby began his next operation on the 8th March, with a raid towards Amman to link up with Lawrence (of Arabia) and the Arab forces. The men of the Yeomanry Mounted Division expected to be moving north soon to join the push to Damascus and it came as no surprise when on the 12th March the East Ridings began their return to the front, moving to first to Mejdel and then a few days later on to the Nahr Sukerier. Private Bill Simpson recalled:

> *"after a spell at Belah we got into our stride again, more equipment, remounts, in fact we were ready to carry on with the campaign, and we were getting nearer the front to take over from other regiments who needed a rest".* [3]

However, events on the Western Front were about to change everything.

THE WESTERN FRONT

The Western Front at the beginning of 1918 was much as it had been when the first trenches had been dug during the autumn of 1914. Despite the huge battles and losses of life on all sides the line had essentially remained static for four years, stretching 450 miles from Nieuport on the Belgian coast south to the Swiss border. However, by the spring of 1918 these defensive systems had grown massively in scale and complexity; a far cry from the first hastily dug positions of 1914.

The numerical superiority of the Germans on the Western Front in the spring of 1918 was a direct result of the revolution and subsequent collapse of Russia towards the end of 1917. The effective withdrawal of Russia from the war (the Brest-Litovsk peace treaty between Russia and the Central Powers was finally signed in March 1918) had allowed the transfer of some 40-50 German divisions from the east to the west. This numerical advantage would not last long however as, following the United States' declaration of war in April 1917, American troops were arriving in Europe at an ever increasing rate; by the end of 1917 there were 300,000, although they were barely trained and totally innocent of the nightmare of trench warfare. But their numbers would continue to grow at a rate that far exceeded anything the Central Powers could match.

Away from the Western Front the Central Powers were on the brink of collapse. The German economy was at full stretch;

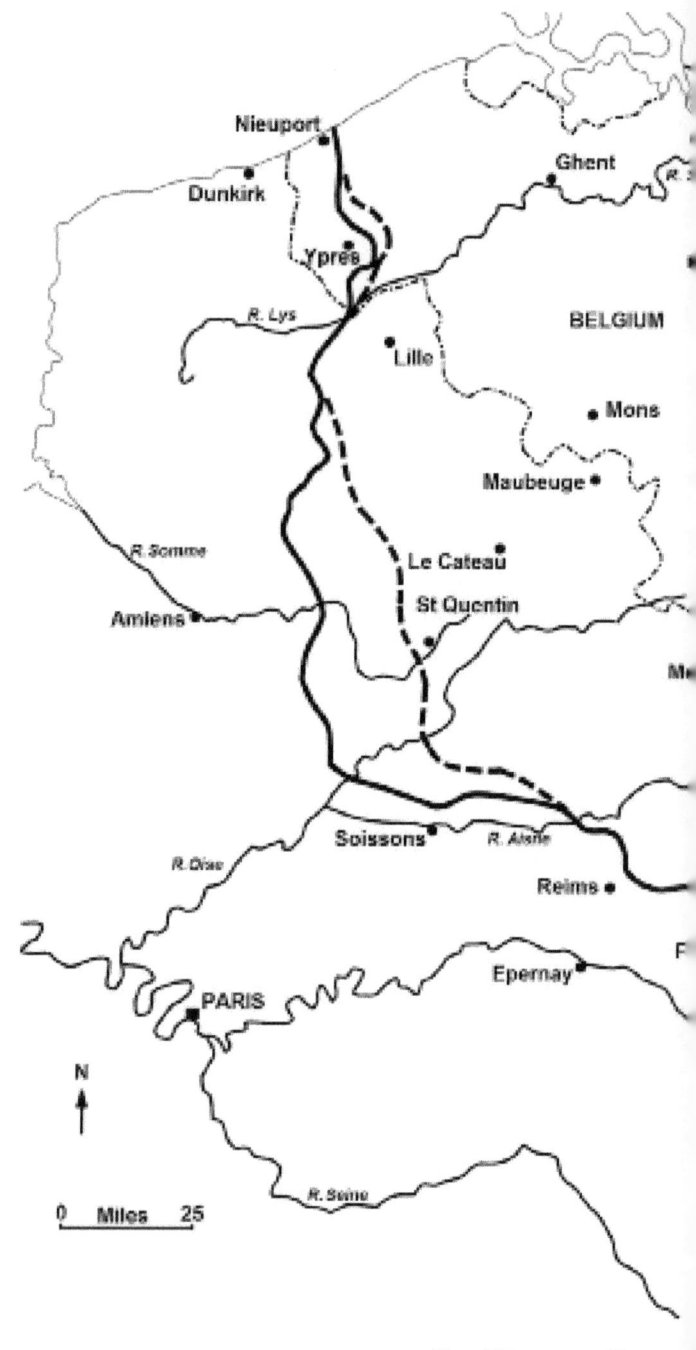

THE WESTERN FRONT

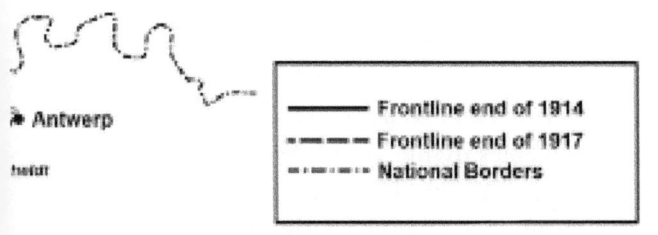

1914–1917

the transport network was crumbling, and manpower was running short in the fields and factories as the Army's demand for men outstripped supply. The Royal Navy's blockade was biting hard and there were food riots across Germany as supplies of food and other consumables dwindled still further.

Germany's major allies Austria-Hungary and the Ottoman Empire were seriously weakened after nearly four years of war and becoming increasingly unreliable. The Turks had suffered a series of defeats in 1917 at the hands of the British and their Arab allies and Austria-Hungary had required German troops to help in the war with Italy.

Germany was therefore faced with a stark choice; strike a decisive blow and win the war before the Americans arrived in sufficient numbers to tip the balance in favour of the Allies, or else risk complete collapse. The war had to be won in 1918 before the window of opportunity was closed.

The Spring Offensives

The Germans, under the command of General Erich von Ludendorff, resolved to attack the British. Ludendorff felt that if the French were defeated the British would continue the war, whereas if the British were defeated the French would surely follow. If Britain could be decisively defeated and the channel ports threatened or captured, then an end to the war might be agreed on terms favourable to the Germans.

With an early offensive in the spring essential to exploit the German's numerical superiority, Flanders, the low lying area of Belgium directly in front of the vital channel ports, would be too wet and any offensive would surely become bogged down, as the British offensives around Ypres had done in 1917. The central section of the British portion of the line, opposite the important city of Arras, was not an attractive place to attack, being atop the Vimy Ridge and commanding the high ground. That left the southern end of the British line in front of the old Somme battlefields of 1916.

It was here that the Germans decided to strike. The plan was to attack in the area of St. Quentin and once the breakthrough had been made, swing northwards towards the channel coast, cutting off the BEF from the French and forcing a withdrawal or surrender.

During the first months of 1918 the Germans began extensive preparations for their planned assault, the *Kaiserschlacht* or Kaiser's Battle. These attacks were to make use of new tactics perfected on the Eastern Front during the battles of 1917. Specialist assault units, the *Sturmbatallions* (Storm Battalions), were created made up of the most experienced and fittest men and commanded by well-trained and experienced NCOs. These *Stosstruppen* (Stormtroopers) were lightly equipped and trained to move forward rapidly, infiltrating the enemy front line following an intense but short artillery bombardment and, bypassing areas of strong resistance, attack and disrupt enemy headquarters, artillery units and supply lines. The pockets of the enemy left behind would be "mopped up" by more traditional and less skilled follow-up units.

In great secrecy, the Germans moved a force of around 75 divisions and over 6,000 guns into positions opposite the British Fifth Army who held the southern portion of the British front. The German troops were well rested, well-trained and well-equipped. In contrast, the 12 divisions of the British Fifth Army were tired, and morale was low; they were under strength and also thinly stretched.

The Fifth Army covered 42 miles of front with 12 divisions; the neighbouring Third Army had 14 divisions to hold 28 miles. They occupied poor positions only recently taken over from the French. General Gough, the commander of the Fifth Army, had yet to improve them by implementing the principles of defence in depth having insufficient men and time to prepare the necessary defences. This meant positioning most of his men forward, well within artillery range of the Germans. In addition, the main British reserve was held away to the north in Flanders.

The German offensive began at 4:40am on the 21st March 1918. Codenamed '*Michael*' it began with a massive artillery bombardment. Over a million shells were fired in five hours, initially concentrated on the rear areas: artillery units, headquarters and supply lines, before shifting to the front lines just before the assault. The barrage included poison gas. What British counter battery fire there was (the German artillery outnumbered the British by more than 2:1) was disrupted by the morning fog.

The 71 divisions of the German 17th, 2nd and 18th Armies, led by the *Sturmbatallions,* attacked the 26 divisions of the British Third and Fifth Armies under the cover of the fog and behind a creeping artillery barrage. The German assault units made rapid progress; no one really knew where the Germans were, communications had broken down (not helped by the fog) and units found themselves surrounded before the even knew they were under attack. Many units were forced to surrender after only limited resistance. Other positions put up more of a fight, but they too soon surrendered when the reality of the situation became apparent. The Germans were soon through the British forward positions and the Fifth Army had begun to retreat in confusion.

The first day of the battle was a disaster for the British Army. The Germans advanced 14 miles and as the Fifth Army began to break up, thousands of men were captured. The Third Army, whilst also forced to retreat, did so in better order. The attack continued and in a week the Germans advanced 40 miles on a 50-mile front and inflicted 300,000 casualties, some 100,000 of them captured. One thousand three hundred guns were lost.

On the 28th March the Germans struck north (Operation '*Mars*'), attempting to capture Arras, but were stopped with heavy casualties by the Third Army. Further to the south progress was still being made, but the rapid advance meant that supplies couldn't keep up. The men were exhausted, and the churned-up countryside of the old Somme battlefields made it difficult to bring supporting artillery up. Allied reinforcements, including some French units, arrived and resistance began to stiffen. German soldiers also became distracted by the plentiful British stores captured in the numerous supply dumps behind the Fifth Army lines, looting and gorging themselves on items in short supply in Germany. Eventually Ludendorff bowed to the inevitable and the offensive was called off on the 5th April.

Unhorsed

With the British Army facing the spectre of defeat on the Western Front, the government ordered General Allenby to postpone his plans for 1918 and to go on the defensive. With the Turks forced out of Jerusalem and the Ottoman Empire teetering on the brink of collapse, the men of the Egyptian Expeditionary Force could be put to better use on the Western Front.

Immediately the 52nd and 74th Divisions were dispatched to France, to be followed by countless other units. In all Allenby was ordered to send some 60,000 troops to France, their places taken by Indian Army formations. Amongst the units ordered to France were nine of the yeomanry regiments, including the East Ridings. Terry Ward noted in his diary for the 31st March:

> *"News of a sudden move. There are very strong rumours that we are going to hand in our horses over to Indian cavalry division and go to France. It will be rotten losing our horses, but I only hope we get some more in France. Never mind, we shall stand a better chance of a "blighty" leave."* [4]

Many of the horses had been with the regiments since August 1914 and a there was a strong bond between horse and rider, after all man and horse were almost inseparable, spending 24 hours a day together. The Lincolnshire Yeomanry, fellow members of the 22nd Mounted Brigade, went as far as to carry out a mock funeral, burying some saddlery and spurs in the desert and erecting a memorial with the following epitaph:

Stranger, pause and shed a tear,
A regiment's heart lies buried here,
Sickened and died through no disorder,
But broken by a staggering order.

Our hearts were warm, theirs cold as Huns,
To take our horses and give us machine guns,
For Cavalry, they said, there is no room,

THE LINCOLNSHIRE YEOMANRY DEPARTING DEIR EL BELAH, APRIL 1918
(Author's collection)

SIDI BASHR CAMP, ALEXANDRIA, APRIL 1918
(ERYC)

So we buried our spurs in a desert tomb.

The Ordnance gave—the Ordnance hath taken away.

On the 1st April 1918, the brigade was ordered to march back to Deir El Belah. After an overnight stop in Deir Sineid the brigade arrived back at Belah on 2nd April. The following day they began the process of handing over their horses and surplus equipment to the various depots there. Private Ward wrote:

> "Handed horses over to remount depot. Handed in saddlery, swords, spurs etc. everybody very 'down' at losing our horses." The following day he noted, "Rotten without horses. Absolutely nothing to do." [5]

Here they learnt their final fate; orders were received that the East Ridings were to be amalgamated with the Lincolnshire Yeomanry to form a battalion of the Machine Gun Corps (MGC), under the command of Lieutenant Colonel the Hon. Guy Wilson DSO of the East Ridings. There was a farewell speech by General Chauvel and the Colonel, and General Allenby paid a visit to the regiment's officers.

Devoid of their horses and equipment the regiment moved by rail to Kantara, on the Suez Canal, during the 7th and 8th April.

Here the provisional machine gun battalion was brought up to strength with a fresh draft of 4 officers and 120 men, but their stay here was short; that same day 'A' Squadron, acting as the Regimental advance party, was sent onto Sidi Bashr, Alexandria. The rest of the regiment followed over the next few days; the move being completed by 11th April.

Training as machine gunners, under instructors from the Machine Gun School at Zeitoun, commenced immediately and four new Vickers machine guns arrived on the 17th.

The regiment now faced a wait for transport to France. Jimmy Seddon during this time thought:

> "life became more or less routine and rather monotonous. As I had a reasonable amount of money, I had some breaks by spending a few evenings in the town with pals where we had meals and wine in the cafes." [6]

Harold Lyon agreed that:

> "*one of the main attractions in Alexandria is a wonderful six course dinner at Madame Serene's*". [7]

The attractions of Alexandria also meant trouble. Leonard May remembered:

> "*we did get quite a lot of leave into town and also did a lot on night patrols in the city streets, as the lads used to get out of hand… the infantry were brought from the front and put straight on board ship and they used to rush the ship police and get into town. When on night patrol we had many rough nights getting them back on-board ship.*" [8]

Terry Ward recounted one such night:

> "*On picket in town. A "picket" consisted of an NCO and four men acting as Military Police. There was a battalion of Irish Guards in town and the owner of a café called us in to deal with 4 wildly drunk Irishmen who were smashing the place up. Having looked them over, we decided the safest way to handle the situation was to go in and drink with them until they were helpless, and then take them away. This we did, but instead of putting them under arrest we dumped them in the next street and left them to sleep it off.*" [9]

OPERATION GEORGETTE

Whilst the East Ridings were coming to terms with the loss of their horses, on the Western Front the Germans launched a new offensive, codenamed *"Georgette"*. Operation *"Michael"* had succeeded in drawing the bulk of the BEF south, leaving only a single division in reserve. This left the Ypres salient in Flanders, already exposed with the Germans on three sides, even more vulnerable. Consequently, on the 9th April, the German 6th Army struck at Neuve Chapelle, with the aim of capturing the strategically important railhead at Hazebrouck, followed a day later by the 4th Army, aiming for Ypres.

Once again they used the tactics of infiltration that had proved so successful in March and once again had the advantage of the cover of early morning fog. The full force of the German assault fell on the two weak and demoralised divisions of the Portuguese Army who quickly broke. The Germans advanced

4 miles almost unopposed to the river Lys on the first day. The British divisions fared better but were forced to retreat as the Germans poured through the gap created by the flight of the Portuguese.

By April the 17th, the Germans had captured most of the ground taken by the British at such great cost the year before, including the emotive Passchendaele Ridge. By the April 25th, the Germans had taken Mount Kemel, the highest ground in the sector, but fresh French reserves and the stubborn resistance of the British divisions finally ground the German offensive to a standstill. The assault was abandoned on 29th April.

Despite the big German gains the British were able to hold on and prevent a major breakthrough. Ypres and the railhead at Hazebrouck remained in British hands. The Allies had suffered 150,000 casualties, the Germans 110,000.

There was now a pause in the German offensives. In spite of the German successes, none of the strategic aims had been met and no general breakthrough had been achieved. Moreover, the Germans had lost a third of million men and needed time to regroup. The conscripts of the class of 1918 were called up early and there were returning prisoners of war from Russia to help make up the losses, but the manpower crisis was becoming more acute. All the while, more and more American troops were arriving in France and British reinforcements were coming from the Middle East. Time was still of the essence.

The Voyage Home

On the morning of the 24th May, the East Ridings began their journey home, entraining at Alexandria's Victoria Station for the journey to Gabbari Docks, where they boarded their troopship, the *Caledonia*. Everyone was aboard by early afternoon but after leaving the dockside the ship sat at anchor in the middle of the harbour whilst the other yeomanry units destined for France were embarked on the other ships.

The *Caledonia*, a 7,558 ton steamer built in 1894 for P&O (for the UK to India route) was commissioned as a troopship in

Training on the Vickers machine gun, Sidi Bashr, April 1918
(ERYC)

A group of East Ridings in the bow of the 'Caledonia', May 1918
(ERYC)

December 1917 and together with five other troopships formed a fast convoy, escorted by Japanese destroyers and trawlers, running between Alexandria and Marseilles, transferring desperately need troops from the Middle East to the Western Front.

Conditions on board were not ideal. The *Caledonia* was originally built for about 540 passengers (365 first and 175 second class) but she was now carrying nearly twice that. The overcrowding made it impossible to hold parades but at least there were no horses to tend to this time.

Finally, with everyone embarked, the convoy finally set sail on the afternoon of 26th May. The *Caledonia* was the fifth ship in the convoy, and she departed at 3:45pm. Once clear of the minefield the convoy formed into line abreast and set course for Marseilles. Due to the threat from enemy submarines (one of the ships had been sunk on an earlier trip) the convoy took precautions to prevent lights showing after dark and as many men as possible were ordered to sleep on deck, especially those billeted on the lower decks.

The night of the 26th/27th May was a clear moonlit night with a calm sea. Just after midnight, about 100 miles from Alexandria, the alarm was sounded, and the men had to parade at lifeboat stations with their life jackets. Leonard May recalled:

> *"At 12pm the ship shook with a big explosion, we thought our ship was torpedoed and got the order to stand to our getaway stations... I was detailed to a boat on the top deck. It was some scramble getting to it. It was a lovely moonlight night and in getting to our posts, we saw a terrible sight. Our ship was lucky but the next ship to us got it."* [10]

That ship was the *Leasowe Castle*, carrying the Warwickshire and South Nottinghamshire Yeomanry machine gun battalion, which was hit by a torpedo on the starboard side, fired by *U-Boat* UB-51. The *Leasowe Castle* launched her lifeboats and the escort sloop *Lily* set her bows alongside the starboard side of the ship so men could directly board her, all under the protection of a smokescreen generated by a Japanese destroyer. Two further torpedoes appear to have been fired, but both missed. At about 2am there was a sudden loud noise and the *Leasowe Castle*, previously fairly stable, sank rapidly. The *Lily* escaped just in time; the ropes connecting her to the sinking ship were cut with an axe at the last minute. However, these actions meant that out of the 3,000 or so men aboard all but 92 were saved. The Captain, Captain Holl, went down with his ship. The survivors were then taken back to Alexandria.

For the rest of the convoy the journey continued although with additional ships and escorts joining en-route from Port Said (Suez Canal) and Malta. Harold Lyon recorded in his diary on the 29th May, as the convoy passed Sicily:

"an aeroplane and 9 motor submarine chasers came up and stayed with us until late afternoon" [11]

The voyage passed without further incident. Although understandably nervous of the submarine threat (*"we were all very upset by this incident* (the *Leasowe Castle*) *and kept to our lifebelts throughout the voyage"*, according to Leonard May[12]), the voyage was generally an enjoyable one, much smoother than the outward voyage and the men were able to enjoy the sunshine and games on deck.

Operation Blücher-Yorck

Ludendorff still saw the British as his main opponents, but *"Michael"* and *"Georgette"* had drawn significant numbers of Allied divisions into Flanders, making a breakthrough there remote. Therefore, Ludendorff now planned to attack the French in the south instead and threaten Paris. He hoped this would draw forces away from Flanders allowing him to renew his offensives in that area.

On the 27th May the Germans launched a new offensive, known as *"Blücher-Yorck"* (after two Prussian Napoleonic generals) against the Chemin des Dames Ridge with a massive artillery bombardment from over 4000 guns, their heaviest concentration yet. Whilst the French Army held this area, the German attack fell heaviest on six shattered British divisions who had been sent to this previously quiet area to recover from their mauling during the March offensive.

With few reserves available, the Germans were able to punch straight through the Allied lines creating a 25-mile wide gap in the front. They reached the Aisne River in just 6 hours and by nightfall had advanced 10 miles. The bridges over the Aisne were captured intact and the Germans quickly crossed the river, taking Soissons the next day and continuing to advance towards the river Marne. This was reached, at Château Thierry, on the 30th, only 50 miles from Paris. Victory seemed to be within their grasp.

However, the Germans were now tired and once again outrunning their supplies, and they had exhausted their numerical advantage. They had lost another 100,000 men, as had the Allies, but whilst Allied reinforcements had started to arrive there were no more German reserves. On 1st June the American Army entered the fray and launched a counterattack at Château Thierry and then at Belleau Wood, forcing the Germans back across the Marne. By the 6th June, the offensive had been halted.

Ludendorff still needed to draw more Allied forces away from Flanders, so on the 9th June he attempted to extend the offensive with the aim of joining the salient captured during *"Blücher-Yorck"* with that captured during *"Michael"*. This would have the effect of straightening his line and releasing more troops for his planned Flanders offensive and would, he hoped, draw further Allied divisions away from the north. The French were however forewarned of the attack (codenamed Operation *"Gneisenau"*) and despite some initial successes (three French divisions were destroyed on the opening day) French and American counter attacks around Compiègne on the 11th effectively ended the attack.

The Yeomanry Return

As the battles raged on the Western Front, the East Ridings landed at Marseilles on the 1st June 1918. They had been away from Europe for two and a half years. After disembarking the regiment marched three miles along the sea front to their camp, a collection of wooden huts with a spectacular view of the Riviera. The men were met on arrival by a huge backlog of nine weeks mail, some only 4 days old, which was warmly welcomed.

After a few days' rest, the regiment entrained on 5th June destined for the British Army's training camp at Etaples, about 15 miles south of Boulogne. The men were packed into French railway wagons, famously designed for '40 men or 8 horses' (40 *Hommes*/8 *Chevaux*) for the long and tedious journey. Leonard May wrote:

> *"we were very cramped up and we used to take it in turns in sitting in the doorway and dangling our legs and getting some exercise".* [13]

For the men, acclimatised to the desert and still dressed in their light Khaki drill uniforms, it was very cold at night. Private Terry Ward recalled:

> *"We halted at one place where men were working on the line and they have a nicely glowing coke brazier. We saw a crowbar alongside it, so just before we moved off, a group of us scrambled out of the truck, thrust the bar through the brazier, and hoisted it into the truck. We were nearly suffocated, but we kept warm for a night."* [14]

The views of the green French countryside were a welcome sight after the dry and dusty desert and the train passed within sight of the Eiffel Tower and the Palace of Versailles as it travelled through Paris. The scenery might have been uplifting but the atmosphere was less so. Corporal Seddon had noticed that the people he encountered in Marseilles:

> *"seemed depressed and war weary. Not much to be wondered at after four years and some appeared to have given up hope."* [15]

This was reinforced by his experiences on the journey:

> *"on the way the train stopped at various places and from what we could see, the morale of the country was at a low ebb and some of the people virtually accused the British of keeping the war on."* [16]

The train finally arrived at Etaples at 5:20am on the morning of the 8th June and the East Ridings marched into No. 9 Rest Camp.

At Etaples were countless transit camps, training camps, general hospitals, depots and convalescent camps stretching for miles; the countryside was covered in tents and huts. The area around Etaples served the whole British Army on the Western Front, housing up to 100,000 men on any given day. Here men heading for the front were introduced to the rigours of life in the trenches though physical training and instruction. It was notoriously harsh.

On the 16th the battalion began the construction of a new tented camp at Cucq (just south of Etaples) into which they moved on the 19th, the day they officially became 'D' Battalion, MGC. The staff work required to bring about the amalgamation of the three squadrons of the East Ridings and three squadrons of the Lincolnshire Yeomanry into the four-company structure of a machine gun battalion commenced immediately.

The Lincolnshire Yeomanry would essentially form 'A' and 'B' Companies, the East Ridings 'C' and 'D' Companies, although apparently men were cross posted to help bind the battalion together. On the 20th a team of specialist instructors (10 officers and 32 men) under Lieutenant Colonel Harper MGC arrived and an intensive machine gun training programme began the next day.

The Machine Gun Corps had been formed in October 1915 to concentrate machine guns that up until that point had been dispersed in small groups amongst the infantry battalions. The early years of the war had shown that machine guns were most effective when used en-masse and grouping them together enabled them to be operated by specialist gunners, using dedicated tactics.

By 1918 the newly formed machine gun battalions were operating in a support role at divisional level, usually one MG battalion per division. Typically, a division would deploy 16 Vickers Guns (comprising one MG company) with the advancing infantry (usually 2 MG sections/8 guns per attacking battalion), whilst the remaining 48 guns (three MG companies) were reserved for barrages and supporting fire.

However, at this stage of the war there were additional MG units available to supplement the divisional MG battalions (such as 'D' Battalion) which could be attached to divisions by Corps

THE GERMAN SPRING OFFENSIVES ON THE WESTERN FRONT, 1918

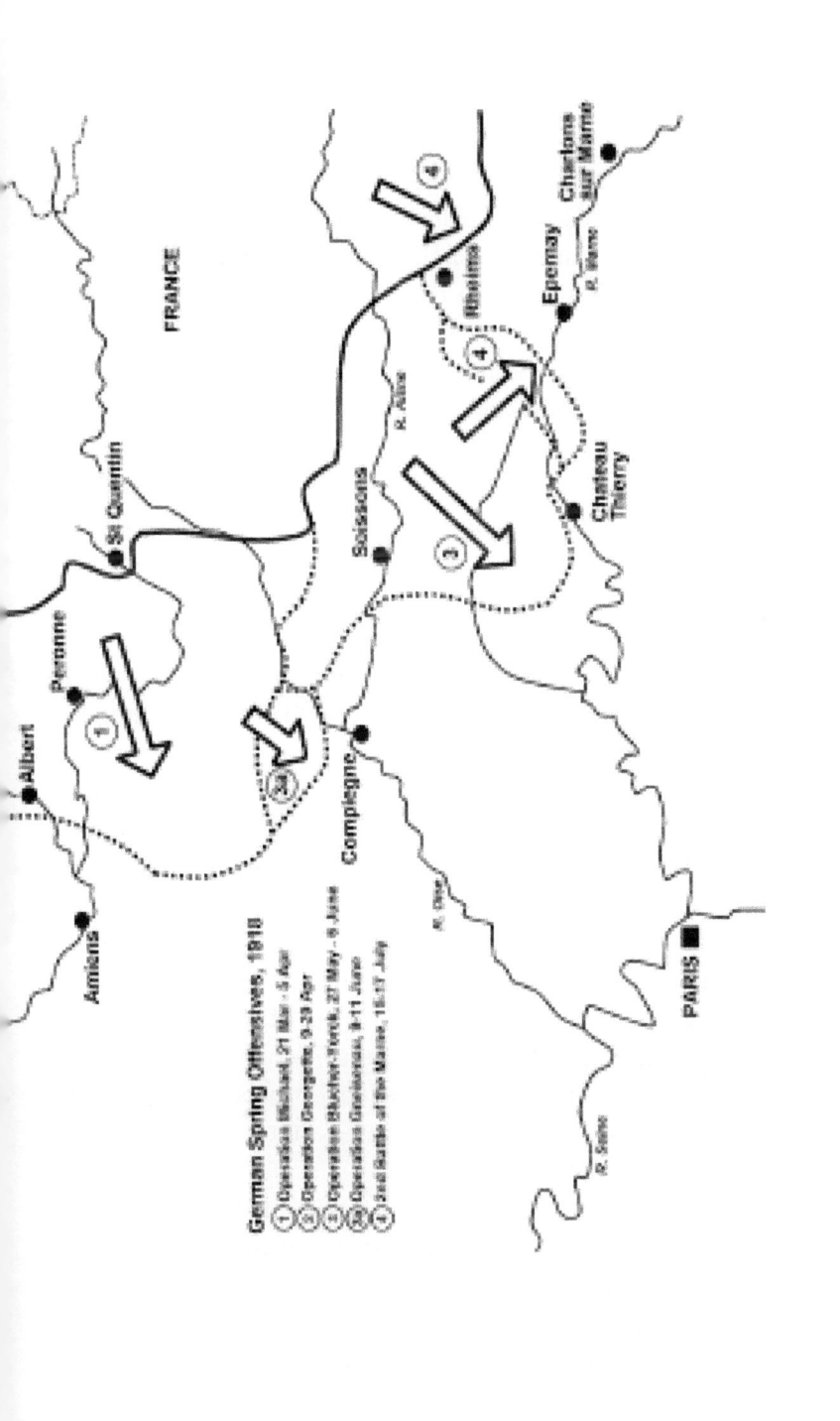

German Spring Offensives, 1918

1. Operation Michael, 21 Mar - 5 Apr
2. Operation Georgette, 9-29 Apr
3. Operation Blücher-Yorck, 27 May - 6 June
3a. Operation Gneisenau, 9-11 June
4. 2nd Battle of the Marne, 15-17 July

Headquarters for specific operations.

Throughout June and July, the training, re-equipment and reorganisation continued apace. Whilst the men were transferred to the Machine Gun Corps the officers remained East Riding Yeomen, simply attached to the MGC. In addition to the training programme of Colonel Harper, men were dispatched to the MGC depot at Camiers (near Etaples) for training and nearly 300 men were transferred to the main MGC Depot in Grantham in Lincolnshire. There were more infantry drills and new skills to learn and new equipment, in particular the 64 Vickers machine guns, to collect and become familiar with.

The belt-fed, water-cooled, 0.303" calibre Vickers machine gun, introduced in 1912, could fire 500 rounds a minute and was renowned for its ruggedness and reliability. In fact, the Vickers was to remain in service virtually unchanged until 1968. The gun weighed around 30lb (13 kg) together with a 50lb tripod (23 kg) and required a team of 6 to 8 men to operate; one to fire the gun, one to ensure the ammunition belt fed correctly and the rest to load the rounds into the cloth belts (by hand) and help carry the gun, ammunition (each 250 round belt weighed 22lbs (10 kg)), water (7½ pints for cooling the barrel) and spare parts. Each section had 4 guns and each company 4 sections for a total of 64 guns per battalion.

Traditionally the machine guns and ammunition had been transported by horse-drawn limber or on pack horses and mules (a typical machine gun battalion would have had more than 200 horses). However, in the new doctrine of defence-in-depth machine gunners needed to be able to deploy more quickly to counter any enemy advance and also be able to follow up successful attacks to protect the ground captured from enemy counterattacks.

And so, in a foretaste of the future, on 8th July 1918 the battalion became mechanised with the delivery of twenty-two 3-ton lorries, a workshop lorry, six touring cars, five 15-cwt boxcars (vans), twenty motorcycle and side car combinations, and eighteen motorcycles. They were now designated a Machine Gun

Battalion (Mobile) and their lorries, operated by Army Service Corps personnel, would be in high demand moving troops in the final months of the war, as a more open form of warfare emerged from the mire of the trenches.

During the summer of 1918 the most important thing in the men's minds was undoubtedly home leave. Most of the men were entitled to at least ten days leave in England. Obviously there had been no opportunity for home leave for the men since they embarked for the Middle East in October 1915 (officers could get home leave however) and so the chance to get home to loved ones, families and friends was very important.

Priority was given to those with the longest service, but all men entitled to leave, with the exception of 32, would receive it by the end of September. But home leave could be a mixed blessing. Frank Seeley, of the Lincolnshire Yeomanry, remembered that:

"it was rather an odd experience, after so long away, to find things so little changed" but that *"the rationing was pretty strict, and warnings of Zeppelin raids were fairly frequent"*.[17]

Many First World War soldiers on leave found that life seemed to be going on pretty much as it had before the war and they felt isolated from those left at home. Many couldn't wait to get back to their units and their friends.

By the middle of July, as the Second Battle of the Marne broke out to the south, the battalion moved closer to the frontline, first to Saulty, near Arras, where they joined the GHQ (General Headquarters of the BEF) Reserve and then at the end of the month to Millian and Bollezeele, near Cassel (a place that would play a significant part in the history of the regiment in the Second World War), just behind the bulge in the Western Front created by Operation *"Georgette"* in April.

Here the serious business began, and small parties of officers and men were attached to the frontline for a week at a time to get experience of the trenches and trench warfare. Leonard May recalled:

"we had not been up long before I, as a sergeant, and twenty or so NCOs were sent up to the front line to get a knowledge of working with machine guns in action. Our trucks took us to some four miles from the front and to a great gorge of a trench called the Hindenburg Line. It was so deep that our sleeping quarters were holes in the sides. We entered small trenches and had to walk miles, the trenches getting deeper until we reached the great front trench… we were detailed to the machine gun sections. To get up to the firing point we had to climb up steps made in the side of the trench. The enemy were very active and gave us some nasty times". [18]

Training would soon be over, and the men of the East Riding and Lincolnshire Yeomanries would return to the war.

The Allied Counteroffensive

The German commander Ludendorff now decided to exploit the gains made during the '*Blücher-Yorck*' offensives and threaten Paris, again hoping to draw reserves away from Flanders. On the 15th July the attack commenced with the usual heavy artillery bombardment and after four hours 52 German divisions attacked; the 7th Army to the West of Rheims and the 1st and 3rd Armies to the East, aiming to link up to the south of Paris.

However, the Allies now had the measure of the German tactics and had also been warned of the impending assault by French intelligence. East of Rheims the good use of defence-in-depth and artillery counter-battery fire stopped the attack on the first day. West of Rheims the Germans broke through the French 6th Army and advanced 9 miles, crossing the Marne before the advance was halted by the French 9th Army, supported by British and American units, on the 17th.

Now came the Allied response. The Germans were clearly spent. Each offensive had been less successful than the last and the losses they had suffered would be almost impossible to replace, particularly the most experienced men in the *Sturmbattalions*. The Allied Supreme Commander, French Field Marshal Foch, now launched a counterattack. On the 18th July, 300 French tanks and some 18 divisions (including 2 American) attacked along the whole of the Marne salient.

Catching the Germans by surprise they broke through and advanced 4 miles on the first day. On the 19th more French and American divisions attacked the eastern flank of the salient and with his forces under threat of encirclement Ludendorff ordered a withdrawal the next day. Soissons was recaptured on the 2nd August and the Germans were back where they started before the spring offensives.

What would turn out to be the final phase of the war, known as the One Hundred Days, began on the 8th August. The British launched a devastating surprise attack in front of Amiens, aiming to push the German lines back outside artillery range of the crucial railway station and to liberate railway lines parts of which now ran through German-held territory. In complete secrecy Haig had assembled a force of 456 tanks, 2,000 guns and more than 20 divisions including the Canadian and Australian Corps, and the French First Army (all under the command of the British Fourth Army). There was a deception plan to ensure the Germans did not learn of the impending attack and be no preliminary bombardment.

The attack was launched at dawn, with 10 Allied divisions on a 14-mile front advancing behind tanks and a creeping artillery barrage. Facing them were 6 weak German divisions. Surprise was complete and having broken through, the British advanced 7 miles on the first day. Over 13,000 Germans and 400 guns were captured—many German units put up only a token resistance before surrendering, something unthinkable only weeks before. Ludendorff described it as "the black day of the German Army".

The British advance continued over the next few days, reaching a depth of 12 miles but as German reserves arrived and the number of tanks available declined the offensive was halted on the 11th.

The French Third Army joined the offensive on the 10th August, on the right of the French First Army, retaking Montdidier. In six days they advanced 4 miles capturing Lassigny. South of them the French Tenth Army launched their attack at Soissons on 18th August and within two days had captured 8,000 prisoners and 200 guns. They now held the Aisne heights at Noyon, overlooking the German positions north of the river Vesle.

Advance to the Hindenburg Line

After a pause to bring up artillery and supplies the British resumed the attack in front of Amiens on the 21st August. The Third Army (supported by 200 tanks and with some American divisions attached) launched an attack on the left of the Fourth Army towards Albert. The advance pushed the Germans back and Albert was taken on the 22nd. The Fourth Army then rejoined the offensive and Bapaume was captured on the 29th.

On the 26th the offensive widened further as the right wing of the First Army attacked along the Arras-Cambrai road. In the face of the Allied attacks Ludendorff ordered a retreat, hoping to form a new defensive position on the river Somme, but with the Allied offensives constantly switching between different sectors he was unable to deploy his meagre reserves effectively. The river Somme was crossed by the Australian Corps on the 30th August. Péronne fell on the 2nd September. On the same day the First and Third Armies breached the strong German position known as the D-Q Line (between Drocourt and Quéant) which meant it was impossible for the Germans to hold their positions to the north and they were forced to retreat back to the Hindenburg Line from whence they had started in March 1918.

On the 28th August the newly re-designated 102nd (Lincolnshire and East Riding Yeomanry) Battalion MGC was placed under the command of the First Army, joining the army reserve (attached to XXII Corps) on 12 hours' notice. Lieutenant Colonel Harper of the Machine Gun Corps and his instructors, their job complete, returned to the MGC depot. Within days the battalion was attached to the 56th (London) Division and took over a portion of the frontline.

As August became September the companies of the battalion took their turn in the trenches, alternating with companies of the various divisional machine gun battalions in XXII Corps (each division having its own machine gun battalion). Corporal

Bill Simpson wrote that he remembered:

> "...*regular stints up the line with his machine gun crew. They would go up for one night and have the next night off and so on, the other sections taking over on his nights off. They were conveyed to and from the line in lorries, two sections to a lorry. They were constantly under artillery fire."* [19]

During the month one officer (Lieutenant W. Grant) and one OR were wounded by shelling, which was an ever-present danger.

Foch now planned a coordinated *Grand Offensive* all along the front to capitalise on the Allied successes. He hoped by maintaining pressure all along the front he could prevent the Germans from forming new defensive positions and he also hoped to capture the main enemy railway lines that ran north-south behind the front, further reducing the capacity of the German armies to fight.

In preparation for the 'big push' on the 12th September the American Expeditionary Force (AEF) launched the first wholly American offensive of the war, when the US First Army attacked the St Miheil salient. The Germans had held this salient since 1914 and it had been the springboard for their Verdun offensive in 1916. The Americans attacked both sides of the salient catching the Germans off guard – they had been in the process of withdrawing to straighten their lines. Despite fierce rearguard actions the salient was cleared by the 16th, the Americans capturing 15,000 prisoners and 250 guns.

The next phase was the clearance of the remaining German positions west of the Hindenburg Line and on the 12th September the British Third and Fourth Armies attacked at Havrincourt and then at Epehy on the 18th. The Germans were forced the 3 miles back to the main Hindenburg Line.

THE GRAND OFFENSIVE

Now the *Grand Offensive* could really begin. In a series of co-ordinated offensives, the Allies would attack along the length of the Western Front. In the south the US First Army attacked first, on the 26th September, in the Meuse-Argonne sector (towards Sedan), supported by the French Fourth Army. Poor logistical organisation and American inexperience, together with difficult terrain and appalling weather, led to chaos and the battle degenerated into a series of slow, bitterly contested advances.

In the centre the attack commenced on the 27th, the British First and Third Armies launching an attack against the Canal du Nord, part of the Hindenburg Line in front of Cambrai. The Canadian Corps (First Army) were chosen to spearhead the attack. Under cover of the creeping barrage the Canadians were able to cross the incomplete canal with little difficulty. In two days the two armies advanced six miles along a twelve-mile front, capturing 10,000 prisoners and 200 guns.

In Flanders the northern element of the attack began on 28th. The British Second Army together with the Belgian Army attacked across the old Ypres battlefields and recaptured all of the ground lost during Operation *'Georgette'*. In three days, the Allies advanced ten miles, but poor weather and overstretched supply lines brought the offensive to a halt.

Following the crossing of the Canal du Nord by the First Army, the Fourth Army attacked the German positions further south along another formidable obstacle, the St. Quentin canal, on the 29th. Two American divisions would lead the assault supported by 150 tanks and the Australian Corps would then pass through the Americans and continue the attack.

Despite initial difficulties and heavy casualties amongst the inexperienced Americans the canal was eventually crossed and by the end of the day a gap nearly four miles wide had been opened in the Hindenburg Line at its strongest point and 5000 prisoners taken. The attack continued and the final (support) line of the Hindenburg Line, the Beaurevoir Line three miles behind the main position, was breached and by the 5th October the British were into open country for the first time since 1914.

BATTLE JOINED

The 56th Division of XXII Corps, First Army, was on the

fringes of the Battle of the Canal du Nord, attacking northwards to protect the flank of the main attack. Supporting them was 'C' Company, 102nd Battalion MGC. Now the yeomen had chance to put their training to use and to prove they had mastered the complexities of the machine gun barrage. The barrage was an artillery tactic adopted and developed by the Machine Gun Corps from 1916 onwards and it was a highly technical operation that required well-trained men and good coordination.

Placed up to 1,000 yards or so behind the frontline, the machine gunners fired over the heads of the attacking infantry, sweeping the enemy's rear areas or targeting specific positions. They were also capable of firing a creeping barrage, a wall of machine gun fire just ahead of the advancing troops which, as the name suggests, crept forward in front of them.

Each gun had to be aimed so that its fall of shot was coordinated with that of the other guns, creating an impenetrable barrier or saturating a particular target area. First, the target would be located on a map and the position of the gun relative to it determined by trigonometry.

Calculations would then be made to determine the gun's 'beaten zone' – the area in which the majority of the rounds fired were likely to fall (no two rounds would ever fall in exactly the same place due to variations in wind, propellant and the condition (and temperature) of the barrel). The trajectory of the rounds would also be calculated (pretty important when firing directly over the heads of friendly troops). A clinometer (hand-held surveying instrument for measuring angles of slope, elevation or inclination of an object) would then be used to set the gun to the required elevation (the angle at which the gun would be fired). For safety a mechanical stop on the tripod was used to ensure that the gun could not fire so low as to hit friendly troops.

Once the gun was set sandbags were placed on the tripod legs to ensure that during firing it would not appreciably move and upset the aim. It was also necessary to ensure that the tripod would not sink into the ground. Wooden stakes, 'aiming posts', would be driven into the ground to allow the gunner to quickly change between different pre-selected targets, either in accordance with the barrage timetable or in response to a pre-arranged SOS signal from the frontline (particularly when being used in defensive positions). Then, once the enemy frontline had been captured the machine gunners were to move up rapidly to be in a position to face any counter attacks.

Leonard May described a typical action:

> "we were with the infantry in front and when they advanced, we fired over them until a safety point was reached. The small artillery was behind us and the bigger ones behind for miles. The noise was terrific; in fact, you could not hear our machine guns firing. We had to notice the position of the crank handles to see what was wrong. The Germans were firing too. The infantry moved forward to take up new positions and we followed just after and dug in". [20]

'A' and 'B' Companies of 102nd Battalion were also involved in supporting the offensive, being attached to the 4th Battalion MGC, but they were not seriously engaged. However, the Germans maintained intermittent shelling all along the front and 1 OR with 'C' Company HQ was killed (Private Alfred Holmes).

The Beginning of the End

By the end of September, the German High Command feared total collapse on the Western Front. On the 28th Ludendorff suffered a nervous breakdown, ranting at everyone and everything, including the Kaiser. The next day the military authorities requested that approaches be made to the Allies for an armistice. On the 3rd October a new, more liberal Chancellor, Prince Max of Baden, was appointed and a request for discussions was sent to President Wilson of the United States on the 4th. President Wilson had proposed his 'fourteen points' in January as a way for peace to be achieved honourably for all the combatants and these would form the basis of the German approach. Now the diplomatic wrangling began. The Germans believed that since they still held parts of Russia, France and Belgium they would be able to secure a peace treaty on equal terms with the Allies.

Time was running out for the Central Powers however. On the same day as Ludendorff lost his nerve, the Bulgarians requested an armistice after the successful Allied offensives on the Salonika front. It came into effect the following day. In the Middle East, the Turks suffered a massive defeat at the Battle of Megiddo at the end of the month, after which Damascus fell on 1st October and Syria evacuated. An armistice would be agreed on the 30th October. Austria-Hungary was also on the brink of collapse. The Empire was breaking apart; by the end of October the Hungarians and what would become the state of Yugoslavia had declared their independence. An armistice would be signed on the 3rd November. There was no to be let up in the Allied offensives on the Western Front either; the Allies sensed that the war could now be won in 1918.

The Final Offensives

After a pause to bring up supplies the attack in Flanders resumed as the British (Second) and Belgian Armies attacked towards Courtrai on the 14th October. By the 17th Lille and Ostend were captured, and Belgian units reached Zeebrugge and Bruges on 19th October, forcing the Germans to abandon the Belgian coast. The Belgian Army would enter Ghent on the 11th November.

In the south the Franco-American attack in the Meuse-Argonne sector resumed on the 4th October and continued to make slow progress, but with more American troops joining from the St Mihiel sector (enough to allow General Pershing, the US Commander, to form the American Second Army) the Argonne Forest was cleared and by the end of the month the Americans had broken through the last German lines and into the open. As the Germans retreated the Americans rapidly advanced up the Meuse valley and they and their French allies had reached the outskirts of Sedan and Meziéres by the 11th November.

It was in the centre where conditions were most favourable for a final, decisive attack, however. Here the British were in open country untouched by the war so far and the terrain was eminently suited to tanks. The British Third and Fourth Armies resumed the offensive on the 8th October, and by the evening 8000 Germans had been taken prisoner and the Germans had evacuated Cambrai. In fact, the German High Command ordered a withdrawal back to new positions on the river Selle. The following day all three British Armies in the centre (the First, Third and Fourth) followed up the retreating German forces, overcoming what little resistance the rearguards could put up. By the 12th October they had reached the line of the river, an advance of over 10 miles in 4 days.

Battle of the Selle

The effort to breach the German positions along the river Selle began on the 17th October. The British artillery had been active since the 12th, attempting to soften up the more strongly defended areas and destroy the German barbed wire entanglements, but at 5am the bombardment increased, signalling the start of the attack. The German positions had been hastily dug and lacked the concrete bunkers and dugouts of the Hindenburg line, although the river itself still had to be crossed. It was thought that the German line was held by 4 weak and exhausted divisions, and it was expected that the Fourth Army would reach the next natural obstacle, the Sambre-Oise Canal, with relative ease.

The lead divisions of the Fourth Army, supported by the French First Army on the left and 4 battalions of tanks, managed to cross the river without serious opposition and casualties were light. However once across the river the attackers found that large swathes of wire remained intact and German resistance stiffened; in fact, the German defenders consisted of nine relatively fresh German divisions and they were able to mount a number of successful counterattacks during the day. The Allies, in particular the US II Corps, part of the British Fourth Army, suffered heavy casualties.

Despite this, by dusk the British had broken though the German defences all along the river Selle and Le Cateau was back in Allied hands. Nevertheless, overall progress had not been as good as expected and the level of German resistance had come as quite a shock after weeks of relatively easy advances. The Fourth Army's attack resumed the following day and after another 2 days of heavy fighting it had advanced up to 2 miles along a 7-mile front and captured 5,000 prisoners.

Now, as a result of the casualties suffered during their assault, the Fourth Army was relegated to a supporting role and the Third and First Armies would take over the attack. And so, at 2am on the 20th October the Third and First Armies launched a joint attack on the German positions along the river Selle to their front.

Under cover of darkness and a heavy artillery barrage (there had been no preliminary bombardment to maximise the chance of achieving surprise) the four corps of Third Army crossed the river without difficulty. Again, German resistance once across the river was fierce but after some stiff fighting Third Army achieved most of their objectives by the end of the day and now occupied the high ground east of the Selle.

On the left flank of the Third Army the lead divisions of XXII Corps, the 4th and 51st (Highland) divisions also attacked a 2am. In addition to the artillery bombardment, the divisions were supported by a machine gun barrage. 'C' and 'D' companies of the 102nd Battalion MGC, (now under the tactical command of the 51st (Highland) Division) fired in support of the Highlanders and 'A' and 'B' Companies supported the 4th Division but were not engaged. There were no casualties amongst the yeomen. The First Army attack in fact met only light resistance as the Germans were already in retreat in response to the advance by the Second Army further to the north in Flanders.

The Approach to Valenciennes

The First Army now found itself facing Valenciennes, a communications hub and the centre of the German defensive plan in the area. On the left of the First Army front VII Corps were advancing over difficult, heavily wooded, country and were lagging behind. In the centre the Canadian Corps faced an assault across flooded marshy ground and the defended Schelde Canal. The most promising axis was that of XXII Corps, where the 4th and 51st (Highland) Divisions were in positions facing the river Escaillon. Whilst it was a small river it had steep and slippery banks and the Germans had placed barbed wire on both banks and also across the river itself. The Germans were dug in on the slope facing the river in trenches that completely commanded the river. It would not be an easy task.

Zero hour was 4am on the 24th October. Under a heavy bombardment by 7 brigades of field artillery and one of heavy artillery, the 51st (Highland) Division attacked on the left with the 4th Division on the right. The divisional history notes "*two companies of machine guns were also detailed to fire a barrage*". These were 'C' and 'D' Companies, 102nd Battalion MGC, under the command of the East Ridings' Captain Pearson and Major White respectively. The barrage was to be a creeping barrage, fired 400 yards in front of the infantry and creeping forward in 200-yard steps. Private Terry Ward wrote:

> "*We moved into the line at 3am onto a railway embankment near Thiant to put up barrage for 51st Division. Spotted by German 'planes in sunken road. They quickly gave our position to their artillery and we were badly shelled. Many casualties and a complete shambles for a time. I think it was here that Captain Mark Sykes won his MC and Corporal Thompson his MM. Digging in til daylight.*" [21]

A machine gun barrage was an awesome demonstration of firepower. The 102nd Battalion war diary notes that 'C' Company fired 3,000 rounds per gun and 'D' Company 4,000 rounds per gun during this barrage. Each company could deploy 16 machine guns, putting a total of 112,000 rounds onto the target in only a few minutes. This required considerable logistics support, 112,000 rounds of ammunition weighed over 3 tons and it had to be transported to the battery positions beforehand and the rounds manually loaded into the canvas belts that fed the guns and although there was a mechanical device to assist them, the men still found it a chore.

Following the bombardment 'C' Company was withdrawn

and 'D' Company took up defensive positions, remaining in the line until relieved by 'C' Company on the 27th. Enemy shelling remained ever present, 'D' Company suffering 1 OR killed (Private Harry Abbis) and 1 Officer (2nd Lieutenant Purnell) and 4 OR wounded in 3 days.

With the support of the artillery and machine guns the infantry of 51st (Highland) Division managed to cross the river, which had been swollen by recent rains, under cover of darkness and attacked the German positions. These were quickly overrun, with more than 1,000 prisoners taken in the process. By the end of the day the division had advanced 3 miles to a line from Trith in the north to Sommaing in the south. The fighting continued for the next two days and by the end of the 26th October the 51st (Highland) Division was in possession of Famars. The Highlanders attempted to take the local high ground of Mont Houy but were repulsed. On the right the 4th Division had reached the line of the river Rhonelle and captured intact a bridge at Artres.

On the 27th the Germans mounted a series of counterattacks and maintained harassing artillery fire, causing a number of casualties, including 1 yeoman killed (Private Charles H Bellamy) and 10 wounded. One such counterattack reached the outskirts of Famars, but it was driven back after bitter street fighting. The next morning the 51st (Highland) Division made a renewed attempt to capture Mont Houy supported by a heavy artillery and machine gun barrage (provided by the 51st Battalion, MGC). The Seaforth Highlanders quickly captured the hill but having suffered heavy casualties were unable to hold the hill in the face of German counterattacks.

During the afternoon of 28th the enemy launched one such counterattack, supported by artillery, along the portion of front where 'C' and 'D' Companies were deployed ('D' Company had returned to the line during the afternoon, relieving a company of the 51st Machine Gun Battalion), but as the 51st Divisional history notes this was "...*easily dispersed with machine gun and Lewis fire*" [22] at the cost of 15 yeomen wounded (10 of them gassed), but by the end of the day the Germans remained in possession of the majority of the hill.

There were further German counterattacks the following day, the 29th; their first attack stalled, and a fresh assault launched at 4pm was repulsed by the Argyll and Sutherland Highlanders supported by the yeomen of 'D' Company. Initially the enemy counterattack, supported by a heavy artillery barrage, succeeded in pushing the Highlanders back, but Lieutenant John Robinson pushed his and a neighbouring machine gun section forward and laid down a protective machine gun barrage which enabled the infantry to recover and defeat the counterattack, at the cost of another 3 wounded from 'D' Company. For his actions, Lieutenant Robinson was awarded the Military Cross.

Lance Corporal Arthur Oldfield was also recommended for a gallantry award for his actions on this day; on hearing that a neighbouring infantry platoon under counterattack lacked any machine guns he immediately volunteered to go out and try to find some enemy guns. He was able to bring in two German guns with several boxes of ammunition and get them in working order. His citation remarked, "He set a splendid example of determination and initiative".

Exhausted, the yeomen and Highlanders were relieved during the night of 29th/30th October and withdrawn, the yeomanry suffering 1 OR gassed. But there was to be little real rest; on the 31st 'B' and 'C' Companies were detached from the battalion and moved into position to support the forthcoming attack on Valenciennes during which time 2 more yeomen were killed by shelling (Private Norman Vertican and Corporal Robert Atkinson).

October had seen the battalion suffer a total of 1 officer wounded, 4 ORs killed and another 35 wounded, 3 of whom subsequently died of their wounds. These losses were made good on the 31st however with a draft of replacements (consisting of 6 officers and 24 ORs).

Battle of Valenciennes

The next attempt to capture Valenciennes was launched on the 1st November. The Canadian Corps (First Army) attacked

Mt. Houy, supported by a massive artillery bombardment from eight field artillery and six heavy artillery brigades, and swept over the hill with only limited opposition, taking 1,800 prisoners. The bridge at Aulnoy was taken intact and the Rhonelle crossed. By the end of the day the outskirts of Marly were reached, but any further advance was prevented by heavy fire from the steelworks, although patrols were able to reach the outskirts of Valenciennes.

To the right of the Canadians the 4th and 49th Divisions of XXII Corps also attacked on the 1st November. Supported by an artillery barrage of 7 field artillery and 1 heavy artillery brigades and a machine gun barrage fired by 'B' and 'C' Companies, 102nd Battalion MGC (reported in the war diary as "most satisfactory"), the leading infantry of the 49th Division succeeded in crossing the Rhonelle with little difficulty and reached the line of the Preseau–Aulnoy road. Here the German resistance stiffened and at 9:30am a counterattack successfully halted the advance. A four-gun section of 'B' Company was sent forward to support the infantry of the 6th Battalion Duke of Wellington's Regiment and the 5th Battalion West Yorkshire Regiment. A second enemy counterattack developed at 4pm and again 'B' Company was called upon to support the infantry, 2 sections being sent forward.

Casualties amongst the yeomen were again light, with only one man wounded. These and similar attacks on the 4th Division were repelled and XXII Corps ended the day only 400–500 yards short of Preseau itself.

On the morning of the 2nd the Germans began withdrawing from Valenciennes and the city was captured by the Canadian Corps. Terry Ward noted in his diary:

> *"Infantry "over top" again. Followed them over and dug in just behind in case of counterattack. Self and one or two men lucky enough to be relieved by reinforcements coming up at night."* [23]

As the battalion followed up the advance, 2 officers (Lieutenant M. J. Piper and Lieutenant B. W. Simpson) and 3 ORs were wounded.

First Army area of operations, October – November 1918

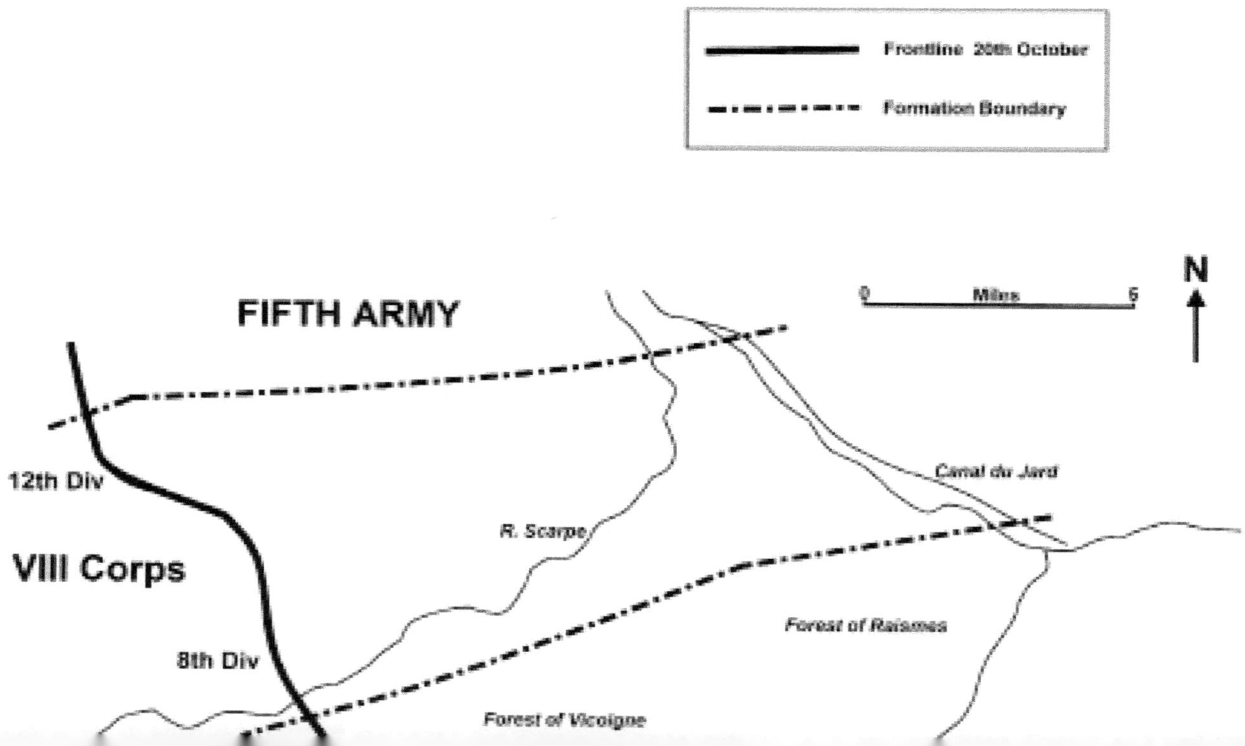

Scheide Canal
Somain
1st Cdn Div
Oisy
Anzin
Valenciennes
Canadian Corps
Marly
St Leger
Aulnoy
4th Cdn Div
Denain
Trith
Mt. Houy
R. Rhonelle
Famars
Preseau
Thiant
Maing
R. Selle
Artres
Maresches
FIRST ARMY
Monchaux
51st Div
Querenaing
Sommaing
XXII Corps
Fleury
Vendegies
Ruesnes
Avesnes
4th Div
R. Escaillon
Le Quesnoy
Saulzoir
THIRD ARMY

Battle of the Sambre

What would turn out to be the final set piece assault of the war began at 5:30am on the 4th November. The British Third and Fourth Armies attacked in the direction of Mauberge on the river Sambre. The Third Army faced open country in the north and the fortified town of Le Quesnoy in the centre and to the south of them the Fourth Army faced the Forest of Mormal and the prospect of crossing the Sambre-Oise Canal. Supported by the now standard artillery barrage the Third Army advanced some 4 miles and captured all their objectives meeting stiff resistance only in a few small villages. At Le Quesnoy the New Zealand Division managed to scale the old 17th Century walls and the German garrison surrendered.

To the south the right wing of the Third Army and the left wing of the Fourth Army overcame some stiff resistance in front of the Forest of Mormal but had almost reached their objectives by nightfall. The crossing of the Sambre-Oise Canal provided the most difficult part of the attack. There was stiff fighting on the approaches to the canal, but the canal was crossed using rafts and a number of intact bridges and the village of Orson the east bank was captured by the end of the day. However, in the canal sector casualties were high, including a certain Captain Wilfred Owen of the Manchester Regiment. All along the front German troops had been surrendering in massive numbers, some 10,000 prisoners being taken, and, in many areas, the German Army was in full retreat.

For the First Army, on whose front to the north of the Third and Fourth Armies the Germans were already in retreat following the fall of Valenciennes, the set piece attack previously planned was abandoned and orders for the pursuit of the retreating Germans issued. In preparation the 4th and 49th Divisions (XXII Corps) were relieved during the night of the 3rd/4th November by the 11th and 56th Divisions respectively.

'A' and 'B' Companies 102nd Battalion MGC now came under the orders of the 11th Division; 'C' and 'D' Companies similarly to the 56th Division, but as part of the reorganisation the battalion was withdrawn from the line, although there was little opportunity for rest as the frontline was moving quickly and they followed along behind, suffering 1 OR wounded as they battled forward along congested roads in an attempt to stay in touch with 11th Division HQ.

By the 6th November the Germans were in full retreat all along the line although the German rearguards continued to put up stubborn resistance on occasions. On the First Army front the 11th and 56th Divisions continued to lead the pursuit, but when they reached the Grande Honnelle their advance was checked by artillery, mortar and machine gun fire. Despite heavy local fighting a slim bridgehead across the river was gained by the 56th Division. In preparation for an attack the next morning, two sections (six guns) of 'B' Company were detached to provide support to the 167 Brigade of the 56th Division, suffering 2 ORs wounded from German shelling. However, opposite the Canadian and XXII Corps the Germans withdrew during the night and the advance, beginning at 9am on the 7th November, made rapid progress meeting limited resistance. The end of the war was in now sight; in Valenciennes there was a formal parade marking the liberation of the city on the 2nd, attended by 1 Officer and 9 ORs of 'B' Company representing XXII Corps.

As the advance continued the 2 sections of 'B' Company deployed with the 167th Brigade were finally withdrawn on the 9th. Since the start of the advance on the 7th the sections had marched across country some 12 miles with the infantry, having to manhandle the guns, ammunition and equipment as there was no transport available. There were no casualties, but the war diary noted, rather understatedly, "the men were much fatigued".

The Armistice

With the Allies rapidly advancing towards the German border and civil unrest and Bolshevik revolutions at home the Germans knew it was the end. Everyone, German and Allied, knew that the war was almost over. Facing revolution at home and knowing that remaining would constitute an obstacle to a peace deal with the Allies the Kaiser abdicated on the 10th November and fled to neutral Holland. The Allied and German delegations met for the final time in a railway carriage in a siding at Compiègne, north of Paris, at 2:05am on the 11th and the armistice terms were agreed at 05:10am. The fighting would stop at 11:00am (the 11th hour of the 11th day of the 11th month), to give time for the orders to be issued.

The Germans would immediately (within two weeks) evacuate all occupied territory in the West, surrender their artillery, machine guns, mortars and aircraft, together with significant numbers of locomotives, railway carriages and lorries. Allied units were to be permitted to cross the Rhine and establish bridgeheads on German soil. The High Seas Fleet was to be interned and disarmed (it was eventually scuttled by the Germans in Scapa Flow) and the U-Boats surrendered. The Treaty of Brest—Litovsk between Germany and the new Russian government was to be repudiated and German forces withdrawn to the 1914 borders. All Allied prisoners of war were to be handed over by the Germans. It amounted to a total defeat.

The war diary of the 102nd Battalion MGC simply noted:

11th Nov 10:45am Following Telegram received from XXII Corps:-
"Hostilities will cease at 1100 November 11th. Troops will stand fast on the line reached at that hour, which will be reported to Corps HQ. Defensive precautions will be maintained and there will be no intercourse of any description with the enemy. XXII Corps."

With a sense of anti-climax, The Great War, the 'War to end all Wars' was finally over.

The 102nd Battalion moved into barracks in Valenciennes on the 23rd November, Leonard May remarking:

"at first we stayed in the barracks, which were in a terrible state and took us days to clean up… we really had a nice time in the town as we had a lot of spare time on our hands, a lot of football etc." [24]

Demobilisation

Life for the men quickly reverted to the peace-time staple of regimental training. In addition to the usual military syllabus there were lectures and classes for the soldiers to prepare them to return to civilian life, under an education scheme organised by the First Army.

The training routine was lightened by ceremonial parades, such as the one in Mons marking the formal entry of the Allies into city (to which the 102nd Battalion provided 6 officers and 94 men), and with official visits, including that of the Commanding Officer of the First Army and HRH The King's visit to Valenciennes.

There was also hard and potentially dangerous work to be done salvaging useful material and equipment from the battlefields. The now Sergeant May remembered:

> *"the town had to be cleared of all dangerous arms, bombs, shells etc. I was given a district to clear, every house, garden etc. was searched and booked down, and when the whole town was finished, lorries went round to collect everything up. It was taken to a large heath and blown up."* [25]

But the overriding issue was demobilisation. The war was won and the men, particularly those pre-War Territorials who had served since 1914, wanted to go home. The men had to endure one last Christmas in the Army, but then demobilisation commenced on the 27th December, when 12 miners and 4 long service yeomen were sent back to England. Throughout January the pace of demobilisation increased and by the middle of February the battalion was reduced to two companies; what remained of 'B' Company was absorbed into 'A' Company under Major C. Wilson of the Lincolnshire Yeomanry and a similar exercise was carried out with 'D' and 'C' Companies under Major Pearson of the East Ridings.

On 7th April 1919 the last 197 men arrived in Calais to hand in their stores and equipment. Those men with significant service left (and 20 volunteers) were transferred to the 200th Battalion, MGC and the remaining Royal Army Service Corps men attached to the battalion were transferred away. And then on the 19th April, the CO, Lieutenant Colonel B Granville DSO, 3 officers and 8 men embarked for the crossing to England, destined for the Old Barracks, Lincoln carrying with them the battalion records. Once there the East Riding Yeomanry entered 'suspended animation' and an uncertain future.

Chapter 6: The Inter-War Years, 1919-1930

The fighting may have ended on the 11th November 1918, but the war wasn't officially over until the various peace treaties were ratified, most notably the Treaty of Versailles, between the Allies and Germany, which was signed on the 28th June 1919. Indeed, many of the yeomen demobilised were not entirely released from military service; they were actually discharged to the 'Class Z' reserve, which meant that although they were able to return to civilian life, they could be recalled to the colours should the need arise. The Class Z reserve was established in December 1918 and was intended as a precaution should Germany reject the terms of any peace treaty and hostilities resume. It was abolished on 31st March 1920.

For many of the men who served the war would never truly be over; those suffering from illnesses and diseases contracted abroad (e.g. malaria, bilharzia), serious physical wounds (e.g. gunshot, shrapnel or gas) and mental injuries (e.g. shell shock) would suffer the consequences for the rest of their lives, which in many cases were quite short.

The first post hostilities death in the East Riding Yeomanry occurred only a week after the armistice. Private John Priestman transferred to the East Riding Yeomanry from the Royal Field Artillery in October 1915. After a spell at home with the 3/1st East Ridings he was sent to join the first line in Egypt in October 1916 and he served with them until he was medically repatriated home with TB, in June 1918. He was discharged as no longer fit for war service in October but died a month later, on 18th November 1918. His TB was declared "attributable to service during the present war owing to strain and exposure of active service".

Private Cyril Clark died in the Hull Royal Infirmary on the 20th January 1919. He died of appendicitis before he could be demobilised. He was 25 and was buried with full military honours in Hull Western Cemetery.

Even more tragic was Lance Corporal Sydney Bonewell. He joined the East Riding Yeomanry on the 31st August 1914 and went to Egypt with the regiment in 1915. He subsequently transferred to the Imperial Camel Corps and saw action in Egypt and Palestine. He died at Hull on 2nd April 1919 whilst on demobilisation leave – he was due to be discharged on the 10th.

Not all the post war deaths were as a result of injuries or illness, however. On 18th March 1919 Company Quartermaster Sergeant Philip Duckels Peacock, serving with the 812th Area Employment Company, Labour Corps, was "killed in native disturbances" in Egypt.

This civil unrest, known as the 1919 Egyptian Revolution, raged between 15th–31st March following the British arrest and exile of several Egyptian nationalist leaders. An estimated 800 Egyptians, 31 European civilians, and 3 British Officers, 17 ORs and 9 Indian Sepoys were killed. CQMS Peacock was amongst the eight people (seven soldiers and one Egyptian) murdered by a mob on the Assiut to Minia train in the incident known as the Deirout train murders.

Philip Duckels Peacock, born Hull in 1892, joined 'A' Squadron in early 1913, arriving in Egypt in November 1915 with the 1/1st East Riding Yeomanry, serving through the Palestine campaign of 1917. He was most likely medically downgraded (on account of injuries or sickness) and compulsorily transferred to the Labour Corps in June 1918 (suggesting he was left behind when the 1/1st ERY relocated to France).

There were a number of other current or former members of the regiment who died in the immediate post war period, but the final 'official' East Riding war death was that of Major Clive Wilson DSO on the 18th January 1921. He was a member of the Wilson shipping family and cousin of the wartime Regimental commander, Colonel Guy Wilson. He had served in the Boer War with the Imperial Yeomanry and then joined the East Riding Yeomanry in 1903, with whom he served until 1912, reaching the rank of Major (although he had reverted to Captain, at his own request, by the time he retired).

He re-joined the regiment as a Lieutenant on the outbreak of war but was forced to relinquish his commission, on the grounds of ill health, in 1916. He subsequently took a commission as a Major, commanding the Beverley Company of the 3rd Battalion, Yorkshire East Riding Volunteer Regiment (part of the Volunteer Training Corps, the First World War equivalent of the Home Guard). His sudden death aged 44 was blamed on apoplexy (a stroke) brought on by the effects of his wartime service.

The cut-off date for 'official' war casualties, set by the Imperial War Graves Commission (today the Commonwealth War Graves Commission) was 31st August 1921. Of course, men continued to die after this date, many due to the effects of wartime service. One example is Corporal Frederick Armitage. He joined the East Riding Yeomanry on 31st August 1914, serving in Egypt with the regiment and latterly with the Imperial Camel Corps. He was demobilised 18th July 1919 but died of malaria, contracted on active service, on 4th September 1922.

Reformation

Throughout 1919 and into 1920 intense debates raged as to the composition of a revived Territorial Force, its role and whether, in fact, it was needed at all. The original *raison-d'être* of the TF had been home defence but now, following the so-called 'war to end all wars', there was no obvious enemy to pose a threat to the mainland. The old foe France was now a solid ally, and Germany was defeated and its military capabilities severely restricted. As a result, the War Office wanted to re-form the TF with an overseas service commitment from the start (rather than asking the force to volunteer, as happened in 1914) allowing the force to act as a reserve to reinforce the (once again much smaller) Regular Army abroad in times of crisis. This plan was strongly resisted by the staunchly independent TF Associations. They feared that the TF would be used simply as a pool of manpower to reinforce Regular units, i.e., that men would be drafted to join Regular Army units rather than being deployed in their own formations. This infringed on the independence of the TF and it was felt that this would have a detrimental effect on recruiting.

If the home service only commitment was to be maintained and with external threats apparently removed, the only realistic role for the TF would be to aid the civil power (i.e., the government). This essentially meant dealing with civil disturbances, in particular strikes and industrial unrest. Britain immediately after the war was in industrial turmoil, and civil unrest, even revolution, was considered highly likely. The short post-war boom was already over, and millions of men were returning from the army expecting to resume their jobs in a new society, 'a land fit for heroes', only to face unemployment and poverty. Unrest was fuelled by the effects of a large increase in union membership during the war and set against the backdrop of the recent Bolshevik revolution in Russia and the government's fear of a similar scenario in Britain.

Precedence was set in January 1919 when the army was called in to help quell a general strike in Glasgow, where the Communist red flag had been raised at one point, and although the strike collapsed before the situation escalated, the government had demonstrated its willingness to use the army to put down or break strikes. Tension remained high throughout 1919 as fears mounted of a crippling strike by the so-called Triple Alliance, formed by the three largest unions: the Miners Federation of Great Britain, the National Transport Workers' Federation and the National Union of Railwaymen. The likelihood of the TF being used to counter such a strike (as opposed to the Regular Army) was increased when the imminent end of conscription, in March 1920, was taken into consideration. The reduction in available manpower that would follow once conscription finished, coupled with the army's extensive overseas commitments, meant that the Regular Army simply did not have sufficient manpower at home to deal with large scale civil disturbances. In the eyes of many this meant that this responsibility would inevitably fall to the units of the TF. Again, the Territorial Associations strongly resisted any such role, fearing that this would alienate the very people from whom they hoped to attract recruits. This left the government pondering the expense of a force that seemingly had no role at home or abroad.

In parallel the military establishment also recognised that the advances in technology and tactics during the war meant that the TF as it existed prior to 1914 would not be wholly appropriate for the new post-war world. It was widely recognised that the advent of the wireless, aeroplanes, tanks and armoured cars, allied to the domination of machine guns and artillery, severely limited the use of cavalry on the modern battlefield. Any reformed TF would need more of the new supporting arms and significantly less cavalry; consequently, most of the 55 pre-war yeomanry regiments would not be needed in any reformed TF. It was suggested that only the most senior regiments would be retained as horsed cavalry, to form a Territorial Cavalry Division, with the rest being converted to artillery or signals units. This was thought likely to deter former members from rejoining however and therefore it was decided that all the yeomanry regiments would be provisionally reformed as cavalry and then be given two years to decide their own fate.

So despite the ongoing debates as to the composition and utility of the force, the TF was officially reconstituted in February 1920. Winston Churchill, the Secretary of State for War, attempted to address some of the concerns of the TF Associations by pledging that units would be mobilised only after an Act of Parliament, and that men would only be sent overseas as formed units and not piecemeal as drafts to Regular units. He also agreed that the TF would not be embodied for the suppression of civil disturbances or labour disputes, except in the case of a grave national emergency (such as an attempted revolution).

The East Riding of Yorkshire Yeomanry was duly reformed at the old Yeomanry Riding School on Walton Street, Hull, in April 1920 and the first officers appointed, including Lieutenant Colonel Guy Wilson CMG DSO, the wartime commander, who was reappointed as the Commanding Officer. The War Office had suggested they become an artillery brigade, but this was resisted by "*those keenly interested in this popular regiment*" (according to the Hull Daily Mail of 13th April) and the regiment initially reformed as a provisional cavalry regiment. The new regiment was to be organised into three Squadrons, 'A' to 'C' (as opposed to the four pre-war squadrons, 'A' to 'D'), centred on Hull, where Regimental Headquarters was to be based, with outlying drill stations at Beverley and Driffield. As a junior regiment there was little hope of retaining their horses and following discussions over the next few months, the regiment chose to convert into an Armoured Car Company. This proposal was accepted by the War Office in August, and the first new recruits to assist in establishing the new unit enlisted in September 1920. They were one of eight yeomanry regiments which chose to mechanize, several years before any Regular Army cavalry units did so. The Lincolnshire Yeomanry rejected conversion of any kind and was disbanded. Other yeomanry regiments became horse artillery or signals units, apart from the fourteen most senior, who retained their horses as traditional cavalry.

The new Armoured Car Company was to consist of four sections, the first two of which were to be formed at Hull, with the additional two sections planned for Beverley and Driffield. General recruitment for the Hull sections opened on the 8th October 1920. The Company were to retain their own pre-war Regimental uniform and insignia and were known as the East Riding Yeomanry Armoured Car Company (ERYACC), coming under the jurisdiction of the Tank Corps. October also saw the official renaming of the Territorial Force as the Territorial Army (TA).

The Company was to be equipped with four armoured cars

for training purposes, with additional vehicles being borrowed for annual training as required. The army faced a shortage of armoured cars however, these being in demand for use in India, Ireland and Iraq, where they were better suited to the Imperial policing role than the larger, heavier tanks. As an expedient measure therefore, 100 'Peerless' armoured cars were built, constructed by fitting armoured bodies (built by Austin) to surplus wartime Peerless 3-ton lorry chassis. Protection consisted of 10mm (0.4") armour plate and the armament comprised two 0.303" (7.7mm) calibre Hotchkiss machine guns mounted in twin turrets, with a crew of 4; the commander, a driver and two gunners. Despite solid rubber tyres, which made them rather unsuitable for use across country or on poor roads, and a low top speed (the 40hp engine gave a top speed of only 18 mph), they were better than nothing.

Recruiting was initially a little slow, perhaps unsurprising with memories of the war still very fresh, but the Armoured Car Company did at least offer the opportunity of learning to drive, and to repair and maintain engines and vehicles, whilst being paid to do so. In these times of economic depression and uncertainly this was an attractive proposition, and of course the old attractions of the annual bounty (£5 for meeting the appropriate training requirements) and the summer annual camp all played their part in attracting new recruits. A number of wartime soldiers, former yeomen and others, re-joined, both for financial reasons and to recapture some of the comradeship of the war years. The armoured cars themselves were also important recruiting tools, motor vehicles still being something of a novelty at the time, often being seen on the roads about town and at recruiting events.

The industrial unrest that had been simmering throughout 1919 and 1920 came to a head in April 1921 and the threat of a general strike loomed. Even though some troops were brought home from abroad, the strength of the Police and Regular Army was considered insufficient to deal with such a situation. Legislation was enacted to enable the Army Reserve to be called out

PEERLESS ARMOURED CARS OF THE 26TH ACC
(ERYC)

should the need arise. Legally, once the Reserve was called out, the TA could also be mobilised, but in discussions with the Territorial Associations the government was advised against calling out the TA for the purposes of breaking the strike, as originally promised.

Consequently, it was decided to create a 'civilian' volunteer force to supplement the Police and the Regular Army, to be called the Defence Force. Men would be enlisted for 90 days service, at normal rates of Army pay, and the force would be under the orders of the War Office. The formation and recruiting of the force was to be accomplished using Territorial facilities (drill halls and barracks) and the TA permanent staff. Although members of the TA who wished to enlist (and it was hoped they would) had to officially resign from the TA, service in the Defence Force would count towards their Territorial obligations and they would automatically be re-enlisted into TA at the end of the 90 day period. Enlistment commenced on the 9th April and lasted for nine days, after which time some 75,000 men had signed up.

Each TA unit was expected to form a corresponding unit in the Defence Force, and the East Riding Yeomanry Defence Force was duly formed at the Walton Street Barracks, under the command of Lieutenant Colonel Wilson. The officers and permanent staff were transferred to the new unit and surviving service records indicate that at least 28 NCOs and men elected to join. This included some members of the Armoured Car Company, but many more had no desire to sign up and be seen as strike breakers or could not get the necessary 3 months off work in the current economic climate. As well as serving Territorials, there were enlistments from former soldiers who were not members of the TA at the time. The loss of the officers and permanent staff to the Defence Force had a detrimental effect on the training and recruitment activities of the TA units and this, added to transport problems and financial pressures, meant that that years' annual camps were threatened with cancellation; a major blow to recruiting and to the efficiency of the

TA (camps typically being the only time the entire unit would train together). In the end camps were made optional, with non-attendance not effecting bounty qualification. The East Riding Yeomanry elected not to hold one due to the embryonic state of the unit.

Ultimately a nationwide general strike did not materialise, and despite some strikes by the miners, the crisis had passed by July. The Defence Force had not been needed, and it was disbanded at the end of the 90 period. A negative consequence of the terms of enlistment in the Defence Force saw men who would have been considered unsuitable for the TA, but who had been accepted into the Defence Force, being automatically enlisted into the TA when the Defence Force was disbanded. This would lead to problems with the recruitment and retention of members in the future.

In December 1921 the Commanding Officer, Lieutenant Colonel the Honourable Guy Greville Wilson DSO CMG TD retired, and was replaced by Lieutenant Colonel James Walker DSO. Lieutenant Colonel Walker originally joined the East Riding of Yorkshire Imperial Yeomanry as Quartermaster (and Honorary Lieutenant) in 1904, before accepting a full commission in 1909, and was the Officer in Charge of the Regimental detachment that attended the Coronation of King George V in 1911. He saw service during the war, being attached to the Royal Artillery and commanding the 32nd (Hull) Divisional Ammunition Column in France. He was awarded the Distinguished Service Order (DSO) in 1916.

A major shakeup in organisation took place in February 1922 when the ERYACC requested permission to concentrate all four sections at Hull, due to the difficulties in training with sections dispersed across the county; this was approved by the Army Council in May 1922. This necessitated the closing of the sections in Beverley and Driffield, and those men not prepared to transfer to the Hull sections were discharged.

By the end of the year the Company had its full complement of vehicles and equipment, possessing four Peerless armoured cars (named 'Tally Ho!', 'Jorrocks', 'John Peel' and 'The Cub'), two motor lorries for spares and ammunition (Albion lorries named 'Huntsman' and 'The Whip'), a self-funded mobile workshop lorry (a Thorneycroft 3-ton lorry called 'The Kennels') as well as a number of motorcycles for dispatch riders. Renovations took place at the old Riding School at Walton Street to make it suitable for the armoured cars, including the concreting of the floor of the riding arena to form a large garage.

Following the disruption to annual camps in 1921 the Company attended their first annual camp since before the war, at Scarborough, in June 1922.

In February 1923, the ERYACC was re-designated the 26th (East Riding of Yorkshire Yeomanry) Armoured Car Company and, in addition, the Tank Corps was granted the title 'Royal' by King George V, who was also the Corps' Colonel-in-Chief, thus becoming the Royal Tank Corps (RTC) in October 1923.

By 1925 the Company was up to its full establishment of 177 men and carving out a formidable reputation as an "efficient" armoured car company. In October 1925 the Company adopted the uniform and insignia of its parent organisation, and the old East Riding of Yorkshire Yeomanry fox badge was replaced with the RTC badge of a First World War 'lozenge' tank surrounded by a crown and laurel wreath, with the motto 'Fear naught', for headdress and collars. The most interesting change was the adoption of the new black beret worn by the Corps. The old peaked service cap was not particularly practical for use in the enclosed spaces of tanks and armoured cars, particularly when looking through viewing ports and periscopes, and after seeing some French troops of the 70th *Chasseurs Alpins*, General Sir Hugh Ellis, the first commander of the Tank Corps, had suggested the beret as an alternative. Black was reportedly adopted so oil stains would be less obvious!

Annual Camp for the TA was cancelled in 1926 due to the General Strike, but life for the Company returned to normal in 1927 and recruitment remained strong, the company only having around 20 vacancies at this time. Annual camp was reinstated and held once again at Scarborough in June, with a full contingent of twelve armoured cars. The Company was commended for its initiative in organising a firing range with moving targets; training consisted of firing the Hotchkiss machine guns whilst on the move at targets mounted on dollies, drawn along rails at ranges of 200 and 400 yards.

After six years at Scarborough, annual camp in 1928 was held at Lulworth Cove, Dorset, located close to the Royal Tank Corps depot and training centre at Bovington. Not only did this provide excellent training opportunities at the nearby RTC schools (gunnery, driving and maintenance) but also provided for numerous excursions to Bournemouth, Poole and Weymouth. The men were able to see and 'joy ride' in some of the latest types of light tanks and armoured cars being introduced into the Regular Army.

It was announced in January 1930 that the Peerless armoured cars of the Company would finally be replaced with the newer, more modern, Rolls Royce model. The Company would receive the Rolls Royce Armoured Car Mark 1 Pattern 1920, which was based on the Silver Ghost chassis, fitted with an armoured body up to 12mm (0.5") thick. The vehicle required a reduced crew of 3 (commander, driver and machine gunner) and was fitted with a single turret mounted at the rear, housing a Vickers 0.303" (7.7mm) calibre machine gun. Performance was much improved, the 80hp 6-cylinder engine giving a top speed of 45mph. The first two cars duly arrived in mid-April 1930.

The issuing of more modern equipment was a welcome development since, as the 1930s progressed, storm clouds began to gather over Europe once again.

Appendix A

THE SECOND LINE-2/1ST EAST RIDING OF YORKSHIRE YEOMANRY

The second-line East Riding of Yorkshire Yeomanry grew out of the Reserve Squadron created from those men who could not or would not serve overseas when the original pre-war regiment was reorganised. The three overseas Service Squadrons went on to form a first-line regiment, the 1/1st East Riding of Yorkshire Yeomanry, and the remaining Reserve Squadron eventually grew into the second-line regiment, the 2/1st East Riding of Yorkshire Yeomanry, under the command of Lieutenant Colonel Philip Langdale, the pre-war Regimental commander, who was deemed too old for overseas service.

The 2/1st East Ridings were grouped together with the second-line of the other Yorkshire yeomanry regiments to form a second-line brigade, the 2/1st Yorkshire Mounted Brigade (a duplicate of the pre-war first-line brigade), commanded by a Colonel W. C. Smithson. The 2/1st East Ridings were initially based at Beverley (home of Regimental Headquarters) where the men were billeted in private homes or public houses (including the Angel Hotel and The Valiant Soldier). Here the new regiment began training the influx of new recruits and weeding out those too old or medically unfit for continued service.

The original intention was for the second-line regiments to provide recruit training and replacements for their first-line regiments, but by the end of 1914 many first-line regiments had been deployed overseas and it was clear that more would inevitably follow. The second-line regiments therefore took over responsibility for Home Defence and a third line was raised to fulfil the training function. Not long after the formation of the 3/1st East Riding of Yorkshire Yeomanry, based at the Regimental Riding School in Hull, the 2/1st was deployed to the coast and given responsibility for the defence of the East Yorkshire coast, centred on Withernsea.

Most of the men were still barely trained and there were only a few old rifles available – they were more of a danger to themselves than the Germans and they spent most of their time digging trenches on the cliff tops. Leonard May, an 18-year-old farmer's son from Brough who enlisted in November 1914 wrote in his memoirs:

> "*after being at Withernsea we had to go to Tunstall a few miles away to patrol the cliff tops. They were steep at that point. We lived in a granary at Lorrimar's farm near Tunstall. This was a very dangerous job if dark and we had a few shocks. Quite a few stakes sticking up were challenged."* [1]

Then one night in the middle of December the alarm was raised, and the men were rudely awoken at midnight and sent out to man the trenches. Bill Austin, another 18-year-old private, who had enlisted in October 1914, remembered:

> "*we had orders to keep quiet, no smoking, no lights, but (we were) never told what to expect. We stayed there starved and hungry until about 10 o'clock in the morning when one of 'B' Squadron's officers came out to tell us that Scarborough had been shelled, and that a submarine had appeared off West Hartlepool. We in our trenches had never heard a sound."* [2]

The 2/1st East Ridings remained on the coast until just after Christmas 1914 when they were recalled to Beverley from where, shortly afterwards, they moved on to Harrogate with the rest of the 2/1st Yorkshire Mounted Brigade. The Harrogate Herald of the 27th January 1915 reported:

> "*on Wednesday and Thursday the first detachments of Yorkshire Dragoons and East Riding Yeomanry appeared. We are expecting a detachment of Yorkshire Hussars as well… now the basin in Low Harro-*

gate is alive with mounted men, and the scene even more exhilarating. Fortunately, we are having splendid weather; not too cold, but bright and fairly dry without frost. The mounted men are smart and capable-looking lot..." [3]

Some of the men were billeted on the top floor of the magnificent Majestic Hotel, although they had to eat in the garages around the back, and when upstairs in the hotel they were under strict orders not to disturb the regular guests. The horses were stabled in the hotel garages and at the Corporation Farm. Training could now get underway in earnest, particularly riding training, there being plenty of room for manoeuvres on the surrounding moors. Leonard May wrote:

"The Stray (at Harrogate) was a good place where thousands of soldiers were being trained. We rode around the beautiful countryside, did night raids etc." [4]

The carving of a fox on Jackdaw Crag, Boston Spa (near Wetherby), which is thought to have been carved by soldiers during the First World War, may well be a lasting testament to the East Ridings presence in the area.

In addition to the usual training of drills and field days the men also attended talks and lectures covering all manner of military subjects, often held in the Opera House or the Winter Gardens. There were also similar events dealing with animal welfare. The Royal Society for the Prevention of Cruelty to Animals (RSPCA) gave lectures and demonstrations, and a Professor W Jones Arisley, a lecturer of farriery at Leeds University, gave a glass lantern lecture on 'The Horse's foot and how to shoe it'. Lectures of this sort were important as many of the new recruits had no experience of riding or horses.

There were also exhortations to temperance, 'manliness', faith and patriotism by the Bishop of Ripon and other members of the clergy at church services and mass meetings.

In late 1915 the 2/1st Brigade was transferred back to East Yorkshire to take over coastal defence duties along the Holderness coast once again; for the 2/1st East Ridings this was a wel-

MEN OF THE 2/1ST EAST RIDING OF YORKSHIRE YEOMANRY,
BRADFORD MOOR BARRACKS C.1915
(Author's collection)

MEN OF THE 2/1ST EAST RIDING OF YORKSHIRE YEOMANRY
NEAR SCARBOROUGH, SEPTEMBER 1915
(Dominic Rogan)

come homecoming as they were headquartered in their hometown of Beverley. The shine was taken off their return home however with the deaths of two yeomen. Private Harold Keller had died at Withernsea on Sunday 28th November and on Tuesday 7th December Private Alfred Featherstone, of 'C' Squadron, which was by then camped at Elmswell Hall near Driffield, died from head injuries sustained when he fell from his mount whilst exercising the horses.

The demand for manpower at the front, the reduction in the threat of invasion and the lack of a role for cavalry in trench warfare meant that many men were transferred to infantry regiments and the 2/1st became a *de facto* infantry training regiment, to the frustration of men who had joined up to fight. Clement Rogan, a Corporal, wrote home in September 1915:

> *"they have been picking out the men today, Corporal Moxon has been picked out and is going. In fact, all the best chaps are. Sergeant Maj. Marshall said if I had been on parade, I should have been picked out for cert. But I wasn't so what does it matter, this regiment will comprise of recruits and unfit men before we're finished and there are a lot of them".* [5]

The regiment was still short of equipment and horses, priority necessarily being given to the units at, or preparing to leave for, the front. On the 19th February 1916 a Driffield Times report on a parade for Lord Nunburnholme, the Lord Lieutenant of the East Riding, noted that:

> *"the regiment was drawn up in line ready to receive the Lord Lieutenant and after the general salute his Lordship inspected the ranks. Those who were not mounted were drawn up in line on the flank"* [6]

This clearly shows that there were insufficient horses to mount the entire regiment, even for a parade for visiting senior officers and dignitaries. The following month, in March 1916, as part of a wider reorganisation of the cavalry, the 2/1st Yorkshire Mounted Brigade (generally referred to as simply the Yorkshire Mounted Brigade following the disbandment of the original 1/1st Yorkshire Mounted Brigade) was re-designated the 18th

Mounted Brigade.

As usual the coastal patrols and picket duties were interspersed with training, including mounted exercises and military skills such as musketry, bayonet drills and grenade throwing (or 'bombing'). During just such a training exercise in April a live grenade fell back into a trench, landing amongst the bombing party and it was only the quick thinking and courageous actions of 1220 Lance Corporal A. S. Smith, who picked up the grenade and threw it out, that prevented a serious incident. As a result of his actions Lance Corporal Smith was promoted to Lance Sergeant.

Sadly, on the 31st May 1916 the 2/1st East Ridings learned of their latest casualty when 2nd Lieutenant Ronald Spicer died of the injuries he sustained in a motorcycle accident in York a month earlier. Riding into St Helen's Square he swerved to avoid two young ladies, lost control and crashed into the wall of Harker's Hotel suffering a broken arm and head injuries.

For relaxation and a break from their duties the men were able to travel to the coastal resort of Withernsea where they could have a bath at the Convalescent Home and take in the prom, although according to Private May, "*the girls were awful, we only tried a few*"![17] There were numerous sporting events and competitions arranged, including billiards and rugby, cricket and boxing matches. Amongst the sporting highlights was a Military Tournament for the Humber Garrison held on 16th June 1916 at the Hull City Football ground (Boothferry Park on Anlaby Road in Hull). Organised as it was by the Northern Command Cross Country and Physical Fitness Association there was a large number of running events, including a marathon, but there was also a bomb throwing competition, a signalling demonstration and also a series of mounted events for the members of the 18th Mounted Brigade. These included tent pegging (a mounted sport in which a horseman riding at the gallop uses a sword or a lance to collect a tent peg or series of pegs from the ground), a 'VC' race for officers (In the "VC" race riders had to race down a course over two fences, pick up dummies (representing casualties) and ride back over the jumps to the finish) and horseback wrestling. The tournament attracted hundreds of entrants and an appreciative crowd of some 4,000 people turned out to watch. According to Lieutenant A. C. Hext:

> "*the ERY licked the heads off the Yorkshire Hussars, but then of course they always do*". [8]

The East Ridings won the section tent pegging race ('C' Squadron), the individual tent pegging for officers (Lieutenant Hext) and the officers' 'VC' race (Major Cadman). Lieutenant Hext wrote to his mother:

> "*I won the tent pegging I think I may say in style (as if I don't blow my own trumpet no one else can). I did not miss a single peg (more swank). I may say I was a hot favourite and started at even money... My luck was out in the VC race however I won my first heat easily but in the final I swung my dummy onto the horse by the arm which pulled off from its body, the crowd howled with joy and thought it a huge joke but it cost me the race. I came in 3rd but no prize*".

Despite the reorganisation of 1916, it was becoming clear that not only was the opportunity for the employment of cavalry limited, but the continuing shortage of horses meant that cavalry and yeomanry units at home could not be fully mounted and that the horses they did have could be better used abroad. As a result, in July 1916, most of the remaining second-line yeomanry regiments at home were converted to cyclist units and thus the 18th Mounted Brigade became the 11th Cyclist Brigade and the East Ridings traded their horses for bicycles.

A Yeomanry Cyclist Regiment

Cyclist units were effectively mounted infantry rather than true cavalry, using their bicycles to move relatively quickly (compared to marching) to the front, where they would fight like normal infantry. They were however, also used for traditional cavalry tasks such as scouting and carrying dispatches and were therefore quite well suited to patrolling the coast. Besides freeing up valuable horses, cyclists offered several advantages over horsed cavalry; they could travel (on good roads at least) further and faster than cavalry and did not have the hindrance of carrying or foraging for fodder.

By November 1916 the 2/1st East Ridings had been moved to billets on the southern edge of Bridlington (in billets described by Private Donald Griffin as "*...cold and draughty... old death traps of boarding houses...*")[10] and the 11th Cyclist Brigade had been re-designated the 7th Cyclist Brigade, now under the command of Brigadier General J. B. Jardine.

For the men life continued to consist of seemingly endless parades, training and guard duties. A typical day would begin with a parade and then breakfast followed by light jobs such as cleaning and straightening up the cycles, followed by classes or training exercises. There were 2 route marches of 6 miles a week, in full marching order (packs, blankets and cycles with 120 rounds of ammunition); shooting practise (on the miniature 25 yard range) and the dreaded assault course; Private Griffin wrote:

> "*yesterday afternoon we went over the bayonet assault course three times with gas respirators on; it nearly killed us because it is bad enough going over once, it is 200 yards long and is full of trenches and shell holes and trip wires, you go over with naked bayonets and stick all sacks you come across*". [11]

For many of the men the result of this infantry training continued to be a compulsory transfer to an infantry battalion. Most were sent to the 3rd Battalion East Yorkshire Regiment with many then posted onwards to any number of different regiments, often with little or no connection with the county. Many of the officers were attached from other regiments; those recently commissioned for training, those considered too old or unfit for front line service or those recovering from illness or injury; few remained with the regiment for long. Lieutenant George Havard-Thomas, of the Sherwood Foresters, who was attached to the regiment for a few months in 1917 following convalescence after being wounded on the Somme, wrote home:

> "*I am getting on quite well here though the majority of the attached officers have gone back to their battalions prior to going out again and the remaining few have an awful lot of work to do*". [12]

He too was impatient to return to the front adding, *"I presume I will be passed general service on my next Medical Board"*. For those officers and men remaining at home life was dreary and frustrations remained. Private Griffin, who by now was a qualified musketry instructor, wrote home that:

> "I am getting a bit fed up and would welcome France as a change for I am sick of wasting time here... I stand no chance whatsoever of going out before the spring and I expect I shall be kept back to train recruits... we are sending lads out now as fast as even they become 19 so we shall be getting shoals of recruits in the spring... then we instructors will have our hands full and be glad of something to do, for as I said we are fed up with hanging about here wasting time". [13]

To help alleviate the boredom there was entertainment available in the form of concert parties (both visiting and regimental), local events such as concerts and recitals held at the Bridlington Spa Hall, tea parties and dances. The Regimental Band, led by the pre-war Bandmaster, Mr. Brocklesby, played an important role, giving concerts and playing at dances. In a letter home Private Griffin wrote, in April 1918:

> "I went on the spa to hear the band. They have not engaged an orchestra for the summer yet but have engaged the combined bands of the ERY and Yorks Hussars for the week". [14]

There was a soldier's canteen run by the Methodist Church in Bridlington that provided games and refreshments and some female company for the men and of course there were also leave passes available, allowing the men the opportunity to return home.

Apart from the revolving door of recruits coming and going and a swap to a hutted camp on the northern side of Bridlington in October 1917 (considered a great improvement), in general the life of the regiment remained pretty much the same throughout 1917 and into 1918 until a crisis in Ireland intervened.

The Irish Crisis

Tensions in Ireland had been simmering for many years. De-

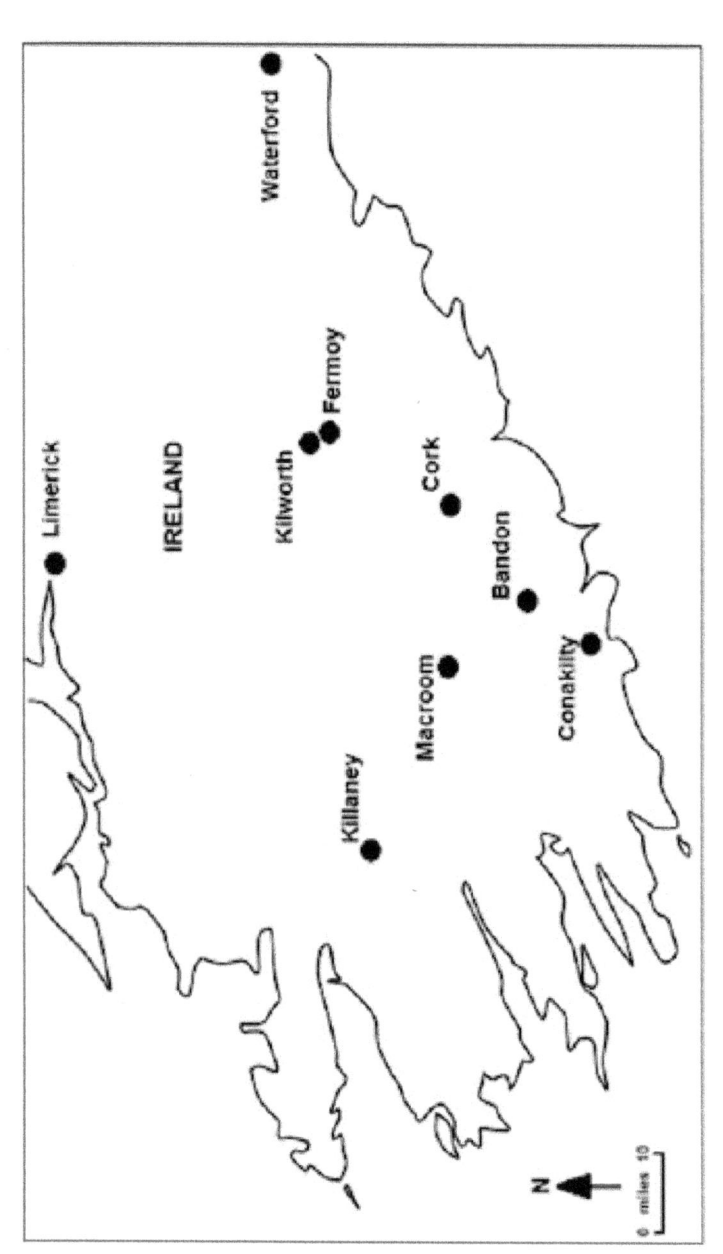

The 2/1st East Riding Yeomanry in Southern Ireland, 1918–1919

spite the Bill proposing Home Rule for Ireland having been suspended in 1914 things were relatively calm for the first few years of the war and many Irishmen joined up to fight for Britain. Then there was the Easter Rising in Dublin in 1916, put down by the British with overwhelming force. Initially not supported by the majority of the population, the heavy-handed handling of the situation by the British and the summary executions of the ringleaders increased support for the Nationalists. To try and counteract this a convention was held in 1917 with the aim of drafting a new constitution for Ireland, but no agreement could be reached, and the more moderate Nationalists began losing ground to more militant elements. Then in March 1918 came the massive German Offensives on the Western Front and huge reverses for the Allies. The army was already short of men and in order to remedy the situation the government proposed introducing conscription in Ireland; until this point compulsory conscription only applied to the mainland. This policy was hugely unpopular and, since the new Military Service Bill was linked to a new Home Rule Bill, managed to alienate both the Nationalists (who opposed conscription) and the Unionists (who opposed Home Rule). An Anti-Irish Conscription Committee was formed to resist the imposition of conscription and on 23rd April 1918 there was a general strike.

In response to this the British moved a large number of troops from the mainland to Ireland in an attempt to maintain order. The 2/1st East Riding Yeomanry and the rest of the 7th Cyclist Brigade was moved to the area around the garrison town of Fermoy in May 1918. Regimental Headquarters was located in Bandon and the regiment was initially camped at Moore Park, Kilworth. The men were rushed over, and it took some time for their kitbags to catch them up. On arrival guards of 25 men were mounted with kit kept close at hand and ammunition was issued, but the tension subsided, and the guard was soon reduced to 8 and the ammunition handed back into stores. Some, perhaps all, of the companies were eventually deployed to neighbouring towns such as Killarney, Clonakilty and Macroom. Guards were

Men of the 2/1st East Riding of Yorkshire Yeomanry at Moor Park Camp, Kilworth (near Fermoy, Ireland) dated August 1918 (Author's collection)

mounted at strategic locations; Donald Griffin, with 'D' Company in Macroom, noted that guards were mounted at four locations, including the Post Office and Railway Station.

The 2/1ˢᵗ East Ridings remained in Ireland until the end of the war, life settling down to the usual routines of training, sports, and recreation. The band accompanied the regiment to Ireland, putting on concerts and performances for the locals, and a Regimental Concert Party, called 'The Forrards' was formed.

The first-line 1/1ˢᵗ East Riding Yeomanry was dis-established (placed in suspended animation) in April 1919 and it seems that the 2/1ˢᵗ East Riding Yeomanry was also disbanded at that time.

Casualties

Although the 2/1ˢᵗ East Ridings spent their war at home (Ireland constituted home service at the time) a number of yeomen lost their lives whilst serving with the regiment:-

Rank	No.	Name	Date	Cause
Pte	51166	P Blair	5/4/1918	Died at home
Maj	-	P S Cadman	31/3/1919	Died at home
Pte	50899	C Clark	20/1/1919	Died at home (appendicitis)
CQMS	50181	R Clough	16/2/1919	Died at home (pneumonia)
Pte	93881	E W Euden	16/2/1918	Died at home
Pte	2200	A Featherstone	7/12/1915	Died at home
Pte	1668	H Keller	28/11/1919	Died at home
Pte	51488	C Pickard	15/4/1917	Died at home
Pte	51139	J E B Scrowston	2/11/1918	Died at home (influenza)
2nd Lt	-	R M Spicer	31/5/1916	Died at home (accident)
Pte	50874	W Stather	13/8/1917	Died at home

Private Scrowston was a victim of the 'Spanish Flu' that swept through Europe (and across the world) at the end of the war. The outbreak started in January 1918 and initially only seemed to affect people for 3 or 4 days, after which they made a full recovery. An example of the impact of the virus is the effect it had on one draft of 80 East Ridings, destined for the East Yorkshire Regiment, which gathered at Regimental Headquarters in Bandon on Thursday 4th July 1918. By the time the party left for Dublin on the 9th there were only 46 men fit due to the 'flu and another 5 became ill during the journey: nearly half of the draft laid low in less than a week. The survivors had to be held up at a rest camp in Dublin before being able to continue on to France. Most of those who fell ill did recover however and were subsequently able to follow on.

Unfortunately, the virus mutated and a second wave of outbreaks in the autumn of 1918 was far more virulent with a much higher mortality rate; in the end it is estimated to have killed between 50 and 70 million people worldwide. Private Scrowston is recorded as having died of influenza at Waterford, Ireland, on 2nd November 1918, sadly less than two weeks before the Armistice.

Appendix B

THE THIRD LINE–3/1ST EAST RIDING OF YORKSHIRE YEOMANRY

In early 1915 a third-line regiment, designated the 3/1st East Riding of Yorkshire Yeomanry was formed under the command of Major Percy Coke, late of 15th Hussars. The increasing likelihood that first-line units would be deployed overseas in the coming year (by the end of 1914 there were already 23 Territorial infantry battalions and 7 yeomanry regiments in Flanders, not to mention those units sent to Imperial garrisons) meant that the second-line would now have to take over the responsibility for home defence. Consequently, a third line was required to take on the role of training depot in order to supply drafts of men to the first and second lines.

Henceforth, after rudimentary military training (basic drill, route marches and arms drill) at the East Riding's Depot in Hull (originally the old Riding School in Walton Street and later at Wenlock Barracks around the corner on Anlaby Road) the recruits were officially posted to the 3/1st East Ridings, camped on the Knavesmere (the racecourse) at York. Here they received their basic training under the auspices of the 5th Reserve Cavalry Regiment (RCR) which was also headquartered there. This regiment provided depot services to the regular cavalry of the line and comprised one squadron each from the 1st (Royal) Dragoons and 2nd Dragoons (Royal Scots Greys). All the third-line regiments of the Yorkshire Mounted Brigade were affiliated to them. These third-line units were purely administrative units, not intended for active service.

Once in York army life for the recruits began in earnest. Private Terry Campbell Ward remembered:

> "*we had our first taste of real army discipline. The NCO's were all regulars and very tough indeed*". [1]

The typical daily routine began with Reveille at 6am followed by an hour of physical training. Then there was an hour of stables when the horses were mucked out, fed, watered and groomed. Breakfast for the men came at 8am after which it was the Riding School, Drill or other training until noon. From 2pm to 4pm it was notionally free time, "into bed or out of barracks". In reality, for the raw recruits this meant time spent cleaning their uniforms, buttons, and riding tack. Boots and brass buttons required polishing and all saddlery buckles, curb chains and bits were steel and also had to be kept highly polished. After tea at 4pm there was a second spell in the stables tending the horses. The main evening meal was taken at 6pm and afterwards, if not on guard duty (duty as stable or main gate guards occurred twice weekly), there was the possibility of a 'pass out' into town, provided your turnout and appearance met the standards of the Sergeant of the Guard.

Private Ward described the Riding School as tough but thorough. The men were initially taught to ride without saddles; all lessons, including jumping, were carried out with blankets only on the horse. Jumping, quite daunting to novice riders, was taught using a 'jumping lane', a series of six jumps of varying height bounded by wooden rails on both sides. According to Private Ward:

> "*you were put on an experienced horse and he just took you down the lane. Reins could not be held and were knotted on the horse's neck*". [2]

After three weeks saddles were allowed, but initially without stirrups. Once the basics of riding had been mastered there was mounted sword drill; the men were taught to thrust to the left and to the right against targets of made of sawdust filled bags.

The recruits would also have completed three weeks shooting instruction at the ranges at Strensall, on the outskirts of York and there would have been infantry training too, including bayonet drills, as the men were expected to be able to fight on foot as well as mounted.

On completion of their training the men would have been posted to either the first or second-line regiment, although as the war progressed, they were more likely to be transferred to an infantry battalion to meet the manpower demands of the Western Front.

The experience of Norman Howarth, a 20-year-old Clerk from Wakefield, is typical of that experienced by many of those passing through the 3/1st. He joined the East Riding Yeomanry at the Hull depot on 1st June 1915 and was posted to the 3/1st East Ridings in York, as 2109 Private N. Howarth, a month later. Following his basic training he was posted to the first-line regiment which was then based in Egypt.

Together with 1 officer and a further 39 men (the first draft sent overseas) Norman embarked on the troopship *Llandovery Castle*, a pre-war Union Castle liner, at Devonport on the 14th January 1916, for the potentially dangerous trip through the Mediterranean. They arrived safely at Alexandria on the 27th, reaching Regimental Headquarters at Deir El Azab, in the Fayoum, on the 8th February 1917; their arrival being duly noted in the Regimental War Diary.

After serving with the regiment through the First and Second Battles of Gaza Private Howarth was transferred to the Machine Gun Corps (MGC) on 27th July 1917, joining a number of other ex-East Riding's in the 18th Machine Gun Squadron MGC (Cavalry). He took part in the final advances into Syria in the last days of the war. Norman survived unscathed and was demobilised on 21st February 1919.

After the initial draft sent out to Egypt in January 1916 the Regimental War diary records the arrival of a number of further drafts from the 3/1st until the end of 1917, but after the 1/1st became a Machine Gun Battalion, replacements would have come through the Machine Gun Corps system.

The 3/1st East Ridings may have been home-based, but they were not completely insulated from the war. On the 2nd May

EAST RIDING OF YORKSHIRE YEOMANRY.

This Regiment was raised twelve years ago, and has been commonly known as **"WENLOCK'S HORSE."**

Its First Line is now at * * * fully armed and equipped with its horses, machine guns, first reinforcements, etc., complete as a fighting unit, and waiting the order to go abroad.

Its Second Line is now at * * * up to full strength, clothed, equipped and undergoing vigorous training, so that its members may also take their place in the firing line.

Its Third Line is now being raised.

FOR THIS AN URGENT APPEAL IS MADE FOR A FURTHER 460 MEN of good education and physique. Applicants should be between the ages of **19** and **35** years.

The terms of service are for the **DURATION OF THE WAR**, and all applicants must be prepared to serve abroad.

Free Railway Warrants are issued to intending Recruits, who should apply to the Depot, Walton-street, Hull (next to the Fair Ground).

God Save the King.

RECRUITING ADVERT FOR 3/1ST ERY, MARCH 1915

1916 Private Leslie Hinson was killed during a Zeppelin air raid on York. During the ten-minute raid by Zeppelin L21 numerous bombs fell across the city, destroying several houses and killing 9 people and injuring another 40. Private Hinson together with another soldier was helping an elderly lady to safety in Peaseholme Green when a bomb fell nearby. All three were killed. Private Hinson was in fact the first East Riding Yeoman across all three regiments to be killed by enemy action.

Then, in April 1917, in the worst day for the East Ridings, 19 yeomen on their way from the 3/1st as a draft to the 1/1st were killed when their troopship, the *Arcadian*, was torpedoed in the Aegean Sea (see Appendix C).

In 1917 there was a major reorganisation of the cavalry reserves, and the Territorial Force third-line regiments were merged with new regular reserve cavalry regiments. This was due in part to a shortage of horses, but by this time the separate identity of the TF had already broken down and it was more efficient to rationalise the training and supply of replacements.

The cavalry was split into Corps; the East Ridings were allotted to the Corps of Lancers and the 3/1st was absorbed into the new 1st Reserve Cavalry Regiment, based at The Curragh in Dublin. Although no longer with their own regiment the men of the reserve cavalry regiments retained their own regimental identities, badges etc. although this was in fact largely nominal by this stage of the war; the regimental system had broken down and the men were more likely to be transferred to the infantry on completion of their training than to their "own" regiment.

The first-line 1/1st East Riding Yeomanry was dis-established in April 1919 and at that time any yeomen remaining with the 1st Reserve Cavalry Regiment would most likely have been transferred to other regiments.

Appendix C

RIDING THE WAVES-THE EAST RIDING YEOMANRY AND THE WAR AT SEA

The war at sea between 1914 and 1918 has been, like many aspects of the First World War, overshadowed by the fighting on the Western Front. This is largely because, despite a few skirmishes at the beginning of the war, the British policy of blockade and the Royal Navy's superiority over the German Imperial fleet meant that there was only one significant fleet action, the Battle of Jutland in 1916, and that was inconclusive.

Faced with this situation the Germans turned to the relatively new and untried submarine in an attempt to counter the Royal Navy. After some successes against naval vessels in 1914, the German submarines (known as *U-Boats*) were turned against civilian ships from early 1915. By attacking merchant ships, Germany hoped to starve Britain out of the war. However, following the American outcry at the sinking of the Cunard liner, *Lusitania,* on the 7th May 1915 with the loss of 1,200 lives, including 123 Americans, the Germans halted unrestricted submarine warfare in September (although attacks against naval vessels continued).

Restricted submarine warfare against merchant ships resumed in 1916 and the restrictions were lifted in February 1917, playing a major role in persuading the United States to join the Allies, which they did in the April 1917. That month the *U-Boats* sank 155 ships totalling over 850,000 tons.

LOSS OF THE ARCADIAN, 1917

In April 1917 the 8,900-ton former cruise ship H.M. Transport *Arcadian* set sail from England accompanied by two Japanese destroyers, her 320 first-class passengers replaced by some 2,000 reinforcements for the Salonika and Palestine fronts in the Middle East. On board was a draft of 42 men of the 3/1st East Riding Yeomanry destined for the 1/1st East Riding Yeomanry in Palestine.

Despite the German U-boat blockade the first stage of the journey, to Malta, passed relatively quietly and at Malta one of the Japanese destroyers remained in port, leaving the *Arcadian* to press on with only one escort.

Just off the North African coast a suspected submarine was spotted and under cover of a smoke screen laid by the destroyer, the *Arcadian* took refuge in the mouth of a river. For several days the *Arcadian* remained there along with another transport that had also taken shelter. On the third day the other transport decided to chance it, only to return later that afternoon badly damaged.

Despite this, the *Arcadian* set out that evening with her destroyer, successfully evading the U-boat and eventually reaching Salonika, where she off loaded about half her compliment of troops for that theatre. That same evening the ship set sail for Egypt.

Once underway there was a lifeboat drill for all followed by a church service on deck, given by an Australian padre who was onboard. About halfway through the service, as the *Arcadian* was steaming down the Aegean about 26 miles north-east of the island of Melos, she was hit forward on the starboard side by a torpedo fired by the U-Boat UC-74 and immediately began to list. Private Reginald Huggins recalled:

> *"without one moment's warning, a terrific explosion occurred, made hideous by the splintering into matchwood of great timbers, the crash of falling glass and the groaning of steel girders wrenched asunder, followed by the hissing rush of escaping steam from the ship's boilers".* [1]

Everyone on board made for the boats on the port side; those on the starboard side that had not been destroyed in the explosion were left hanging against the side of ship by the list.

According to Private Huggins,

> "*the great ship began to settle down on her port side with the loose deck paraphernalia slithering about in all directions and dropping into the sea*". [2]

Fortunately, the boat allocated to the East Riding's draft was on the port side and many of the men were able to get into it. They were unable to cast off quickly enough however and as the ship rolled over it pushed the boat under, crushing those who remained inside. The ship then partly righted itself and dived, dragging down those boats still tied to it and sucking down any men in the sea near the ship. It was all over in about 4 minutes.

With daylight fading the survivors found themselves lost in a cold sea seemingly without much hope of rescue. Sometime around midnight lights were seen in the distance but it was another few hours before a naval officer, who had a torch, was able to attract the attention of the rescue ships, and the bedraggled survivors could be hauled out of the sea. They were taken to Crete and put on a torpedoed transport ship that had been grounded in one of the bays. Eventually a fresh transport arrived to take them onwards to Alexandria.

Over 200 men were lost with the *Arcadian*, nineteen of them from the East Riding Yeomanry, the regiment's highest single death toll for the entire war. The majority of those killed are commemorated on the Mikra Memorial at Thessaloniki (Salonika) in Greece, including all those of the East Riding Yeomanry except for Private Herbert Kendal, who is buried in Syra British Cemetery on the island of Syros. This cemetery holds many men who were lost with the *Arcadian* and whose bodies washed up on the many islands in the vicinity.

Loss of the Leinster, 1918

The war at sea touched the East Riding Yeomanry again in 1918. On the 10th October the 2,640-ton mail boat R.M.S. *Leinster* left Kingstown, Ireland, on the regular mail run to Holyhead. On board were over 750 passengers, most of them servicemen along with about 180 civilians, 76 crewmen and 22 mail workers.

Only 12 miles outside the harbour, and without warning, a torpedo fired by UB-132 struck the post room at the forward end of the ship. Despite the damage the ship did not seem to be in imminent danger of sinking and there was little panic. A few minutes later however, as the passengers and crew began to launch the lifeboats, a second torpedo struck the engine room. The torpedo hit caused the boilers to explode and many people were killed in the blast or from the large amounts of debris thrown up. One lifeboat, full of people, was being lowered on the starboard side at the time the torpedo hit, and it was blown to pieces. Within 15 minutes the *Leinster* had sunk.

Many of the lifeboats were capsized in the rough sea, and the survivors clung onto the upturned boats, life rafts and whatever debris they could find until the first rescue ships from Kingstown arrived on the scene. The rough sea conditions made it difficult to haul the exhausted survivors onto the ships and many succumbed to the cold and the sea in sight of safety. In total more than five hundred people had died. To this day it remains the greatest loss of Irish life at sea, surpassing the *Titanic* and the *Lusitania*. One of the victims was Josephine Carr, a 19-year clerk in the newly formed Women's Royal Naval Service, known as the Wrens. She was the first Wren to die on active service. Of the postal workers aboard only one survived.

Also onboard were at least eight members of the 2/1st East Riding Yeomanry, at that time based in Southern Ireland around Cork. These men, like so many others aboard that day, were travelling back to the mainland for leave; a small number of men were granted eight days leave in England every week. They were permitted to catch the evening train the day before their official leave began which allowed them to catch the morning sailing from Kingstown on their first day of leave. Private Stephens, who was drowned, had been sent a telegram informing him of the arrival of his cousin on home leave from France and it is thought he was travelling home to see him. Only one of the East Ridings survived, a Private Atkin Emerson; the remaining

THE FINAL MOMENTS OF THE ARCADIAN
(Charles Cole)

seven being lost.

The dead of the disaster are commemorated on a memorial in Dun Laoghaire (as Kingstown is known today) and it is possible to dive the wreck. Many of the victims are buried in Grangegorman Military Cemetery in Dublin.

Appendix D

BATTLE HONOURS OF THE EAST RIDING YEOMANRY, 1914–1918

Egypt 1915 – 1917
The Campaign Honour awarded for service in the defence of Egypt during the early years of the war. In addition to Turkish attacks from 1915, the British faced an uprising of the pro-Turkish Senussi tribe on the Libyan border. The 1/1st East Riding of Yorkshire Yeomanry garrisoned the oasis of Fayoum west of Cairo from November 1915 until December 1916.

Palestine 1917 – 1918
The Campaign Honour commemorating the British advance into Palestine that commenced with the 1st Battle of Gaza in March 1917 and continued until the end of the War; Jerusalem fell in December 1917 and Damascus on 1st October 1918.

Gaza
This Battle Honour was awarded for participation in the attacks on the main Turkish defences in Palestine, which ran from Gaza to Beersheba. The British broke through during the 3rd Battle of Gaza in November 1917. The 1/1st East Riding of Yorkshire Yeomanry took part in all three battles as part of the ANZAC Mounted Division (1st and 2nd Battles) and the Yeomanry Mounted Division (3rd Battle), largely in supporting roles.

El Mughar
This award was authorised for participation in the battle on 13th November 1917 that resulted in the capture of 'Junction Station' (an important railway hub north of Jerusalem) and the severing of Turkish communications between Jerusalem and

Jaffa. The battle is notable for some of the last British cavalry charges in action, including one by the 1/1st East Riding of Yorkshire Yeomanry at Akir.

Nebi Samwil

This award covers the fighting to the north-west of Jerusalem in November and December 1917 which led to the capture of the Nebi Samwil ridge, dominating the approaches to the Holy City. The 1/1st East Riding of Yorkshire Yeomanry, part of the 22nd Mounted Brigade, were at one time the most forward regiment of the advance, taking part in bitter fighting in the Judean Hills.

France and Flanders 1918

The Campaign Honour France and Flanders 1914 – 1918 commemorates the main theatre of the First World War, the Western Front. By the spring of 1918 manpower shortages meant that the 1/1st East Riding of Yorkshire Yeomanry was amalgamated with the Lincolnshire Yeomanry to form the 102nd Battalion, Machine Gun Corps, taking part in the final British offensives of October and November 1918. The East Riding of Yorkshire Yeomanry were bestowed this honour with '1918' only.

Selle

The regiment was awarded this honour for participating in the battle that commenced on the 17th October 1918 along the line of the River Selle near Cambrai. The 102nd Battalion MGC, of which the East Riding Yeomanry formed a part, was in action supporting the 51st (Highland) and 4th Infantry Divisions (1st Army) from the 20th October.

Valenciennes

This honour was awarded for the participation in the actions fought during the advance of the First Army along the line of the River Scheldt towards Valenciennes. Following the successful advance towards the city 20th – 31st October, Valenciennes fell on 2nd November 1918. The 102nd Battalion MGC, of which the East Riding Yeomanry formed a part, was once again in action in support of the 51st (Highland) and 4th Infantry Divisions.

Sambre

The honour awarded for the final phase of the British offensives. The attack on the German defences on the River Sambre by the British Third and Fourth Armies began on the 4th November 1918 and by the end of the day the Germans were in full retreat. It was to be the last offensive of the First World War. The 102nd Battalion MGC, of which the East Riding Yeomanry formed a part, was in action in support of the 11th and 56th (London) Infantry Divisions.

Appendix E

Awards and Decorations, 1914–1918

The following Officers and men of the East Riding of Yorkshire Yeomanry were decorated for their bravery or service during the First World War. The ranks are given as those at the time the award was made.

Distinguished Service Order
Major E D Moore

Distinguished Conduct Medal
50057 Squadron Sergeant Major (WO II) T H Duffield
50582 Sergeant V L Lamplugh (8th Company Imperial Camel Corps)
50588 Corporal J Freeman (10th Company Imperial Camel Corps)
50590 Lance Corporal S Leaf (10th Company Imperial Camel Corps)
150330 Lance Corporal A Oldfield (102nd Battalion MGC)
50146 Private F W Sherwood
50243 Private (Acting L/Cpl) F Smales
50255 Private (Acting L/Cpl) C V S Tesseyman

Order of Saint Michael and Saint George
Companion – Lieutenant Colonel The Hon. G G Wilson DSO

Member of the British Empire
Lieutenant (Acting Captain) C Burgoyne
Lieutenant Arthur Charles Hext (attached 2nd Battalion, East Yorkshire Regiment)

Military Cross
Major P H Parker (attached 18th Squadron MGC)
Captain J F M Robinson
Captain N C M Sykes
Lieutenant H D P Francis
Lieutenant J D Robinson (102nd Battalion MGC)
2nd Lieutenant W Featherstone (102nd Battalion MGC)
Hon. Lieutenant and Quartermaster G W Piercy

Military Medal
150164 Sergeant E W Wilson (102nd Battalion MGC)
150185 Corporal H Beverley (102nd Battalion MGC)
150173 Corporal (L/Sgt, A/Sgt) S Thompson (102nd Battalion MGC)
95908 Lance Corporal T Steel (18th Squadron MGC (Cavalry)
150440 Private J Young (102nd Battalion MGC)
50813 Private H Young
50801 Private C Myers

French *Ordre du Mérite Agricole* (Order of Agricultural Merit)
Chevalier – Lieutenant (Acting Captain) J Reah

French *Croix De Guerre* (War Cross)
50354 Private Harold D Hart

Meritorious Service Medal
150162 Company Sergeant Major (WO II) A Skilbeck (102nd Battalion MGC)

Khedive's Sudan Medal
Captain T G N Bardwell, with 'Darfur 1916' Clasp

Mentioned in Dispatches
Lieutenant Colonel The Hon. G G Wilson DSO
Major E D Moore
Major C E Reynard
Captain E Bromet (RAMC, attached)
Captain C G Lloyd
Captain N C M Sykes

Mentioned in Dispatches cont'd
Lieutenant G Eustace Smith
Lieutenant H D P Francis
Lieutenant A C Hext (attached 2nd Battalion, East Yorkshire Regiment)
Lieutenant J F Rolland
505 Acting Regimental Sergeant Major T Rickaby
50057 Squadron Sergeant Major (WO II) T H Duffield
50029 Squadron Quartermaster Sergeant R W Clokie
1390 Sergeant E Dunning
50017 Sergeant A Skilbeck
95920 Sergeant B C Witty (18th Squadron MGC (Cavalry))
50613 Private A Fanthorpe

Appendix F

ROLL OF HONOUR, 1914–1921

The following officers and men of the East Riding of Yorkshire Yeomanry lost their lives during the First World War.

Rank	No.	Name	Date
Pte	150336	Abbis, H	26/10/1918
Pte	1054	Addy, T	20/11/1918
Cpl	165964	Atkinson, R	31/10/1918
Pte	16485	Auty, F	10/10/1918
Lt	--	Bailey, R N M	1/12/1917
Pte	16639	Barradell, E	10/10/1918
Cpl	18209	Bell, D	15/4/1917
Pte	50294	Best, A B	14/11/1917
Pte	50331	Best, E H	16/11/1917
Pte	51166	Blair, P	5/4/1918
Pte	150347	Blowman, E	30/10/1918
Pte	150350	Brooks, A J	8/11/19158
2nd Lt	--	Bryson, W M	1/9/1918
Pte	16641	Bugg, E	10/10/1918
Pte	50413	Burgess, L C	21/11/1917
A/L/Cpl	50081	Byass, B	14/11/1917
Maj	--	Cadman, P S	31/3/1919
Pte	18235	Cawkill, S	14/11/1917
Sgt	50581	Clark. G P	28/3/1918
Pte	2077	Clark, W	7/8/1916
Pte	50299	Clarke, W	21/4/1917
2nd Lt	--	Coates, J	15/8/1918
Pte	50230	Cook, J W	6/6/1919
Sgt	50380	Craggy, J S W	31/3/1918
Pte	50415	Cross, C	15/11/1917
Pte	2224	Deakin, F	20/11/1917
Pte	2481	Dosdale, W	15/4/1917
Pte	93881	Euden, E W	16/2/1918

Rank	No.	Name	Date
Pte	2200	Featherston, A	7/12/1915
Cpl	50588	Freeman, J	18/8/1918
Pte	50647	Freer, J	26/6/1918
Pte	18233	Garside, R W	15/4/1917
Pte	2597	Goldie, H C	3/12/1917
2nd Lt	--	Gresham, L S	7/5/1918
Pte	150383	Grice, A	26/10/1918
Pte	18247	Groves, W	15/4/1917
Cpl	1284	Harrison, J	17/5/1916
Pte	18606	Hawes, J	5/4/1917
Maj	--	Haworth-Booth, B B	8/11/1918
Pte	2213	Hetherton, A	14/11/1916
Pte	2106	Hill, F	15/4/1917
Pte	2094	Hinson, L	2/5/1916
Pte	50616	Howard, S I	27/3/1918
Pte	16471	Hunt, A E	10/10/1918
Pte	1668	Keller, H	28/11/1915
Pte	18254	Kendal, H R	15/4/1917
Pte	2469	Kitching, H	15/4/1917
Pte	50033	Lofthouse, A	4/5/1917
Cpl	18214	Lofthouse, C A	15/4/1917
L/Cpl	50596	Lyth, W	31/3/1918
L/Cpl	50601	Maynard, H R	27/3/1918
Pte	18476	Miles, G A	15/4/1917
Pte	18614	Moore, P	15/4/1917
Pte	18260	Moore, W E	15/4/1917
Pte	14344	Parker, J W	16/3/1920
CQMS	1190	Peacock, P D	18/3/1919
Pte	51488	Pickard, C	15/4/1917
Pte	18266	Pickering, C	15/4/1917
Pte	50802	Priestman, J W	18/11/1918
Pte	50819	Richardson, W	14/11/1917
Pte	18269	Salvidge, W	15/4/1917
Pte	51139	Scrowston, J E B	2/11/1919
Pte	40414	Sketchley, G H A	17/11/1917
Pte	1013	Smith, C A	3/9/1921
2nd Lt	--	Spicer, R M	31/5/1916
Pte	18273	Stabeler, H	15/4/1917
Pte	50626	Stanton, W O	27/3/1918

Rank	No.	Name	Date
Pte	50874	Stather, W	13/8/1917
Pte	9660	Stephens, N R	10/10/1918
Pte	18271	Storry, O	15/4/1917
Saddler	50359	Throssel, R B	26/3/1917
Pte	16473	Turner, T H	10/10/1918
Pte	150277	Vertican, N	31/10/1918
Pte	50303	Walker, H	19/6/1918
Pte	18280	Warcup, C	15/4/1917
Sgt	1935	Webb, J	22/2/1915
Sgt	18205	Webster, E	15/4/1917
Pte	18279	White, E	15/4/1917
Pte	16484	Whitlam, C	10/10/1918
Pte	50911	Wigglesworth, R N	13/11/1917
Pte	10601	Wilkins, W H	24/6/1918
Maj	--	Wilson, C H A	18/1/1921

Notes

The author has made every effort to contact the copyright holders of the material used in this book. If any errors or omissions are brought to our notice, we will be happy to make the necessary corrections in future editions.

Chapter 1

1. A Call for Imperial Yeomanry, Hull Daily Mail, Monday 3rd March 1902, p4
2. Imperial Yeomanry Training 1902 (Provisional), HMSO, London, p7
3. Letter from J. B. Stracey-Clitherow, dated 20th April 1905 (Author's Collection)
4. Letter from Lord Wenlock to Deputy Assistant Adjutant General (DAAG), Northern Command, dated 8th January 1905 (contained in NA WO 32/6641)
5. 'Mail' Mustard & Cress.; "The Territorial horse is a noble animal…", Hull Daily Mail, Thursday 9th May 1912, p1
6. Harold W. Lyon Lecture Notes (ERYMS)
7. 'Mail' Mems; "While at Salisbury Plain…", Hull Daily Mail, Monday 10th June 1912, p4
8. Postcard from unidentified 'D' Squadron Trooper, 28th May 1912 (Author's Collection)
9. The Racecourse Camp, Hull Daily Mail, Tuesday 19th May 1914, p5

Chapter 2

1. Excitement in Driffield, The Driffield Times, Saturday 8th August 1914, p3
2. Memoirs of Lt Frank Wood (ERYMS)
3. Excitement in Driffield, op. cit.
4. Memoirs of Lt Frank Wood (ERYMS)
5. Letter from Private Norman Green to his brother, Stanley, Wednesday 12th August 1914 (Europeana1914-1918)
6. Midnight Turnout, The Hull Daily Mail, Wednesday 12th August 1914, p4

7. Green letter, op. cit.
8. Memoirs of Lt Frank Wood (ERYMS)
9. Death of E.Y.Yeomanry Officer, The Hull Daily Mail, Tuesday 25th August 1914, p3
10. Harold W. Lyon Lecture Notes (ERYMS: 2001.98)
11. Memoirs of Lt Frank Wood (ERYMS)
12. Ibid.
13. Postcard from Private W. H. Hairsine, 11th September 1914 (Author's Collection)
14. Recollections of J B Seddon (Liddle Collection)
15. Diary of Frederick Whitmore Burch (Liddell Hart Centre)
16. Memoirs of Lt Frank Wood (ERYMS)
17. Ibid.
18. Ibid.
19. Seddon, op. cit.
20. Memoirs of Leonard May (ERYMS)
21. Seddon, op. cit.
22. Wood, op cit.
23. The Royal Visit, The Newcastle Daily Journal, Friday 21st May 1915, p5
24. Seddon, op. cit.
25. May, op. cit.
26. Recollections of W H Austin (Liddle Collection)
27. Seddon, op. cit.
28. May, op. cit.
29. Austin, op. cit.
30. Seddon, op. cit.
31. May, op. cit.
32. Postcard from unidentified Private, 6th August 1915 (Author's Collection)
33. Postcard from unidentified Private, 3rd September 1915 (Author's Collection)
34. Austin, op. cit.
35. Seddon, op. cit.
36. May, op. cit.
37. Austin, op. cit.
38. Ibid.
39. May, op. cit.
40. Seddon, op. cit.
41. Ibid.

42. Austin, op. cit.
43. Seddon, op. cit.
44. Austin, op. cit.
45. Ibid.
46. Seddon, op. cit.

Chapter 3

1. Recollections of J B Seddon (Liddle Collection)
2. Harold W. Lyon Lecture Notes (ERYMS)
3. Seddon, op. cit.
4. Memoirs of Leonard May (ERYMS)
5. Peter Thornton Papers (IWM)
6. Seddon, op. cit.
7. Ibid.
8. May, op. cit.
9. Seddon, op. cit.
10. Thornton, op. cit.
11. May, op. cit.
12. Seddon, op. cit.
13. Letter from Captain J F M Robinson to his mother, 26th December 1915 (Tom Robinson)
14. May, op. cit.
15. Seddon, op. cit.
16. Ibid.
17. May, op. cit.
18. Thornton, op. cit.
19. Letter from Captain J F M Robinson to his future wife, 14th April 1916 (Tom Robinson)
20. Ibid.
21. Ibid.
22. May, op. cit.
23. Seddon, op. cit.
24. Quoted in unidentified newspaper clipping (Author's collection)
25. Letter from Lt. R. N. M. Bailey, 10th April 1916 (Parliamentary Archives)
26. Thornton, op. cit.
27. Ibid.
28. Robinson, op. cit.
29. Letter from Lt. R. N. M. Bailey, 16th May 1916 (Parliamentary Archives)
30. Thornton, op. cit

31. Letter from Lt. R. N. M. Bailey, 6th March 1916 (Parliamentary Archives)
32. Thornton, op. cit
33. Letter from Lt. R. N. M. Bailey, 10th June 1916 (Parliamentary Archives)
34. Recollections of T C Ward (Liddle Collection)
35. Diary of Harold Lyon (ERALS)
36. Seddon, op. cit.
37. Lyon Diary, op. cit.
38. Thornton, op. cit.
39. Thornton, op. cit.
40. Thornton, op. cit.
41. Thornton, op. cit.
42. Letter from Lt. R. N. M. Bailey, 28th October 1916 (Parliamentary Archives)
43. May, op. cit.
44. Lyon Diary, op. cit.
45. Ward, op. cit.
46. Thornton, op. cit.
47. Wood, op. cit.
48. Seddon, op. cit.
49. Wood, op. cit.

Chapter 4

1. Diary of William 'Wass' Reader (YORCM)
2. Recollections of J B Seddon (Liddle Collection)
3. Memoirs of Lt Frank Wood (ERYMS)
4. Reader, op. cit.
5. Ibid
6. Ibid.
7. Wood, op. cit.
8. Reader, op. cit.
9. Ibid.
10. Ibid.
11. Diary of George Lancaster (ERYMS)
12. Reader, op. cit.
13. Lancaster, op. cit.
14. Reader, op. cit.
15. Wood, op. cit.
16. Lancaster, op. cit.
17. Wood, op. cit.

18. Ibid.
19. Wood, op. cit.
20. Memoirs of Leonard May (ERYMS)
21. Wood, op. cit.
22. Ibid.
23. Recollections of W H Austin (Liddle Collection)
24. Reader, op. cit.
25. Wood, op. cit.
26. The Distinguished Conduct Medal 1914-20 Citations – Yeomanry, p86
27. Reader, op. cit.
28. Ibid.
29. Ibid.
30. Lancaster, op. cit.
31. Reader, op. cit.
32. Recollections of T C Ward (Liddle Collection)
33. Reader, op. cit.
34. Seddon, op. cit.
35. Austin, op. cit.
36. Letter from Lt. R. N. M. Bailey, 13th September 1917 (Parliamentary Archives)
37. Ibid.
38. Reader, op. cit.
39. Ibid.
40. Seddon, op. cit.
41. Ibid.
42. Ibid.
43. Lancaster, op. cit.
44. Reader, op. cit.
45. Recollections of T C Ward (Liddle Collection)
46. Lancaster, op. cit.
47. Ward, op. cit.
48. Ibid.
49. Unpublished account by Captain (Acting Major) J F M Robinson (Tom Robinson)
50. Seddon, op. cit.
51. Ward, op. cit.
52. Robinson account, op. cit.
53. Ibid.
54. Ibid.

55. Austin, op. cit.
56. Robinson account, op. cit.
57. The Beverley Guardian, Saturday 2nd March 1918, p4
58. Ward, op. cit.
59. Seddon, op. cit.
60. Ibid.
61. Lancaster, op. cit.
62. Ward, op. cit.
63. Ibid.
64. Seddon, op. cit.
65. Ward, op. cit.
66. Harold W. Lyon Lecture Notes (ERYMS)
67. Austin, op. cit.
68. Lyon Lecture, op. cit.
69. Lancaster, op. cit.
70. Austin, op. cit.
71. Seddon, op. cit.
72. Ibid.
73. Ibid.
74. Diary of Harold Lyon (ERALS)
75. Seddon, op. cit.
76. Ibid.
77. Lancaster, op. cit.
78. Ward, op. cit.
79. Seddon, op. cit.
80. Wood, op. cit.

Chapter 5

1. Memoirs of Lt Frank Wood (ERYMS)
2. Diary of William 'Wass' Reader (YORCM)
3. Recollections of Bill Simpson (Liddle Collection)
4. Recollections of T C Ward (Liddle Collection)
5. Ibid.
6. Recollections of J B Seddon (Liddle Collection)
7. Diary of Harold Lyon (ERALS)
8. Memoirs of Leonard May (ERYMS)
9. Ward, op. cit.
10. May, op. cit.
11. Lyon (Diary), op. cit.
12. Ibid.
13. May, op. cit.

14. Ward, op. cit.
15. Seddon, op. cit.
16. Ibid.
17. With the Lincolnshire Yeomanry in Egypt and Palestine 1914-1918, J. W. Wintringham, p85
18. May, op. cit.
19. Simpson, op. cit.
20. May, op. cit.
21. Ward, op. cit.
22. The History of the Fifty First (Highland) Division 1914-1918, F. W. Bewsher, p402
23. Ward, op. cit.
24. May, op. cit.
25. Ibid.
26. N5

Appendix A

1. Memoirs of Leonard May (ERYMS)
2. Recollections of W H Austin (Liddle Collection)
3. To Our Boys on Service, Harrogate Herald and List of Visitors, Wednesday 27th January 1915, p4
4. May, op. cit.
5. Postcard from Private Clement Rogan, 19th September 1915 (Dominic Rogan)
6. Inspection of the Yeomanry, Driffield Times, Saturday 19th February 1916
7. May, op. cit.
8. Letter from Lt. A. C. Hext, 18th June 1916 (Author's collection)
9. Ibid.
10. Papers of Donald Griffin (IWM)
11. Ibid.
12. Papers of George Havard-Thomas (IWM)
13. Griffin, op. cit.
14. Ibid.

Appendix B

1. Recollections of T C Ward (Liddle Collection)
2. Ibid.

Appendix C

1. Torpedoed in the Aegean Sea, True World War 1 Stories, pp406-410
2. Ibid.

Bibliography

East Riding Archives and Local Studies Service (ERALS):
DDX824/1 Diary of Harold W. Lyon of Market Weighton (typescript) 1915-1919
DDX1698/1 East Riding Yeomanry in Egypt photograph album (R. S. Stephenson)
DDYC/1/7/1 Photographs of East Riding of Yorkshire Imperial Yeomanry pre-Second World War
DDYC/1/7/2 Photographs of soldiers in the Middle East during World War One
DDYC/1/8/11 East Riding Yeomanry Roll of Honour Lists and a history of related events

The East Riding Museums Service (ERYMS):
Transcript of the diary of Private George Lancaster, East Riding of Yorkshire Yeomanry
Memoirs of Leonard May of the East Riding of Yorkshire Yeomanry
Transcript of the diary of Lt Robert Stephenson of the East Riding Yeomanry, 1917
Memoirs of Lt Frank Wood of the East Riding Yeomanry
Transcript of a series of lecture notes, by Harold W Lyon, Sergeant, East Riding Yeomanry

europeana1914-1918
(http://www.europeana1914-1918.eu/en/):
17034 Harry Stanley Green's letters and medals

National Archives (NA):

WO 32/6641 Approval of Full-Dress uniform for East Riding of Yorkshire Imperial Yeomanry

WO 32/7278 Formation of East Riding of Yorkshire Imperial Yeomanry

WO 95/247 War Diary 1/1 East Riding Yeomanry amalgamated into 102nd (Lincs & East Riding Yeo) Battalion MGC, 1st Jun 1918–30th Apr 1919

WO 95/4445 War Diary 1/1 East Riding Yeomanry, Mediterranean Expeditionary Force 26th Oct 1915–31st Jan 1917

WO 95/4507 War Diary 1/1 East Riding Yeomanry 1st Jun 1917–30th Apr 1918

WO 95/4548 War Diary 1/1 East Riding Yeomanry 1st Feb 1917–31st May 1917

WO 95/2857/2 War Diary 51st (Highland) Battalion MGC, 1st Mar 1918–28th Feb 1919

Imperial War Museum (IWM) Collections:
Documents:
2230 Private papers of Sergeant Donald Edward Griffin
1880 Private papers of Lieutenant George Havard-Thomas MC
16285 Private papers of Lieutenant Peter Thornton

Liddell Hart Centre for Military Archives:
GB99 KCLMA Burch: Papers of Maj. Gen. Frederick Whitmore ('Eric') Burch (1893- 1977) pertaining to "account of service with York Troop, East Riding of Yorkshire Yeomanry, 1914"

York Castle Museum:
YORCM: TD15.1 Shorthand diary written during the Palestine Campaign in 1918 by William (Wass) Reader, East Riding Yeomanry (transcript)
YORCM: TD17 Shorthand diary written during the Palestine Campaign in 1917 by William (Wass) Reader, East Riding Yeomanry (transcript)
(Copyright York Museums Trust (York Castle Museum))

Liddle Collection, Leeds University Library:
LIDDLE/WW1/EP/055/20 Private Papers of William (Bill)

Simpson, Trooper, East Riding Imperial Yeomanry
LIDDLE/WW1/EP/062/02 Private Papers of Austin, W. H., Trooper, 1st East Riding Yeomanry
LIDDLE/WW1/EP/075 Private Papers of Seddon, J. B., Trooper, East Riding Imperial Yeomanry
LIDDLE/WW1/EP/084 Private Papers of Ward, C. Terry, Trooper, East Riding Imperial Yeomanry
(Quotes from the above reproduced with the permission of Special Collections & Galleries, Leeds University Library.)

UK Houses of Parliament: Parliamentary Archives:
BAI/5 & 12 Private Papers of Robert N. M. Bailey, East Riding Imperial Yeomanry

Crimlisk Fisher Archive, Filey
Various photographs of the East Riding Yeomanry at Filey, 1915

Author's Collection
Letters of Lieutenant A. C. Hext, 2/1st East Riding Yeomanry
Photograph Album, Private F. H. Wilkin, 1/1st East Riding Yeomanry
Photograph Album, Private J. Pritchard, 1/1st East Riding Yeomanry
Research Folders, Yorks East Riding Yeomanry 1794-1814 and East Riding of Yorkshire Yeomanry, 1st & 2nd West York Yeomanry, originally compiled by the late R. J. Smith
East Riding of Yorkshire Imperial Yeomanry Bazaar Souvenir, Walker and Brown, Hull 1906
Various Postcards, photographs, and ephemera

Veterans and their families
An account of the Charge at El Mughar Ridge, by Major Robinson – courtesy of Tom Robinson
Photographs/Postcards of Private John Stanley Cole – courtesy of Charles Cole
Photographs/Postcards of Clement Rogan – courtesy of Dominic Rogan

Published Works:
Anglesey, The Marquess of, *A History of the British Cavalry*

1816-1919, Volume 5: 1914-1919 Egypt, Palestine & Syria, Leo Cooper, London 1994

Anon., General Staff Manual, *Infantry Machine Gun Company Training (Provisional)* 1917, Naval & Military Press, nd (reprint)

Anon., *Officers Died in the Great War*, HMSO, 1919

Anon., *Soldiers Died in the Great War*, HMSO, 1919

Anon., *The Distinguished Conduct Medal 1914-20 Citations – Yeomanry*, London Stamp Exchange, c.1980s

Anon., *The Territorial Year Book*, 1909, Ray Westlake Military Books, Newport 1988 (reprint)

Anon., *The Territorial Year Book*, 1910

Anon., *Through Palestine with the 20th Machine Gun Squadron*, Project Gutenberg eBook edition, (retrieved from https://www.gutenberg.org/files/17109/17109-h/17109-h.htm)

Athawes, P. D., *Yeomanry Wars*, The Scottish Cultural Press, Aberdeen 1994

Attwood G. M., *The Wilsons of Tranby Croft*, Hutton Press, Beverley 1988

Baker A., *The Genealogy of the Regiments of the British Army, Volume 2, The Yeomanry*, The Military Press 1999

Beckett I. F. W., *Territorials – A Century of Service*, DRA Publishing, Plymouth 2008

Bewsher F. W., *The History of the Fifty First (Highland) Division 1914-1918*, Naval & Military Press, nd (reprint)

Brown, R., A *Yeoman's Story – The Diary of Trooper Raymond Brown Staffordshire Yeomanry 1915 – 1919*, Trustees of the Staffordshire Yeomanry Museum, Stafford 1994

Bruce A., *The Last Crusade: The Palestine Campaign in the First World War*, John Murray, London 2003

Clark L., *World War I – An Illustrated History*, Helicon, 2001

Cook, H. C. B., *The Battle Honours of the British and Indian Armies 1662 – 1982*, Leo Cooper, London 1987

Crutchley C. E., *Machine Gunner 1914-1918*, Bailey Brothers & Swinfen, Folkstone 1975

Dennis, P., *The Territorial Army, 1906-1940*, RHS, London, 1987

Dudley Ward C. H., *The Fifty Sixth Division 1914-1918*, Naval & Military Press, nd (reprint)
Edmonds J. E., *Military Operations France & Belgium 1918, Volume 5, 26th Sept – 11th Nov, The Advance to Victory*, Imperial War Museum, London (reprint)
Fegan T., *The Baby Killers: German Air Raids on Britain in the First World War*, Leo Cooper, Barnsley 2002
Freeman, R., *The Inter War Years (1919 – 1939): The Best One-Hour History*, Kendall Lane, April 2014
Granger John D., *The Battle for Palestine 1917*, The Boydell Press, Woodbridge 2006
Harris J. P., *Amiens to the Armistice*, Brassey's, London 1998
Hart P., *1918 – A Very British Victory*, Weidenfield & Nicolson, London 2008
Hatton S. F., *The Yarn of a Yeoman*, Hutchinson & Co., London 1930
Hewison R. N., *The Fayoum: History and Guide*, The American University in Cairo Press, Cairo 2008
James E. A., *British Regiments 1914-1918*, 5th Edition, Naval & Military Press 1998
Keegan J., *The First World War*, Hutchinson, London 1998
Lecane P., *Torpedoed! The RMS Leinster Disaster*, Periscope Press, Penzance 2005
Lewis J. E. (Introduction), *True World War 1 Stories*, Robinson, London 1999
Livesey A., *The Viking Atlas of World War I*, Viking, London 1994
MacMunn G. & Falls, C., *British Official History of the War, Military Operations in Egypt and Palestine, Aug 1914 to June 1917*, HMSO
Massie R. K., *Castles of Steel – Britain, Germany and the Winning of the Great War at Sea*, Pimlico, London 2005
McGuirk R., *The Sanusi's Little War: The Amazing Story of a Forgotten Conflict in the Western Desert, 1915–1917*, Arabian Publishing, London 2007
Mitchinson K. W., *Defending Albion, Britain's Home Army 1908-1919*, Palgrave MacMillan, Basingstoke 2005

Norfolk, R.W.S., *Militia, Yeomanry and Volunteer Forces of the East Riding 1689–1908,* East Yorkshire Local History Society, 1965

Sellwood, A. V., *The Saturday Night Soldiers,* White Lion Publishers, London 1974

Stone N., *World War One – A Short History,* Penguin, London 2008

Sumner, I. and Wilson, R., *Yeomanry of the East Riding,* Hutton Press, Beverley 1993

Westlake R. & Chappell M., *British Territorial Units 1914-1918,* Osprey Men-At-Arms Series No. 245, Osprey, London 1991

Willmott H. P., *World War I,* Dorling Kindersley, London 2008

Wilson R., *The East Riding Yeomanry (Wenlock's Horse) 1902–1947,* Military Modelling Magazine, Vol. 13 No. 4 & 5, April & May 1983

Wintringham J. W., *With the Lincolnshire Yeomanry in Egypt and Palestine 1914-1918,* Lincolnshire Life, Grimsby 1979

Woodward D. R., *Forgotten Soldiers of the First World War,* NPI Media, 2007

Index

11th Cyclist Brigade, 247, 248
11th Division, 224
18th Mounted Brigade, 246, 247,
18th Squadron MGC(C), 114, 119
1st Reserve Cavalry Regiment, 259
22nd Mounted Brigade, 99, 103, 108, 114, 117, 120, 128, 139, 143, 146, 154, 159, 169, 173, 179, 186, 193
26th Armoured Car Company
Designation of, 238
2nd Northumbrian Division, 56, 63
51st (Highland) Division, 217, 218, 219
56th (London) Division, 210, 212, 224, 225
5th Reserve Cavalry Regiment, 255
7th Cyclist Brigade, 248, 251
Abu Gandir, 89, 93, 95, 97, 99
Ain Arak, 171
Akir, 158, 159, 161, 163, 165, 166
Aldborough, 42
Alexandria, 79, 81, 82, 85, 104, 105, 195, 196, 199, 200, 257, 262
Ali Muntar, 122, 123, 124, 125, 133, 152
Amwas, 168, 169
Annabeh, 180, 181
Annual Camp
1909, 27
1912, 29-33
1914, 33-35
1922, 239
1926, 239
1927, 240
1928, 240
ANZAC Mounted Division, 118, 120, 122, 123, 124, 131, 135, 137, 139, 142, 148, 153, 154, 158, 166, 167, 177
Armitage, F., 231
Ashlin, C. H. N., 95

Atkinson, R., 98, 220
Austin, W. H., 65, 68, 74, 75, 77, 78, 125, 145, 163, 177, 179, 242
Bailey, R. N. M., 97, 101, 103, 104, 107, 145, 146, 167
Bandon, 251, 254
Bardwell, T. G. N., 74, 95
Barr, F., 98
Bedlington, 56
Beersheba, 129, 137, 139, 140, 141, 145, 146, 149-153, 166, 168, 175
Beit Ur El Foka, 178, 179, 180
Beit Ur El Tahta, 169, 174, 175, 179, 180, 182
Best, A. B., 165
Beverley, 12, 13, 15, 16, 41, 44, 48, 234, 236, 241, 242, 245
Bilharzia, 142, 229
Bir El Abd, 116, 117, 118
Bir El Melalha, 120
Bireh, 169, 173, 174
Black Beret
adoption of, 239
Blackhall Rocks, 59
Boer War, 11, 13, 15, 18, 21, 45
Naming of units, 15
Bollezeele, 207
Bonewell, S., 230
Bridlington, 13, 16, 28, 43, 248, 249
Brown, Wilkinson, 44
Bulford Camp, 29
Burch, F. W., 53
Cadman, P. S., 247
Cairo, 82, 87, 101, 104, 108, 139, 167
Calvert, C. A., 16
Cap Badge
Change, 27
Origin, 17-18
Cassel, 207
Chatby Camp, 81
Clark, C., 230
Clonakilty, 251

288

Coke, P., 255
Costessey Hall, 67, 68
Costessey Park, 75
Cucq, 203
Defence Force, 237-238
Deighton, S., 34
Deir El Azab, 87, 88, 89, 90, 93, 105, 107, 257
Deir El Belah, 121, 122, 125, 131, 135, 141, 185, 186, 195
Deirout Train Murders, 230
Demobilisation, 226-227
Diss, 67
Dixon, C. F., 98
Dodgson, K., 95
Driffield, 13, 15, 16, 28, 41, 42, 234, 237, 245
Dueidar, 108, 109, 114
Duffield, T. H., 65
East Cottingworth, 16
Egyptian Revolution 1919, 230
El Arish, 118, 129, 141
El Buggar, 144, 147
El Fukhari, 138, 142
El Gharaq El Sultani, 88, 91, 93, 95
El Mughar, 155, 158, 159, 161, 165
El Shauth, 143
El Shawashna, 88, 90
Emerson, A., 263
Escrick, 12, 16
Esdud, 155, 183
Etaples, 202, 203
Fayoum, 85, 87, 88, 91, 93, 99, 108, 257
Featherstone, A., 245, 253
Fencehouses, 56
Fermoy, 251
Filey, 64, 65
Flamborough Head, 42
Fulford, 16, 41
Gaza, 120, 121-129, 131, 133-134, 137, 139, 140, 141, 147, 149, 152, 158, 185, 186

George V, 64, 238, 239
Gharack South, 91, 93, 99, 143
Gharack West, 93
Goz El Geleib, 151
Green, N. W., 43
Gresham, L. S., 135
Griffin, D., 248, 249, 253
H.M.T. Arcadian, 135, 259, 260-262
H.M.T. Caledonia, 197, 199
H.M.T. Victorian, 75, 76, 78, 79, 81
Hagar Mashguk, 93
Hairsine, W. H., 51
Hall, C. O., 16, 28
Harrison, J., 101
Harrogate, 242, 243
Hartlepool, 57, 60, 242
Havard-Thomas, G., 248
Haworth-Booth, B. B., 16
Hedon, 15
Helmsley, 65
Herries, Lord, 12, 16, 27
Hetherton, A., 108
Hexby, 16
Hext, A. C., 247
Hinson, L., 259
Hornsea, 16
Hotchkiss machine gun, 115, 117, 131, 161, 235, 240
Hotham, 16
Howarth, N., 257
Howden, 15
Hudson, B., 65
Huggins, R., 261
Huj, 149, 153, 154, 177
Hull, 12, 13, 15, 16, 18, 19, 42, 230, 234, 238, 242, 246, 255
Hunmanby, 16
Imperial Camel Corps, 95, 106, 122, 131, 137, 139, 152, 168, 230, 231
Imperial Service Badge, 29
Imperial Yeomanry, 11, 12, 17, 23

289

Junction Station, 155, 158, 165-168
Kantara, 108, 115, 141, 195
Kasr El Gebali, 90
Kasr Karun, 91, 106
Keller, H., 245
Khalasa, 137, 144, 145
Khan Yunis, 119, 120, 121, 138, 139, 142
Khargat, 106
Killarney, 251
Kilnwick Percy, 44, 47, 48, 51
Kilworth, 251
Lancaster, G., 118, 119, 137, 152, 155, 167, 175, 178, 183
Langdale, P. J., 16, 33, 34, 49, 241
Lloyd, C. G., 182
Lofthouse, A., 135
Ludd, 158, 166, 167, 169, 177, 181
Lulworth Cove, 240
Lyon, C. G., 60, 165, 167
Lyon, H. W., 31, 48, 81, 98, 105, 108, 113, 171, 174, 178, 181, 196, 200
Macroom, 251, 253
Malton, 16, 28
Market Weighton, 13, 15, 33
Marseilles, 199, 201, 202
May, L., 59, 64, 67, 68, 75, 82, 83, 88, 89, 95, 108, 122, 196, 199, 202, 207, 214, 226, 227, 242, 243, 246
Medinet Madi, 99, 104, 105, 106
Mejdel, 153, 183, 184, 187
Mena House Camp, 82
Milliam, 207
Mobilisation 1914, 41–42
Moore, E. D., 161, 177
Naane, 166, 167, 168
New Akir, 161, 165, 166
Newbald, 33
Newport, 16, 19

North Cave, 16
North Midland Mounted Brigade, 64, 67, 74, 75, 85, 87, 91, 93, 99
Norton, 16
Nunburnholme, Lord, 56, 245
Oldfield, A., 220
Patrington, 16, 42
Peacock, P. D., 230
Pearson, H. W., 144, 146, 218, 227
Peerless armoured car, 235, 239, 240
Pickering, 65
Piper, M. J., 221
Pocklington, 13, 15, 16, 28, 44, 56
Priestman, J., 229
Purnell, P. J., 219
R.M.S. Leinster, 262-265
Ramleh, 158, 166, 167, 168, 178
Reader, W., 115, 116, 117, 118, 119, 121, 128, 135, 137, 138, 147, 154, 186
Reformation, 231
Regimental band, 34, 249, 253
Riccall, 16
Riddlesworth Hall, 67
Riding School, 19, 234, 239, 242, 255
Rifle, Short Magazine, Lee-Enfield, 120, 139
Robinson, J. D., 220
Robinson, J. F. M., 89, 93, 101, 143, 144, 159, 161, 163, 165
Rogan, C., 245
Rolls Royce armoured car, 240
Rolston, 16
Romani, 106, 115, 116
Salisbury Plain, 29, 31
Sanderson, O, 28
Saulty, 207
Scarborough, 57, 59, 239, 240, 242
Schlieffen Plan, 39, 53, 54
Scrowston, J. E. B., 25, 254

290

Seaham Harbour, 56, 57
Seddon, J. B., 51, 59, 60, 64, 67, 68, 74, 75, 76, 77, 78, 81, 82, 83, 87, 88, 90, 95, 105, 109, 115, 138, 149, 151, 161, 166, 171, 179, 180, 181, 183, 195, 202
Seeley, F., 207
Selby, 15
Senussi, 83-87, 91-95, 107, 108
Sewerby Park, 43
Sheikh Zowaiid, 118
Shellal, 131, 133, 135, 141, 147, 149, 151
Sherwood, F. W., 128
Shilta, 169, 178
Shotton Hall, 56, 59
Simpson, B. W., 221
Simpson, W., 187, 211
Sledmere, 15
Slingsby, A. P., 28
Smales, F., 117, 128
Smith, A. S., 246
Southampton, 75
Spicer, R. M., 246, 253
Spurn Point, 42, 43, 44
Stephens, N. R., 263
Stephenson, R. S. S., 169, 185
Stracey-Clitherow, J. B., 16, 17, 19, 23, 27, 29, 33
Strensall, 256
Suez Canal, 62, 69, 83, 85, 108, 146, 195
Sykes, N. C. M., 59, 161, 218
Tel El Fara, 133, 135, 137, 143, 146
Tel El Marakeb, 138, 146, 147
Tel El Sheirn, 152, 153, 154
Territorial Army, 234
Territorial Force
Formation of, 23–24
Renaming, 234
The Curragh, 259
Thetford, 67
Thornton, P., 82, 87, 90, 99, 101, 103, 105, 106, 107, 109

Tomlinson, W., 114
Treaty of Versailles, 229
Valenciennes, 217, 220-221, 224, 225, 226, 227
Vickers machine gun, 195, 203, 206, 240
Wadi Ghuzze, 120, 122, 125, 134, 141
Wadi Muellih, 93
Wadi Raiyan, 93
Walker, J., 238
Ward, T. C., 104, 109, 154, 155, 161, 166, 167, 169, 173, 183, 193, 195, 196, 202, 218, 221, 256
Warter Priory, 28, 53, 56
Wenlock, Lord, 12, 13, 15, 16, 19, 21, 22, 27, 33
Whitby, 57, 59
White, J. D., 119, 218
Wilkinson, P. C., 95
Wilson, A. S., 16, 28
Wilson, C. H. A., 28, 231
Wilson, G. G., 28, 49, 56, 75, 174, 195, 231, 234, 237, 238
Withernsea, 42, 43, 242, 245, 246
Wood, F., 42, 43, 44, 48, 53, 56, 57, 60, 110, 115, 116, 119, 120, 121, 123, 124, 128, 184, 185
Woodhouse, G. H., 182
Wright, W. C., 149
Yeomanry Mounted Division, 139, 140, 145, 153, 154, 159, 166, 167, 168, 169, 173, 174, 175, 177, 178, 180, 182, 186
York, 12, 16, 33, 34, 41, 42, 43, 67, 246, 255, 256, 257, 259
Yorkshire Mounted Brigade, 25, 27, 29, 42, 56, 116, 241, 242, 245, 255
Zeitoun, 195

ALSO FROM LEONAUR
AVAILABLE IN SOFTCOVER OR HARDCOVER WITH DUST JACKET

THE FALL OF THE MOGHUL EMPIRE OF HINDUSTAN *by H. G. Keene*—By the beginning of the nineteenth century, as British and Indian armies under Lake and Wellesley dominated the scene, a little over half a century of conflict brought the Moghul Empire to its knees.

LADY SALE'S AFGHANISTAN *by Florentia Sale*—An Indomitable Victorian Lady's Account of the Retreat from Kabul During the First Afghan War.

THE CAMPAIGN OF MAGENTA AND SOLFERINO 1859 *by Harold Carmichael Wylly*—The Decisive Conflict for the Unification of Italy.

FRENCH'S CAVALRY CAMPAIGN *by J. G. Maydon*—A Special Correspondent's View of British Army Mounted Troops During the Boer War.

CAVALRY AT WATERLOO *by Sir Evelyn Wood*—British Mounted Troops During the Campaign of 1815.

THE SUBALTERN *by George Robert Gleig*—The Experiences of an Officer of the 85th Light Infantry During the Peninsular War.

NAPOLEON AT BAY, 1814 *by F. Loraine Petre*—The Campaigns to the Fall of the First Empire.

NAPOLEON AND THE CAMPAIGN OF 1806 *by Colonel Vachée*—The Napoleonic Method of Organisation and Command to the Battles of Jena & Auerstädt.

THE COMPLETE ADVENTURES IN THE CONNAUGHT RANGERS *by William Grattan*—The 88th Regiment during the Napoleonic Wars by a Serving Officer.

BUGLER AND OFFICER OF THE RIFLES *by William Green & Harry Smith*—With the 95th (Rifles) during the Peninsular & Waterloo Campaigns of the Napoleonic Wars.

NAPOLEONIC WAR STORIES *by Sir Arthur Quiller-Couch*—Tales of soldiers, spies, battles & sieges from the Peninsular & Waterloo campaigns.

CAPTAIN OF THE 95TH (RIFLES) *by Jonathan Leach*—An officer of Wellington's sharpshooters during the Peninsular, South of France and Waterloo campaigns of the Napoleonic wars.

RIFLEMAN COSTELLO *by Edward Costello*—The adventures of a soldier of the 95th (Rifles) in the Peninsular & Waterloo Campaigns of the Napoleonic wars.

AVAILABLE ONLINE AT www.leonaur.com
AND FROM ALL GOOD BOOK STORES

ALSO FROM LEONAUR
AVAILABLE IN SOFTCOVER OR HARDCOVER WITH DUST JACKET

WINGED WARFARE *by William A. Bishop*—The Experiences of a Canadian 'Ace' of the R.F.C. During the First World War.

THE STORY OF THE LAFAYETTE ESCADRILLE *by George Thenault*—A famous fighter squadron in the First World War by its commander..

R.F.C.H.Q. *by Maurice Baring*—The command & organisation of the British Air Force during the First World War in Europe.

SIXTY SQUADRON R.A.F. *by A. J. L. Scott*—On the Western Front During the First World War.

THE STRUGGLE IN THE AIR *by Charles C. Turner*—The Air War Over Europe During the First World War.

WITH THE FLYING SQUADRON *by H. Rosher*—Letters of a Pilot of the Royal Naval Air Service During the First World War.

OVER THE WEST FRONT *by "Spin" & "Contact"* —Two Accounts of British Pilots During the First World War in Europe, Short Flights With the Cloud Cavalry by "Spin" and Cavalry of the Clouds by "Contact".

SKYFIGHTERS OF FRANCE *by Henry Farré*—An account of the French War in the Air during the First World War.

THE HIGH ACES *by Laurence la Tourette Driggs*—French, American, British, Italian & Belgian pilots of the First World War 1914-18.

PLANE TALES OF THE SKIES *by Wilfred Theodore Blake*—The experiences of pilots over the Western Front during the Great War.

IN THE CLOUDS ABOVE BAGHDAD *by J. E. Tennant*—Recollections of the R. F. C. in Mesopotamia during the First World War against the Turks.

THE SPIDER WEB *by P. I. X. (Theodore Douglas Hallam)*—Royal Navy Air Service Flying Boat Operations During the First World War by a Flight Commander

EAGLES OVER THE TRENCHES *by James R. McConnell & William B. Perry*—Two First Hand Accounts of the American Escadrille at War in the Air During World War 1-Flying For France: With the American Escadrille at Verdun and Our Pilots in the Air

KNIGHTS OF THE AIR *by Bennett A. Molter*—An American Pilot's View of the Aerial War of the French Squadrons During the First World War.

AVAILABLE ONLINE AT **www.leonaur.com**
AND FROM ALL GOOD BOOK STORES

ALSO FROM LEONAUR

AVAILABLE IN SOFTCOVER OR HARDCOVER WITH DUST JACKET

THE 9TH—THE KING'S (LIVERPOOL REGIMENT) IN THE GREAT WAR 1914 - 1918 *by Enos H. G. Roberts*—Mersey to mud—war and Liverpool men.

THE GAMBARDIER *by Mark Severn*—The experiences of a battery of Heavy artillery on the Western Front during the First World War.

FROM MESSINES TO THIRD YPRES *by Thomas Floyd*—A personal account of the First World War on the Western front by a 2/5th Lancashire Fusilier.

THE IRISH GUARDS IN THE GREAT WAR - VOLUME 1 *by Rudyard Kipling*—Edited and Compiled from Their Diaries and Papers—The First Battalion.

THE IRISH GUARDS IN THE GREAT WAR - VOLUME 1 *by Rudyard Kipling*—Edited and Compiled from Their Diaries and Papers—The Second Battalion.

ARMOURED CARS IN EDEN *by K. Roosevelt*—An American President's son serving in Rolls Royce armoured cars with the British in Mesopatamia & with the American Artillery in France during the First World War.

CHASSEUR OF 1914 *by Marcel Dupont*—Experiences of the twilight of the French Light Cavalry by a young officer during the early battles of the great war in Europe.

TROOP HORSE & TRENCH *by R.A. Lloyd*—The experiences of a British Lifeguardsman of the household cavalry fighting on the western front during the First World War 1914-18.

THE EAST AFRICAN MOUNTED RIFLES *by C.J. Wilson*—Experiences of the campaign in the East African bush during the First World War.

THE LONG PATROL *by George Berrie*—A Novel of Light Horsemen from Gallipoli to the Palestine campaign of the First World War.

THE FIGHTING CAMELIERS *by Frank Reid*—The exploits of the Imperial Camel Corps in the desert and Palestine campaigns of the First World War.

STEEL CHARIOTS IN THE DESERT *by S. C. Rolls*—The first world war experiences of a Rolls Royce armoured car driver with the Duke of Westminster in Libya and in Arabia with T.E. Lawrence.

WITH THE IMPERIAL CAMEL CORPS IN THE GREAT WAR *by Geoffrey Inchbald*—The story of a serving officer with the British 2nd battalion against the Senussi and during the Palestine campaign.

AVAILABLE ONLINE AT www.leonaur.com
AND FROM ALL GOOD BOOK STORES